Effective
Group
Discussion

D0402331

Effective Group Discussion

Fourth Edition

John K. Brilhart
University of Nebraska at Omaha

ⱳcb
Wm. C. Brown Company Publishers
Dubuque, Iowa

Book Team

Louise Waller
Editor

Maxine Kollasch
Production Editor

Barbara Grantham
Designer

Faye Schilling
Visual Research Editor

Mavis M. Oeth
Permissions Editor

wcb group

Wm. C. Brown
Chairman of the Board

Mark C. Falb
Executive Vice President

wcb **Wm. C. Brown Company Publishers, College Division**

Lawrence E. Cremer
President

Raymond C. Deveaux
Vice President/Product Development

David Wm. Smith
Vice President/Marketing

David A. Corona
Assistant Vice President/Production Development and Design

Janis M. Machala
Director of Marketing Research

William A. Moss
Production Editorial Manager

Marilyn A. Phelps
Manager of Design

Mary M. Heller
Visual Research Manager

Photo Credits: *147, 267* James Ballard/*59* Bob Coyle/*49* EKM–Nepenthe: Robert Eckert/*11* EKM–Nepenthe: John Maher/*12* National Institute of Mental Health/*71, 197, 257, 307* Jim Shaffer

Library of Congress Catalog Card Number: 81–691–01

ISBN 0–697–04194–8

Printed in the United States of America

Second Printing, 1982

contents

contents

preface

Effective Group Discussion, Fourth Edition, is written for those persons who want to understand what is happening in small groups in order to be the most effective member of the group. The book provides a balanced presentation of empirically grounded theories of the dynamics of small group communication and techniques that have proven useful in a wide variety of discussions. Written primarily for the beginning student in small group communication, discussion, and group dynamics courses, the book should also serve as a reference source for experienced practitioners and designated leaders. Instructors in such academic fields as speech communication, social psychology, business communication, and education will find it an appropriate and highly teachable textbook.

The needs of the student were kept uppermost in mind while writing. Many examples and short case studies are provided to enrich the limited small group experience of some undergraduates. The illustrations are designed to teach rather than entertain. Although the freshman should find the text quite understandable, theory and research are developed at a level that should satisfy the needs of students in upper-division courses.

A general model of open systems, which the author believes is the best model available for understanding the small group, is used for the first time in this fourth edition to give a coherent structure to the contents. Yet the complexity and jargon of general systems theory is avoided. The first six chapters are designed to develop the reader's understanding of the small group as an open system of input, process, and output variables.

The importance and nature of members' attitudes as input variables is greatly expanded over the third edition. The chapter on communication among group members is simplified, even while the section on nonverbal cues is appreciably enlarged. The process of group development is clarified by the inclusion of Tuckman's four-phase model. Decision-making is more sharply differentiated from problem-solving, in part by making it the substance of a separate chapter. The approach to problem-solving in small groups is much more descriptive than it was in previous editions. While the outline sequences for organizing problem-solving discussions are retained, more flexibility in their application is encouraged.

Theories of leadership applicable to small groups engaged in discussion are developed in more detail than in the third edition, without taking away practical advice for those new to the role of discussion leader. The chapter on observing and evaluating small group discussions is enriched with additional instruments for observing individual behaviors and group processes.

The "special methods" and group techniques formerly included in two chapters are reduced and incorporated into a single final chapter. This chapter may be omitted in teaching; appropriate sections of it may be woven into various units; or it may be a useful reference source for both student and practitioner.

To understand any field of study, one must acquire the specialized vocabulary of the field. To this end I have included a list of definitions of *key concepts* in each chapter. *Study objectives* point to the importance of these concepts. The combined lists provide a comprehensive glossary.

I believe that a course in small group communication should be in large part experiential. Therefore, the most useful exercises from the third edition are retained and many new ones added.

Acknowledgments

Credit and appreciation are due numerous persons who have made contributions to my work as author of this book; I can name only a few of them. First, I am reminded of how much I owe to such instructors and writers as Kenneth Hance, J. Donald Phillips, Elton S. Carter, Sidney J. Parnes and Robert F. Bales. Many colleagues in the study of small group dynamics and communication have expanded my vision through their papers and research reports. Andy Barela of the Audio Visual Center at the University of Nebraska at Omaha was most helpful in creating original drawings, and photographers from this center helped me capture on film some of the flavor of small group meetings. The University Administration granted the leave time necessary to complete the manuscript. Several editors of Wm. C. Brown Company Publishers gave invaluable advice, and prodded me when other activities began to interfere; special thanks is due to Patricia M. Schmelling. My colleagues in numerous small groups played vital roles, unknown to them at the time, as I remained the constant participant-observer. Students enrolled in my small group courses over the past twenty years have given me more of the understanding necessary to write such a book than has any other group of people. My wife, Sue, provided constant support, even when the preparation of this book greatly diminished our time together. To all these persons, and many not mentioned, my heartfelt thanks.

J. K. B.

Effective
Group
Discussion

1 everybody does it: communicating in small groups

Study Objectives

As a result of your study of chapter 1 you should be able to:

1. Explain why it is important that you understand the basic dynamics of small groups as systems and be able to participate effectively in small group discussions.

2. Define and use the terms presented in this chapter: group, small group, discussion, small group discussion, group dynamics, and small group communication.

3. Classify any small group on the basis of its major purpose and source.

Key Terms

Activity group   a group to which members belong in order to participate in some collaborative activity.

Committee   small group of people given an assigned task or responsibility by a larger group (parent organization) or person with authority.
   ad hoc or special—given a specific task to perform, and goes out of existence when this job is completed.
   standing—continues indefinitely with an area of responsibility that may include many tasks.

Composite discussion program   a combination of types of public discussion formats, such as symposium-panel-forum, or symposium-forum.

Conference   discussion by representatives from two or more groups in order to find ways to coordinate efforts, reduce conflict, etc.

Discussion (small group discussion)   a small group of people talking with each other face to face in order to achieve some interdependent goal, such as increased understanding, coordination of activity, or solution to a shared problem.

Forum discussion   large audience interacting verbally, usually following some presentation.

Group   two or more persons united for some purpose(s) and interacting in such a way that they influence each other.

Group dynamics   a field of inquiry concerned with the nature of small groups, including how they develop and interact, and their relationships with individuals, other groups, and institutions.

Interaction   mutual influence by two or more persons via communication process.

Learning group (growth group)   groups that discuss in order to enhance the knowledge, perceptions, and interactions of the members.

Panel discussion   a small group whose members interact informally and impromptu for the benefit of a listening audience.

Primary group   small group in which the major purpose is to meet the members' needs for affiliation.

Problem-solving group   a group that discusses for the sake of deciding what course of action to take in order to resolve a choice or solve a problem.

Public discussion group   a small group that plans and presents before an audience a discussion-type program such as panel, interview, or symposium.

Public interview   one or more interviewers asking questions of one or more respondents for benefit of listening audience.

Small group   a group of a size such that members can all perceive each other as individuals with awareness of the role of each member, who meet face to face, share some identity or common purpose, and share standards for governing their activities as members.

Small group communication   the scholarly study of communication among small group members, among such groups, and between them and larger organizations; the body of communication theory produced by such study.

Symposium   series of brief public speeches on a single major problem or topic, with no direct interaction among speakers.

Small groups are the very warp and woof of daily living in the 1980's. The most basic unit of society is the small group. We do not exist as humans alone, but in groups of from as small as two to as large as ten or more members. Although we dramatize the loner such as the mountain man in television fantasies, no one really lives or works alone. Most people spend a major portion of each day in small groups. A careful examination of any organization reveals many separate but interdependent work groups, task forces, committees and councils. Looking ahead to the year 2000, communication futurist Robert Theobald foresaw a political order with innumerable decision-making groups in which citizens would serve for definite periods of time. From this he argued that

As the diversity of age and style in decision-making groups increased in the eighties, all those involved needed to develop a far more conscious understanding of the basic communication styles that are required if decision-making groups are to function successfully.[1]

Vital to such groups, he said, will be abilities in communicating with larger constituencies of the small groups that make decisions, development of mutual perceptual patterns, and knowing how to work together so that groups are not merely a "conglomeration of individuals acting out of their narrow motivations, and clashing . . . in their behavioral patterns." Even now, the higher a person goes in any organizational hierarchy, the more time the person spends in meetings of small groups and the greater the need for the skills and abilities Theobald described.

Communicating in small groups is so much a part of our lives that most of us take it for granted, failing to perceive and understand what is happening in these groups or how to make them more effective. We need to understand how to communicate more effectively in them, or we are doomed to unsatisfying and ineffectual discussions *ad nauseum.*

Stop reading for a minute, and answer the following questions (to yourself or on paper):

1. Can you name or describe all the small groups in which you participated during the past week?
2. How satisfied are you with these groups and your participation in each of them?

How many groups did you list? What problems in these groups and with your roles in them did you identify? If your list does not include at least eight or ten groups, probably this indicates some unawareness on your part of the fabric of communication in your life. Does your list resemble either of the following examples? A student: family, Bible study group, sorority, executive committee of sorority, discussion group in psychology class, volleyball team, props committee for *Macbeth,* car pool. A faculty member: family, collective bargaining team, arrangements committee for professional convention, research team, executive committee of state historical association, steering committee of AAUP, two committees of academic department, gourmet club, two graduate student committees, and numerous informal discussions among groups of acquainted faculty members and students. These are not exceptionally long lists.

The amount of time spent in *formal* groups alone can be overwhelming. Kriesberg found that executives spend an average of ten hours per week in formal committee meetings.[2] Goldhaber found that at the University of New Mexico the average tenured faculty member served on six committees simultaneously, with eleven hours per week spent in committees and other scheduled meetings.[3] Add to these figures the amount of time spent in formal discussions, and you can see that the importance of small group discussion in our lives cannot be overstated.

It would be delightful if we could say that most of the talk in these ubiquitous small groups is productive of personal satisfaction for the participants, achieves the purposes to which the discussions were addressed, and makes for a sense of unity among the members. But it is hardly so. Our folklore contains many sayings that indicate that something is less than adequate in the way many small groups communicate: "The way to kill anything is to give it to a committee." "Committees are groups that keep minutes and waste hours." "A committee is a group of people none of whom is capable of doing anything about the problem deciding collectively that nothing can be done about it." "A group can make a mess of anything." Both popular and scholarly journals carry numerous articles about serious problems in families and other primary social groups, and how vital these are to our personal and societal well being. As Giffin and Patton wrote,

Since the individual today is experiencing a growing dependency on groups of all descriptions, it is important that people be familiar with the dynamics of group interaction. Once a person has acquired an understanding of the nature of groups, the bases of their development, and their interrelationships with individuals and other groups he has the basis for prediction and control.[4]

We humans need membership in small groups for many reasons. First, we need them *to meet distinctly human needs*. Schutz summarized these as needs for *inclusion, affection* and *control*: the need to belong or be included in groups with others, a need for love, and a need for power in relation to both other persons and our environment.[5] Second, we need small groups because they are *more effective problem solvers in the long run* than are individuals. Group members can see the blind spots and biases in each other's thinking, eliminating many faulty solutions and leaving as a remainder an idea that is better than any one member alone could devise. For many of the decisions we must make there is no "correct answer at the back of the book"; only the judgment of our peers arrived at through consensus can guide us in choosing among alternatives. Third, participation in work planning or problem solving has been proven to be a great motivator of effort. People work harder and better when they have helped decide what to do. No plan of action is good if the people who must carry it out don't like it and work halfheartedly. A long line of investigations has shown that groups are powerful persuaders of their members, leading to more personal change than study, lectures, or a one-to-one pitch. Even our self-concepts and personalities are largely formed by interaction in small groups.

You may have studied small groups in a sociology course, especially their role in establishing and maintaining social organization as the link between the individual and society as a whole. In psychology you may have studied how the small group modifies the individual's personality and self concepts, and how various types of small groups can be therapeutic for their members. In the field of speech communication and in this book we focus on the process of communication among the members of small groups, especially how you can influence this process to make the groups in which you participate more satisfying to the members, efficient, and productive of quality decisions. Findings from scholars in many fields will be reported and applied, but throughout the book the central objective will be to help you understand what is happening as members talk and work together, and how to make your own communicating as productive as possible. Small group discussion, the talk among members of a group, cannot be reduced to a set of simple formulas, for it is far too complex.

A *systems* concept has been used to organize the book. *System* implies interdependence among components in an ongoing process. In a small group this means that everything that happens in any part of the system makes a difference in every other component of the group. Because the only person you can directly influence and control is yourself, this book is designed to help you develop an awareness of your own behavior in small groups and its implications for other members of the groups in which you are an active member. Put another way, we will aim at developing the art of communicating effectively in a variety of types of problem-solving and learning groups.

Before going further some definitions are needed. Misunderstanding of what I have written, of your fellow students, and of your instructor is likely to be frequent if we do not use certain key terms to refer to the same kinds of events and behaviors. Learning any new subject is to a large degree a matter of learning the special language of the field of study. Throughout this book lists of *key terms* are included at the beginning of each chapter. To start off you need to understand how I have used several terms found throughout the pages that follow.

Discussion and Related Concepts

Group is the first term we must consider. Groups have been defined by various writers with reference to members' perceptions, goals, structure, interdependence and interaction among members. The following definition was chosen as the one most suited to a study of small group communication:

A group is defined as two or more persons who are interacting with one another in such a manner that each person influences and is influenced by each other person.[6]

This definition emphasizes interaction and mutual influence. Interaction implies *communication,* the exchange of signals between or among persons who belong to the group, and that at least some of these signals are perceived and responded to in such a way that each group member makes some difference in how each other member acts in the future. By this definition, persons collected in one place would not constitute a group unless and until there was reciprocal awareness and influence. Group members could be widely scattered geographically, interacting through formal channels such as newsletters, telephone conversations, closed circuit TV, or radio, and never see each other face to face. Each member would have some reason(s) for belonging to the group and a sense of membership, but the reasons could be widely different from member to member.

This brings us to a very basic concept in this book: *small group.* Many attempts have been made to define the small group on the basis of the number of members, but this has never worked. *Small* is at best a metaphor; as used in "small group." Perhaps "small" is an unfortunate word choice with which we seem to be stuck, for the essence is not one of number but of a sense of being able to include all members in one's perception. Perceptual studies have shown definite limits on how much information we can take in at a glance and keep organized in memory.[7] At one glance most of us can perceive a number of similar units from one to about eleven at the maximum. When that number of units is exceeded, we have to begin counting, as "one, two, three . . ." or "three, six, nine. . . ." Attempts to develop category systems for instantly observing and classifying behaviors of people in face-to-face discussion groups revealed that with considerable training most people can learn to handle up to about 12 or 14 categories, but not more.[8] In this sense, the *small group* is one in which members can perceive at least peripherally all the members at once, with some awareness of who is and is not in the group, and the role each is taking. I have arbitrarily eliminated the dyad (two persons) from specific consideration in this book, for there is a lot of evidence that dyads function considerably differently from groups of three or more members. Perhaps the most usable definition of the small group was formulated by Crosbie: ". . . a collection of people who meet more or less regularly in face-to-face interaction, who possess a common identity or exclusiveness of purpose, and who share a set of standards governing their activities."[9] I will also use the term *small group* to refer to groups that meet only once, provided that a sense of shared purpose, face-to-face interaction, and some standards for governing their activity also exist within the group.

Small group indicates what is often called a "pattern property" or non-additive dimension. "Groupness" emerges from the relationships among the persons involved, just as "cubeness" emerges from the image of a set of planes, intersects, and angles in specific relationships to each other. One can draw a cube with twelve lines (try it), but only if they are assembled in a definite way. Any other arrangement of the lines gives something other than a cube. Likewise, one can have a collection or set of people without having a group or a discussion group. A robber and three policemen may interact orally, but they do not constitute a group (lacking an interdependent purpose, shared norms, and procedures). A "promotively interdependent purpose" exists when all members succeed or fail together. The success of each is dependent upon the success of all. Each member promotes the success of the others.

Discussion is another key term in this book. "Discussion" has been used in a variety of ways: the "discussion" section of a research report in which inferences and conclusions are drawn; the "body" or major part of a public speech; any oral interaction among persons, including even a verbal fight; and interaction among several persons following some preselected procedure. In this book, *small group discussion* refers to *a small group of persons talking with each other face to face in order to achieve some interdependent goal, such as increased understanding, coordination of activity, or a solution to a shared problem.* This definition implies several characteristics of small group discussion:

1. A small enough number of members for each to be aware of and have some reaction to each other (from three to rarely more than fifteen members).
2. A mutually interdependent purpose so that the success of each member is contingent upon the success of the entire group in reaching this goal.
3. Each person has a sense of belonging, of being a part of the group.
4. Oral interaction, involving speech communication via both verbal and nonverbal symbols. This interaction is continuous during a discussion so that the members are constantly reacting, adapting, and modifying their actions in response to each other. Impromptu speaking, rather than prepared speeches, is the essence of small group discussion; in common terms, discussion entails "give and take."
5. A sense of *cooperation* exists among the members. There may well be disagreement and conflict over information, ideas, and activities, but all members perceive themselves as being engaged in a search for a group outcome that will be as satisfactory as possible to all. Argument is viewed as a means for testing ideas so the best ones can be selected, rather than as a way of winning. Thus it is possible for representatives of competing groups to discuss if they seek means to coexist in peace rather than defeat each other.

The term *small group communication* will be used in this book to refer to the study of interaction among small group members, and to the body of communication theory produced by such study that can be used to produce more effective discussion among the members of small groups. Later in this book we will take up a detailed study of this body of theory and principles.

Group dynamics is another term that you may have heard in conjunction with the study of small groups. Although to the layman this term may imply a set of tricks or gimmicks to stimulate interaction, in this book "group dynamics" will be used to refer to a field of study much broader than that of small group communication: ". . . a field of inquiry dedicated to advancing knowledge about the nature of groups, the laws of their development, and their interrelations with individuals, other groups, and larger institutions."[10] We must examine the knowledge gained by scholars of group dynamics if we are to understand the communication going on in small groups, and thus make our discussions as effective as possible.

Being an effective discussant in a variety of types of small groups calls for an understanding of the dynamics or forces at work in the group, both an understanding of and skills in the processes and means by which communication is effected, and a personal involvement or commitment to the group as well as knowledge relevant to the purpose of the group. One could be an effective public speaker, but a poor member of small groups, and vice versa.

Types of Small Groups that Discuss

Small discussion groups exist for many purposes and have their origins in many sources. The student of small group communication and discussion needs a simplified scheme for classifying small groups. A way to classify groups will help in observing, analyzing, and talking about the discussions that he or she will observe and in which he or she will participate. The classification system presented here is based on the group's purpose. It has proven useful to many beginning students of the arts of discussing. It is important for you to develop an image and definition of the characteristics of each major type of discussion group so that you can communicate efficiently with your instructor and classmates.

Primary Groups

These are groups of people who are together for the human need of affiliation rather than to accomplish some specific purpose. All are long-term groups. Examples include the family, the gang that regularly shares cokes in a student center, four girls who eat lunch and often attend movies together, two or three couples who often dine and bowl together, friends who share most coffee breaks, and college professors who regularly drop into each other's offices for a chat. Such groups *may* take on specific tasks and often make decisions, but more often they provide personal support, chat about a variety of topics, "let off steam," and generally enjoy each other. Their talk will often be disorganized and informal—for talk is not the means to an end so much as the end in itself, a part of human companionship.

The information and advice given in this book for making communication effective in the small group will apply to primary groups, but they will not be a major concern of ours; rather, we will focus on problem-solving and certain types of learning and personal growth groups.

Figure 1.1 A primary group enjoys a casual conversation.

Therapy and Encounter Groups

All therapy and encounter groups are called collectively "personal growth" groups. They are composed of persons who have come together to develop personal insights, overcome personality problems, and grow as individuals from the feedback and support of others—to engage in personal learning and growth. Members of such groups do not choose each other. They usually have some authority figure present, such as psychiatrist, therapist, transaction analyst, facilitator, or trainer. No *group* product is sought, but each member needs the presence of others to accomplish personal aims. Such groups are highly artificial and have a limited term of existence. At times your class in speech, discussion, or group dynamics may become this sort of group. It is formed in much the same way as an encounter group: several persons with a desire to learn for individual reasons but needing others for such learning to occur, come together under the guidance of an authority figure probably called the "instructor."

Study or Learning Groups

These groups are similar to encounter and therapy groups to the extent that they are formed as a medium for the learning and growth of the participants. If you are reading this book for a course concerned with small group discussion, your class may be organized into several learning groups. Such groups, rather

Figure 1.2 An encounter group helps members with personal problems.

than seeking growth in the personality as the primary end (although that may be one objective), primarily meet to understand a subject more thoroughly by pooling their knowledge, perceptions, and beliefs. While they are exchanging information the participants also gain practice in speaking, listening, critical thinking, and other communication skills.

I hope you have participated in learning groups in such courses as literature, social science, and philosophy. I have had the pleasure of being in innumerable such groups. As a breeder and trainer of hounds, I have learned an immense amount from discussions with friends while driving to field trials for our dogs. Much of my appreciation of painting came from extensive discussions with others of what we saw in paintings. On my campus, posters advertise the Women's Resource Center, inviting any interested person to drop in for "rap" sessions to explore feelings, beliefs, and values about sex roles in our society. Other posters announce Bible study groups, meditation groups, philosophy discussion groups, and many others.

The "round table" is a type of learning group sometimes sponsored by organizations as a way for people sharing some common interest to come together to exchange information and ideas. Churches, libraries, colleges, and many volunteer organizations produce such informal learning groups.

Problem-Solving Groups

There is a wide variety of problem-solving groups, but all of them discuss for the general purpose of reaching a decision about what course of action to take in the face of some difficulty. Their work may be highly involved, taking many steps, or may be limited to choosing among alternatives already provided. The concept "problem" will be explained in detail in chapter 8. Problem-solving groups may or may not be empowered to take action (sometimes they can only recommend or report the results of an investigation).

Activity Groups

These are groups formed to enable members to engage cooperatively in some activity, often both for the sake of doing the activity and for the affiliation provided by doing the activity with others. Members of such groups must invariably solve problems and make choices among alternatives about such matters as when and where to meet, how to pay for their activities, how to conduct the activities, and all the other decisions that must be made in co-ordinating the efforts of several persons. A few examples may clarify the concept of "activity groups": a dinner group of people who meet at intervals to eat together at a new restaurant; game-playing groups, such as bridge, poker, backgammon, pinochle, and chess clubs; a road rally club; dog, cat, or other animal interest groups; and hunting groups.

Committees

These are groups of persons who have been given an assignment by a parent organization or some person in authority. A committee may be formed to investigate and report findings, to recommend a course of action for the parent group, to formulate policies, or to plan and carry out some action. All such tasks require discussion among the members. Boards, councils, and staffs are special types of committees. For example, the board of directors is often called an executive committee. Such groups represent a larger organization, often with very extensive power to make and execute policy.

Committees are usually classified as either *ad hoc* or *standing*. The *ad hoc* or special committee has a defined task to perform, and when that has been accomplished it goes out of existence. Such groups may have one, few, or many meetings. *Ad hoc* committees do such things as evaluate credentials of job applicants, draft constitutions, hear student appeals, plan social events, investigate and recommend what to do about special problems, and evaluate programs of study, departments, or even entire schools. Standing committees continue indefinitely even though the membership may change periodically. Such groups are usually given a definite scope of responsibility by their parent organization, usually described in the constitution or bylaws. Every organization has them.

Figure 1.3 A committee of nurses preparing a recommendation.

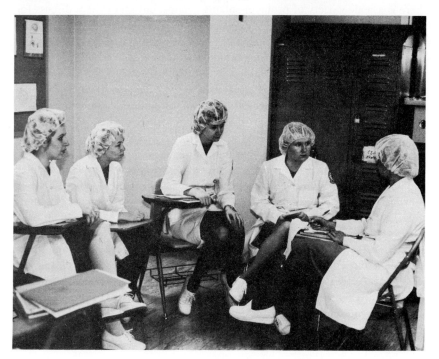

Some special committees empowered to act are called "task forces." A task force is usually appointed by an administrator or larger parent organization, as is any committee, to carry out a detailed assignment with a specific objective, such as a "Mayor's task force to develop a human relations program for the police division" or a task force to design a radically new type of fuel.

Conference Groups

This term is widely used to refer to almost any type of face-to-face communication; for example, a secretary will often say that her boss is "in conference" when he is talking with other persons in his office. At times "conference" is used to refer to a large gathering of persons who hear speeches, study various topics, and perhaps engage in small group discussions.

In this book, *conference* will be used to refer to a meeting of representatives from two or more other groups; since every large organization contains within it many small functioning groups, conferences are very important for coordination within and among organizations. The conferees communicate information from one group to another, perhaps coordinating their efforts. Intergroup conflicts and competition must be mediated to work out a solution acceptable to all groups represented. For example, representatives of various charitable organizations meet to coordinate the efforts of their respective groups and to exchange information and ideas. The various crew heads, designers, and directors must confer periodically to plan and coordinate the efforts of the many people involved in producing a play. Conferences between delegates of the Senate and House of Representatives attempt to resolve differences in legislation bearing on the same issue. Representatives of business and labor meet to decide on wages, working conditions, and fringe benefits. Conferences are frequently held with representatives from the various campuses in a university system to resolve differences in policies, coordinate academic programs, etc. Such conferees must often report their decisions for approval by the groups they represented.

Public Discussion Groups

All public discussions are planned for the enlightenment and influencing of a listening audience. Hence, every public discussion is a "show," and may have the elements of showmanship and detailed planning needed for efficiency and heightened impact. At the same time, spontaneity and the dynamic emergence characteristic of all discussions must be present. To bring about such a balance takes careful selection of members, preparation, and a special style of moderating. In a sense a public discussion group is a committee or task force empowered by some authority or parent group to plan and present a collective public speech.

Panel Discussion

A *panel* is a type of public discussion in which several participants, guided by a designated moderator, interact directly with one another in a relatively spontaneous way for the benefit of an audience. The participants should be knowledgeable and articulate representatives of varying points of view bearing on a question of public interest. Although panel members need an agreed-upon outline of questions to follow, the speaking should be impromptu and relatively informal, with direct responses to each other's remarks. Panel discussion provides an excellent format for presenting programs to relatively small audiences, such as a class. Your instructor may assign groups in your class to prepare and present panels. Public television and educational radio stations carry many panel discussions. The lively interchange can make for intellectually stimulating listening and viewing.

A *public interview* may be conducted by one or more interviewers of one or more interviewees at a time. "Meet the Press" and "Issues and Answers" are well-known interview programs on both radio and television that you may have witnessed. So-called "press conferences" are interviews conducted by news correspondents with spokesmen of major institutions and organizations; presidential news conferences are common examples. Interviewers and interviewees may agree in advance on a list of major questions or topics to be discussed, or the show may be entirely spontaneous. The interviewer's responsibility is to represent the audience by asking questions she thinks they would most want or need to have answered. Obviously, the interviewee is selected because of a special role or position in society.

Forum Discussion

A *forum* refers most often to a period of time when the audience to a panel discussion, lecture, film, or other presentation is invited to ask questions or express opinions. This term is also used to refer to a discussion held by a large gathering of people, such as a hearing on a proposed change in zoning laws or a public hall meeting in which a political official or administrator goes before all interested persons to discuss with them any of their concerns about the office or agency he represents. Mayors, legislators, county commissioners, and other officials schedule "town hall" forums in many communities.

Symposium

A *symposium* consists of a series of brief public speeches on a single major problem or topic, with each speaker selected because of his position, point of view, or expertise. Although some writers still insist on classifying symposia as discussions, there is no direct interaction among the speakers; each prepares his remarks carefully; and there is little direct reference, if any, by the speakers to what the others have said.

Members of a symposium group discuss among themselves in advance of the program, sharing what each is likely to say and developing an overall outline for the program so their speeches will not overlap but still provide the coverage of the subject needed by the audience. In so doing they are engaging in problem-solving discussion in advance of their symposium presentation. Hence the symposium is not discussion, and will not be considered further in this book.

Composite Discussion Programs

Frequently programs for public meetings contain a number of phases, some discussion and some not. Thus we may have a brief symposium in which each participant talks for several minutes, followed by a panel discussion, followed by a forum period.

Summary

In this opening chapter we have considered the vital roles small groups play in our lives—the very source of our identity, the vehicle for satisfying many of our most basic human needs, and a means to decision making and problem solving in a complex society. Yet there is much evidence that small groups are frequently ineffectual and frustrating to their members. Understanding the basic dynamics of small groups and the available theory about communication within them is essential if one is to be effective in the arts of small group interaction.

Key terms in the study of small groups and discussion have been defined to facilitate communication. Finally, a scheme for classifying small groups according to purpose and source was presented: primary groups, therapy and encounter groups, study or learning groups, problem solving groups, activity groups, committees, conference groups, and various types of public discussion groups.

With your understanding of these key terms and concepts we can now proceed to a more detailed consideration of the dynamics of small groups. Chapter 2 presents the small group as a system and how you can be both a component part of such a system and at the same time an observer of it. Chapters 3 and 4 describe the major input variables to a small group as a system: members and their attitudes, physical environments, and knowledge. Beginning with chapter 5 the various major processes, or process variables, are explained, with recommendations for improving them: communication (chapter 6), decision making (chapter 7), problem solving (chapter 8), and leadership (chapter 9). Chapter 10 focusses on output variables of member satisfaction and productivity via evaluation of the components and process dynamics leading to them. The final portion of the book is devoted to special techniques for discussion in organizations, learning and public settings.

Exercises

1. Keep a journal of your experiences in small groups, with at least one entry for each class meeting. Date each entry, writing it as soon as possible following each class or small group meeting. Include descriptions of what happened in small groups of which you were a member, evaluations of each class session, principles or guidelines that you formulate about how to participate in small group discussions, insights into your personal behavior as a small group member, and anything else that is important to you as a student of small group communication. Be sure to use the terminology presented in this book for talking and thinking about small groups. Make your entries concise, yet clear and thorough. Try to be completely honest, frank, and open; no one but you and your instructor will see the journal unless you choose to show it to someone else. Your instructor will establish specific dates on which to collect, read, and respond to your journal.

2. For one week keep a list of all the small groups in which you actively participate during the week. See if you can classify these groups according to the scheme for doing so in this chapter. Next, rate your personal satisfaction with each group, from "1" (very dissatisfied) to "7" (very satisfied). Compare your list with those made by other members of your class. What do you conclude? Use the format that appears at the top of page 18.

1.
2.
etc.

3. *Icebreaker.* This exercise is designed to help you get acquainted with classmates and to reduce tensions and formality that exist within a collection of strangers. The entire class should sit in a circle for this exercise, so that each member can see each other face to face. While doing the exercise, each member should have his or her name on a card or name tag large enough to be read across the circle.

1. First, complete the following sentences with the first thing that comes to mind. Each person should answer question 1 before proceeding to question 2. Begin each set of answers with a different person; your instructor will indicate who should lead off, then proceed clockwise until all have answered.

The three adjectives that best describe me are ___ , ___ , and ___ .

Three persons most important to me are ___ , ___ , and ___ .
When I meet someone I like, I _____ .
When I meet someone I initially dislike, I _____ .
Being in a small group makes me feel _____ .
I'm taking this course because _____ .
Ten years from now I see myself as _____ .
My favorite place in the whole world is _____ .
My favorite activity is _____ .
The thing I am most proud of about myself is _____ .

2. Briefly discuss the following:
Who is most like you?
How do you now feel about your class?
Who impressed you most? Why?
What have we learned from this exercise?

Bibliography

The bibliography at the end of each chapter provides sources you may want to consult for more detail about concepts or ideas presented in the text of the chapter. These bibliographies are purposefully limited to the few writings likely to be most interesting and helpful to you as a beginning student.

Cathcart, Robert S., and Samovar, Larry A. (eds.). *Small Group Communication: A Reader,* 3rd ed. Dubuque: Wm. C. Brown Company Publishers, 1979. The opening section and 3 articles on pp. 1–25 provide an excellent development of the concept "small group."

Shaw, Marvin E. *Group Dynamics: The Psychology of Small Group Behavior,* 3rd ed. New York: McGraw-Hill Book Company, 1981. On pp. 12–14 Shaw answers the question "do small groups really exist?"

Theobald, Robert. "The Communications Era from the Year 2000," *National Forum* 60 (Summer, 1980):17–20.

References

1. Robert Theobald, "The Communications Era from the Year 2000," *National Forum* 60 (Summer, 1980), p. 20.
2. M. Kriesberg, "Executives Evaluate Administrative Conferences," *Advanced Management* 15 (1950), pp. 15–17.
3. Gerald Goldhaber, "Communication and Student Unrest," unpublished report to the President of the University of New Mexico, undated.
4. Bobby R. Patton and Kim Giffin, *Problem-Solving Group Interaction* (New York: Harper & Row, Publishers, 1973), p. 6.
5. William C. Schutz, *FIRO: A Three-Dimensional Theory of Interpersonal Behavior* (New York: Rinehart, 1958).
6. Marvin E. Shaw, *Group Dynamics: The Psychology of Small Group Behavior,* 2nd ed. (New York: McGraw-Hill Book Company, 1976), p. 11.
7. Robert S. Woodworth and H. Schlosberg, *Experimental Psychology,* rev. ed. (New York: Henry Holt and Company, 1954), pp. 90–94.
8. Robert F. Bales, *Interaction Process Analysis* (Cambridge, Mass.: Addison-Wesley, 1950).
9. Paul V. Crosbie, ed., *Interaction in Small Groups* (New York: Macmillan Publishing Company, 1975), p. 2.
10. Darwin Cartwright and Alvin Zander, *Group Dynamics: Research and Theory,* 3rd ed. (New York: Harper & Row, Publishers, 1968), p. 7.

2 the small group as a system

Study Objectives

As a result of studying chapter 2 you should be able to:

1. Consciously and intentionally adopt a participant-observer perspective when engaged in discussions.

2. List and explain the major input, process, and output variables in a small group as an open system.

3. Describe the characteristics of an ideal discussion group.

Key Terms

Input variable an observable source of energy and "raw material" to any open system.

Interdependent goal a goal such that achievement of it by one member is dependent upon achievement by all.

Issue a question for which there is not a single, simple answer; a point in discussion for which there are two or more positions or answers provided by members.

Open system a system in interaction with its environment requiring constant adjustment and balancing with external forces.

Output variable any observable consequence or change resulting from the functioning of a system, including changes in the inputs, the components of the system, products it creates, and its environment.

Participant-observer active participant in a small group who is at the same time observing and evaluating its processes and procedures.

Principle of least-sized groups formulated by Thelen, states that a group should be no larger than necessary to include all needed information, skills, etc. within the members.

Process variable a characteristic of the *functioning* of a system as it modifies inputs during the internal interactions of living, adapting, and working.

System a structured complex of interdependent components in constant interaction requiring adaptation among its parts to maintain its organic wholeness.

Variable an observable characteristic of anything.

"Why should I study group dynamics?" you might ask. Why indeed! This is a highly complicated field of study with bibliographies of books and articles dealing with research and theory numbering in the thousands. Parts of this literature are often the subject matter for upper-division and graduate level courses. If your purpose is just to be a more effective participant in discussion groups, why tackle all that? We certainly cannot deal with all of group dynamics, but to understand small groups enough to develop personal discussion skills depends on being able to perceive at least several of the major forces influencing the groups in which you discuss.

The Participant-Observer Perspective

A major purpose of this book, and of the course for which you may be reading it, is to develop a *participant-observer* perspective.

The participant-observer is a regular member of the group, engaging actively in its deliberations but who at the same time is observing, evaluating, and adapting to its processes and procedures. A participant-observer directs part of his or her attention to doing the work of the group, whatever that may be, and part to how the group is functioning, trying always to be aware of what the group needs at the moment. Such a member makes a conscious effort to be aware of the adequacy of the group inputs and its process variables in relation to the desired outputs. This sort of member can supply needed information, ideas, procedural suggestions, and interpersonal communication skills *when needed,* or seek them from other members of the group who may not realize what is needed at the moment. Lacking such an orientation, the member may be a drag on the system, like a parasite, or an inconsequential appendix that the group could well do without.

Some "members" of groups are participants in name only. They add almost nothing to the inputs of the group, though they may detract little from its energy and resources. Such is the observer who watches and listens, but does little or nothing. This may be the result of lack of knowledge and abilities relevant to the purpose of the group, lack of skills in communicating within small groups, or a lack of sophistication in small group processes and procedures. Doubtless you can think of examples you have known of observer-like members: the committee member who adds nothing to solving the problem assigned to the committee, the classmate in a group discussing a short story who has not read the story, or the knowledgeable classmate who doesn't speak up.

Some members are valuable because of their personal knowledge or skills, but have little understanding of process variables in a small group. So long as the group is operating well they can make a real contribution when asked to do so, but they are of no help in resolving conflicts, reducing misunderstandings and confusion, coordinating the work of others, and helping out when the group gets into trouble.

The members with a highly developed knowledge of small group dynamics and communication theory may be of great value in establishing harmonious relationships among members, verbalizing ideas to unite the group, calling attention to process variables reducing the effectiveness of the group, and suggesting procedures and discussion techniques. To be an all-around valuable member of the group one must have both a participant-observer focus and information and ideas that are needed by the group to achieve its objectives. For example, if members of a group are meeting to develop a traffic plan for a large campus, there will undoubtedly be wide differences in the beliefs about what is desirable and what ought to be done. These differences could lead to destructive conflicts within the group or to the sort of argument that can lead to a truly outstanding solution to their problem, *if* members have the necessary information about the traffic on campus and about small group processes and communication.

Throughout the rest of this book we will be examining the major variables in the small group as a system so you can become a more knowledgeable participant-observer member; gaining the resources of knowledge and skills needed to accomplish the task of the group in which you participate will be up to you. At this point as a beginning student of small group discussion you need an overall image of the "ideal" small group, which you can begin to use at once as a standard against which to compare the groups in which you participate and as a general framework on which to assemble all the experiences and information you will be gaining in this course. For these reasons I have first developed a model of the small group as an open system, then a composite of an ideal group.

The Small Group As an Open System

You have probably noticed that when a new person joins a group there is a major change in the group, not just a simple addition of a new member. This illustrates the idea of a "system." The small group can best be understood as a system of interdependent components and forces. General systems theory is built on an analysis of living things, which attempt to remain in dynamic balance with an environment by constant adjustments throughout the entire organism. Any system is active, "living," dynamic—constantly changing. No system is ever static: a change in any part of an organism or its immediate environment reverberates throughout the entire system. For example, a "head cold" affects your whole body and its functioning to some degree, not just your head. High blood pressure, as a response of your body to some stress experience with the environment, affects everything in your body, including how you feel, your thinking, and all you do even though the changes may not be immediately perceptible.

One benefit of thinking of the small group as a system is that this emphasizes the notion of multiple causation, which is to say that whatever happens is not the result of a single simple cause, but the result of a complex interrelationship among many forces. Another benefit of the systems concept is that it leads us to look for multiple outcomes of any change in the group as a system. With a systems perspective we are more likely to consider all of the characteristics of a group when trying to understand and improve its functioning, rather than look at only one or two of them and thus possibly miss what is most important at the moment.

The variables (characteristics) of a small group can be classified into three broad categories: input variables, process variables, and output variables. "Input variables" are the components from which the small group is formed out of a larger structure or environment. These include the members of the group, the reason(s) for forming the group, any other groups or organization to which it relates, the resources available to the group (knowledge, money, tools, etc.), and the immediate setting or physical environment in which the group is functioning. "Process variables" refers to how the group functions internally, or how the members relate to each other, procedures they follow, how they communicate among themselves, and how they do their work as a group. "Output variables" are results of the group processes, including tangible work accomplished (such as things built, policies developed, solutions to problems), changes in the members themselves, the effects the group has on its environment, and changes in the group's processes. As you can already tell, these are not separate, but as was previously stated, everything influences and is influenced by everything else in the small group—it is a *system*. Another way of stating this is that all components and variables interact with each other in a small group.

Figure 2.1 is a diagrammatic model of many of the variables in each of the three sub-systems of a small group. The arrows indicate the interaction among these sub-systems, as well as among the variables in each sub-system. The list of variables in each box could be greatly extended; those listed are included because they are usually important to any small group. The arrows at the top indicate a feedback system, in which part of the output modifies the future inputs and the operations of the system. A simple illustration of this can be seen in a successful basketball team. The output of repeated winning will produce more enthusiasm and commitment to the team by the players, a continually more polished way of performing together, more liking of the members for each other and their coach, greater attendance at games, the likelihood of more funds and better equipment, and so on.

This model of a small group is an *open* system model, meaning that the group interacts with its environment rather than in social isolation. Gross described four characteristics of any open system that apply to the small group[1]:

1. the membership may be changed, but the group continues to exist as a group even though some outsiders become members and some former members become outsiders;

Figure 2.1 A model of the small group as an open system of sub-systems.

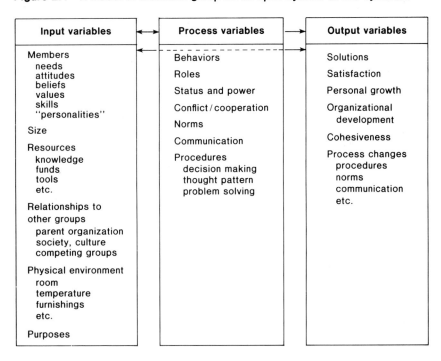

Input variables	Process variables	Output variables

Members
  needs
  attitudes
  beliefs
  values
  skills
  "personalities"
Size
Resources
  knowledge
  funds
  tools
  etc.
Relationships to
other groups
  parent organization
  society, culture
  competing groups
Physical environment
  room
  temperature
  furnishings
  etc.
Purposes
	Behaviors
	Roles
	Status and power
	Conflict / cooperation
	Norms
	Communication
	Procedures
	  decision making
	  thought pattern
	  problem solving
		Solutions
		Satisfaction
		Personal growth
		Organizational
		  development
		Cohesiveness
		Process changes
		  procedures
		  norms
		  communication
		  etc.

2. members are also members of other groups that may produce conflicting loyalties, demands on time and energy, or even lead some members to leave the group;
3. resource exchange, which means that resources are used and changed by the work of the group, and outputs are produced that will become further resources to the group or to other individuals or groups with which it interacts;
4. reciprocal influence between the members and outsiders to the group.

An Ideal Discussion Group

Before presenting an abstract model of an ideal discussion group, I have selected two small groups from the hundreds in which I have participated or observed as outstanding in their inputs, processes, and outputs. These examples are intended to give a sense of concrete reality to the ideal model. One is a problem-solving committee with authority to recommend to a parent group. The other is a self-improvement learning group.

A committee of five faculty members of a college of Arts and Sciences, elected by their colleagues and charged with preparing a draft of a constitution for the college, comprised the problem-solving group. The college is part of a university. It previously had no constitution, but a new by-law of the university Board of Regents authorized the colleges to develop constitutions for their internal governance. The five members each came from different academic disciplines, representing the humanities, social sciences, physical sciences, and fine arts. The dean acted as chairman *pro tem* at the first meeting to explain what he understood the charge of the committee to be, than asked the committee to elect a chairperson. The group then discussed the duties of that position such as calling meetings, seeing that detailed records were kept, providing tentative agendas for meetings, seeing that multiple copies of all the writing the committee had done were prepared, and providing equal opportunity for each member to speak. Following that discussion a secret vote was taken, and Professor Orin Miller elected. Fortunately, all members knew each other from previous groups over the past several years, and the correct choice was made. This group never manifested any doubt that the chair was the real choice of the group for leader. No one ever showed the least dissatisfaction with Orin as leader. The dean then left the group, asking that if possible a completed constitution be presented to the faculty of the college at a meeting to be held six months later.

Orin asked the group how they viewed their job, and how they might go about it. The following discussion ensued:

Paul Steiner: This is a tremendous opportunity to create a model of democratic academic governance. We've never had anything like this at our university, so the constitution we write will be a ground-breaking thing. We have a great challenge, and a great responsibility.

Joan Brightly: Amen! I really feel that this is important, and that we must and can do a great job. If we do our job well, the faculty will adopt the constitution we propose, and it will serve them well.

Tom Mulbach: Yeah, that's how I see it, too. I'm not much of a lover of committees, but this one matters. I can't think of a finer group of people to work with on drawing up our first constitution.

Ray Stone: And how—this is the cream of our faculty. I'm sure we can work well together, and do a fine job. But I think we ought to plan out how we will go about this.

Orin: I'm pleased that we all feel that our task is so important, and that we have such a fine group. Okay, Ray, why don't we discuss what the problems are that we face in writing a constitution, then how we might go about it, and come up with a general plan for our meetings.

Group: Fine. Yes. Good. Let's do it. [etc.]

Orin: Well, then what do we need in a constitution? I suggest we make a list of all the things we think need to be addressed in it.

Ray: Definitely it must state the purpose of the faculty as a group such as setting standards, approving degree programs, examining courses and evaluating them, advising the dean on recommendations for promotion and tenure of faculty, and similar academic matters.

Joan: It will need a committee structure, with the purposes, selection, and organizing of standing committees to do all these things.

Paul: And a section on how the constitution is both adopted and amended as needed at a later date.

This listing of possible component sections of a constitution for the college went on for about twenty minutes, with the chair asking a few questions to clarify ("Do you mean have the departments represented on a rotating basis?"), asking if there was anything else anyone could think of, and writing everything down. Then:

Orin: "Well, that's quite a list! Let me read it all over to you, and see if I've left anything out. Then we might discuss whether this is all we need, and if we need it all. Before we end this discussion, I think we should decide how to proceed from here.

Following nods of approval, Orin read the list, thus summarizing the group output to that time. This summary provoked further discussion:

Joan: We don't have anything about membership. We need to define how one qualifies for voting in the faculty.

Paul: Right.

Orin: Okay, it's added to the list. I think we've made a good beginning on setting our goals. I'll have this typed, run off, and send each of you a copy so you can think it over and maybe suggest additions or deletions at our next meeting. Also, I guess we should put these in some order. Would anyone be willing to try that?

Joan: Well, I've done a lot of work on constitutions in the past, so I guess I could do that. But I'm now anxious to get to talking about what we need to do and how to go about it in the months ahead.

Others: Yes. Me, too. Let's.

Orin: Okay, I think one of the first things we ought to do is draw up a list of similar institutions, then divide up the list among us and everyone write to several of them for copies of their constitutions, then note things we have overlooked as possible topics in our constitution, and sections that especially impress you.

Tom: Good idea. We sure ought to write to Iowa State and Penn State.

Roy: And Michigan State and Western Michigan. I heard they have a fine set-up there.

Orin: Those all sound like good places to get examples, but before we get further into that I think we should plan out our long range agenda, the general procedure to follow through our meetings. Is that all right with all of you? [Nods of agreement from all.] First, when should we meet and how often?

Ray: This is as good a time as any for me. How about the rest of you?

Paul: Well, I can make it, but because of having no classes on this day I'd rather keep it free for research and writing. How about another time? Could we all compare schedules?

The group members then did so, and chose unanimously to meet every Wednesday from 2:00 p.m. until as late as necessary.

Orin: We have an awful lot of work to do, so I think we ought to meet every week, at least at first, until we are sure we will have a draft ready for the faculty meeting in April. What do the rest of you think?

Paul: I agree wholeheartedly, but I think we should skip a week or two until we get back the copies of constitutions we request and have time to analyze them.

Joan: I guess I agree Paul, but I think we should meet next week to finish up our list of possible topics and maybe write a sort of preamble to help us get our sights set and our values in order as to what we want to achieve from or through a constitution.

Paul: Yeah, I hadn't thought of that, but you're right.

Orin: Is that agreeable to you fellows [to Tom and Ray]?

Both replied that it was.

Orin: Why don't we each write down what we think is the purpose of our constitution, and what we think the preamble ought to say about those things?

Group: Fine. Okay. I'll do what I can. That's a good place to start.

Orin: Now let's get on with our long range plan. We get a list of schools, then divide it up and write to them for copies, then revise our outline of a constitution and take it up a section at a time, one or two sections per meeting, being sure we have time to go over it as a whole and get it prepared before the faculty meeting. How does that strike you as a procedure?

Paul: That sounds good to me, but I've noticed how easy it is. if we begin in a group with something to shoot at. So why don't we form one- or two-person sub-committees to write tentative drafts of the various articles and sections?

Joan: I think that's a good way to proceed, if we can choose what sections we begin work on and agree that each of us is to do about the same amount of work.

Tom: That's fine by me, if we can write other tentative sections than those we are assigned when we don't agree with what has been presented to us.

Ray: Yes. I think it is vital that we be very open with each other on what we think and believe, and that we don't have to agree with what someone wrote. It's too important not to bring out all the pro's and con's on each issue.

Orin: I certainly would hope we examine everything we propose from all angles. How do the rest of you see that?

There was general consensus expressed that this was necessary, and that they could disagree openly, yet remain friends, working in cooperation. The committee then set up its list of schools from which to request copies of constitutions.

Throughout their entire eighteen meetings this group followed the general procedure and agenda laid out at the first meeting. Sometimes a proposed article would be accepted with minor revisions, sometimes it would be argued in depth and with strong feelings, but never in the approximately fifty hours of discussion did any name calling occur. Orin sent out an outline agenda for each meeting, along with a copy of articles to be considered at the meeting so members could look it over in advance. At the next to last meeting the following discussion occurred:

Orin: I think we now need to talk about how we introduce this constitution to the faculty and get them to vote for it. I'm really proud of us and the constitution we have drafted, and don't want it to get chopped up or beaten down by people who don't understand it so well as we do.

Joan: Right, Orin. As chairman, you will make the motion for adoption, and explain what we designed it to accomplish, and why.

Paul: Yes, and now I think we should consider all the things people might raise as objections, or what they might want to change, and how we can argue against those.

Orin: Do you all agree? (everyone did, so they proceeded, dividing up the main responsibility for thinking up rebuttals on each section).

At the final meeting of the group:

Orin: I'm really sort of sad to see our "Ben Franklin" committee come to an end, though I can sure use the time to get back to some research I had to put aside. This has been the finest group to work with I've ever been in. As chairman, I can't thank you enough.

Tom: I feel the same—we've been a great group. But, Orin, you've been a model chairman, by far the best I've ever seen.

To this there were strong expressions of agreement, a tribute to Orin, and to themselves for how proud they were of their work. The college was given the constitution, discussed it in great detail section by section, made two relatively minor amendments to it, and then adopted it by a unanimous vote, something very exceptional for a group of 160 people with strongly held beliefs from a wide divergence of backgrounds. This constitution is still in effect, with some amendments over the years, and is regarded as the best college constitution in the university where I am employed. This was, I think, the finest problem-solving group I ever observed. Why? The dynamics and components are many, but especially important were the sense of committment each member brought to the task, the availability of needed resources (information in the form of constitutions from elsewhere and many informal polls of fellow faculty members; ideas; writing skills; members' skills in cooperation and communication; an ideal setting in which to work—a quiet, comfortable conference room with chairs in a circle around a table—and a systematic procedure that all had helped to develop. All decisions were made by consensus, which helped build the sense of teamwork throughout. Orin never acted bossy or dogmatic in his role, but he worked very hard to keep the group following its procedures, to see that all points of view were heard and respected, and that consensus was reached. Tom was especially skilled at bringing a sense of good humor and calm to the group when anyone seemed to get upset over a conflict of ideas. As the group succeeded on each different part of the document, that success added to their enthusiasm and ability to work well, including being open about any doubts or disagreements they held. The final products included not only a fine constitution and ready adoption by the faculty, but also a sense of unity and satisfaction among the members. Orin made a statement of tribute to the whole group, saying they deserved the credit for what was accomplished for the faculty, not he. Several years have passed since then, but all are still members of the faculty, and share a remarkable sense of pride and friendship.

The learning group to which I alluded earlier was composed of 14 people, ranging in age from about 20 to possibly 60, who had joined to study and discuss contemporary religious beliefs and problems in an informal course called "Great Western Faiths." The leader had participated in a weekend training program for study-discussion leaders, and like most such leaders was not in any sense an expert on the subject matter of the discussions. They met once a week for two hours in a library room. I was privileged to observe this group as a researcher, and to tape record its discussions (20 hours in all) for later analysis. This is a typical bit from one of their discussions. The leader I will call Helen.

Helen: Tonight we are discussing symbolism in religion. I hope you all had time to do the readings carefully, and enjoyed them as much as I did. What topics and questions in these readings would you most like to discuss?

Mark: I'd like to talk about the differences in the symbols of Catholic and Protestant faiths, especially the Catholic use of icons and statues.

Betty: Let's discuss what we think the major similarities are in symbols of the Jewish and Christian religions.

Sam: Yes, and how different churches use crosses.

Maia: Communion as a symbol versus the idea of transubstantiation—I'd like to talk that over, especially with my Catholic friends.

Helen: What else?

A total of seven different major issues was raised, which Helen wrote on the board as each was presented and then she added one more. Then she suggested discussing these eight issues in the order in which they were raised in the readings all had done. I was impressed with Helen's addition—it ensured that every major subject in the readings would be addressed by the group. This agenda-setting took about six minutes.

The group then proceeded to discuss these issues. When someone would get on a different topic, Helen would say something like "Charlie, I think that is getting us away from the topic of the uses of crosses and into vestments. Why don't you save that for later—it fits under our sixth topic." Here is a typical excerpt from one of their discussions:

Mark: I really don't understand why Catholics have all those statues of Mary, Jesus, angels, saints, and so on. That seems pagan to me.

Sam: I'm no Catholic, as you know, but I thought Monsignor Knox had a really good explanation of those. He said on page 427 that. . . ."

Mary: Let me explain what those mean to me as a practicing Catholic, and how they were explained to me in catechism. I feel a. . . .

Mark: Well, that does make a difference, Mary. I really couldn't understand what Knox meant before you said that. I still don't like them, but I can at least see that you aren't an idol worshipper, and I guess in a way it is like we looked on our big old family Bible in its place on the top of our bookcase when I was a boy. We almost worshipped it, yes, and it served to remind us of the presence of God and to be humble. Hm!

At one point Gene said this:

Gene: I think that's a poor way to do things. After all, as we discussed last week, everyone can be his own priest. You should really consider changing that, Selina. Now in my church. . . .

Helen (interrupting Gene): Hold it, Gene. I think you are telling Selina she is wrong, and that you are trying to convince or convert her. We agreed that our purpose would be just to understand each other, and not to argue who was right or wrong, and that there would be no proselytizing in this group.

Gene: Oops! Guess I got carried away. You are right Helen, and I'm sorry, Selina. Everyone to his own, I guess—mine's different, and I can't buy yours, but I accept that all I have a right to do here is get you to understand what I think and believe about symbolism, not to try to make you like my beliefs.

Thus a source of disintegration was stopped—competition and winning each other over—and the group reaffirmed its most basic of all norms. At the final session, all the members were present. As the meeting was ending, Sam made a little speech to Helen on behalf of the entire group, and gave her a necklace as a token of their appreciation. They voted her "the best darn leader in Dubois," and then had a party (also a surprise to Helen, complete with cake and coffee). When a subsequent course in cultural anthropology was announced in Dubois, Helen was again selected as leader and many of the same people joined the group.

I could go on telling you of other groups, such as the committee in my department that never got its work done and ended with a bitter fight between two members, or of the study-discussion group that began with 17 members and had 5 at the last session, none of whom voted (on a secret ballot) for the same leader if they should ever meet again. But about now you may want to discuss with your classmates what you think were the best and worst small groups you ever belonged to, and why you think so.

Characteristics of the Ideal Discussion Group

The ideal discussion group can only be determined from its outputs, its effectiveness. The very title of this book is indicative that it is about how to achieve desired outputs (see figure 2.1). Of course, outputs can only be evaluated against purposes or goals. Given the reason(s) for the group being formed, then one can say against those standards that the group has been relatively effective in its discussion processes. However, environmental constraints must also be taken into account. For example, no matter how skilled a team of veterinarians may be, if they are trying to treat a disease of unknown origin or for which there is no known therapeutic procedure (as rabies) they cannot effectively do so. Then a realistic goal would be only to eliminate as much suffering as possible. The organization establishing a committee may limit what it can do despite the excellence of its functioning. The interdependence of all components of a system is again demonstrated as we seek to define the characteristics of an ideal discussion group. Since "discussion" is the name of the communication process involved in which a small group works face to face, the emphasis here is on the process variables listed in figure 2.1, rather than on the input and output variables.

Input Variables

1. **Members**—members share basic values and beliefs relevant to the purpose of their being a group and toward each other. For instance, if one member believes deeply that abortion is a venial sin and another member believes it is an excellent way to prevent children from being born into a family situation likely to be damaging to them, the group is not likely to reach consensus on what the law should be governing abortions. Ideally, members' attitudes toward the group and toward each other would *at least* be described as positive. Each member expects that the others will do a fair share of the work, has something important to offer the group, places trust and confidence in the

statements and actions of the others, and has a spirit of inquiry toward the goal (no pre-determined belief about what the group must do, or what is the "truth" about the subject of learning). The members expect to cooperate and compromise. None has a need to dominate or win over the others. They have the skills needed to think systematically and logically from evidence to a conclusion, and to communicate so that mutual perceptions are developed through their speaking and listening.

2. **The principle of "least-sized groups"** is exemplified by the group with a number of members sufficiently small for all to be active participants and perceptually aware of each other as unique individuals (not stereotypes), yet large enough to supply the variety of knowledge and skills needed to achieve high-quality outputs. A divergence of backgrounds and perspectives will be characteristic of an ideal discussion group, yet a similarity of goals and values will underlie these differences if decisions must be made and actions taken.

3. **Resources** to achieve the objectives of the group will be available. Reliable *facts* are known or accessible to members, and they have or can generate reasoned opinions and ideas about the topic or problem. They have physical resources of tools, communication media, funds, and any other needed objects. For instance, one group of which I was a member could not do its work until a highly detailed set of data on computer tapes was made available from a government agency, and a member with computer programming skills was added to the group. We also had to gain access to computer time and that required money to pay for the time.

4. The ideal discussion **group's relationships to other groups** are such that the mission of the group is clear and realistically achievable with the available material and human inputs and, if there are competing groups, it has relatively equal or superior power to them in effecting decisions. For example, an advisory group of workers whose suggestions are never accepted and acted upon is meaningless.

5. To function optimally, a discussion group must have **a place to meet** that provides for members' needs and the discussion process to occur without disruption. A committee that has no adequate room in which to meet regularly will expend much energy just finding and changing meeting places, and trying to get members to those places. A committee assigned to decide which of several candidates for a position to hire could not function in a room where secrecy was compromised by the constant coming and going of strangers.

6. **The group's purpose is clearly defined and accepted by all members.** There is adequate perspective on the external structure, including an understanding of the area of freedom. The group makes constant adaptations to the changes in conditions facing it. All members give the group goal priority over personal goals or needs not in harmony with the group objectives.

Process Variables

1. **Behaviors of members are predictable to each other.** A member who undertakes an assignment can be counted on to carry it out, such as gathering certain needed information, typing up and distributing a report, or doing something as part of the application of a solution to a problem. Members can be counted on to attend scheduled meetings, or notify the group if this is not possible.

2. **Roles of members are relatively stable, mutually understood, and accepted by all members.** Each finds satisfaction of personal needs and motives in his or her role. Although there is sufficient role definition to permit members to predict each other's behavior, there is also sufficient flexibility to permit anyone to make any needed contribution to the task or group maintenance. The leadership position has been settled in the minds of all members, and the leader has a group-centered orientation. Leadership functions are optimally shared by all members.

3. **Members have relatively equal status,** so that all can exert influence based on their contributions of knowledge, skills, and ideas, not on the basis of status in groups or organizations external to the discussion group. Teamwork is evidenced by sharing of rewards, mutual support, and decision making by consensus. Members expend their energy in achieving the goals of the group, not in competing for power and position over each other. Thus cooperation is maximized and conflict is limited to the evaluation of ideas in a search for the best possible solutions.

4. **Norms and the values underlying them are understood and adhered to,** or else discussed openly and changed when found not to be productive. The group has a culture of beliefs, values and standards that encourages thorough searching for and testing of facts and ideas, open conflict over the merits of ideas, and displays of affection, support, and solidarity.

5. **The flow of communication reveals an all-channel network,** with a high proportion of remarks being directed to all members, and few cliques or dialogues between two persons. Members are skilled in expressing their knowledge and ideas in ways that evoke similarity of understanding of facts and ideas, without inducing defensiveness (threat) in each other. Statements are formulated in ways to make the relationships among statements by different members readily apparent.

6. In an ideal group, **all members understand and share procedures that are efficient, prevent overlooking important issues and facts, and lead to goal achievement.** In a problem-solving group, this means that all members understand and follow a thought sequence that is based on scientific methods of problem solving. They share in exercising control over this procedure; procedures are decided upon by the group, not imposed on it. Specific discussion techniques appropriate to the purpose

of the group are known and accepted by all members. In learning groups, the sequence of issues is decided by the group, with changes made only by consent of all.

Output Variables

1. **The purpose of the group will be perceived by all members as having been achieved.** Decisions (and solutions to problems) will be supported by members as the best possible, and all will demonstrate an affective commitment to enact decisions made by the group.
2. **Members will experience personal satisfaction** with their respective roles in the group, the ways in which the discussion process and group work occurred, and their relationships to the other group members.
3. **Cohesiveness will be high,** with each member having a strong sense of identification with the group and giving it high priority among competing demands for his or her time and energy. Affectively, members will have a sense of "we-ness" and so express their attitudes toward the group both in action and word. A high degree of interpersonal trust exists among members.
4. **There is consensus on the role and leadership structure of the group.** If asked independently, each would name the same person(s) as leader of the group, and as choice for leader in the future. There is perceptual similarity among members on the duties of any designated or acknowledged leader, and on what behavior is expected from each member.

Summary

In this chapter I have presented a model of the small group as a system with certain input variables including members, skills, knowledge, and other resources. The group is a system that processes these resources via interaction involving speech communication as the primary medium, and produces outputs of physical products, solutions to problems, perceptions, and changes in members attitudes, knowledge, and skills. From a description of real groups a model of the ideal discussion group was formulated. In the next chapter we will examine in detail the input variables of member attitudes and information.

Exercises

1. Discuss the following issues with a small group of classmates, or with the entire class sitting in a circle.
    A. How important is it to develop a participant-observer focus?
    B. How could you tell if a discussion group member had such a focus?
    C. How might we develop such a focus while doing the work of this class.

2. Compare a small group as a living system to a living animal as a system; to a hive of bees, pack of wolves, or other group of social animals with which you are familiar. Identify the smallest and largest living systems you can think of.

3. In this chapter a number of input, process, and output variables of small discussion groups were identified. What others do you think should be included, and why? Your answer should include a modification of figure 2.1.

4. Write a brief discription of the "best" small group of which you have ever been a member. Why do you think it was the best? What characteristics of its process and components seem to have made a difference? Now compare your ideas about what made for an outstanding group with those of your classmates.

5. Study carefully the script of excerpts of the discussion from the constitution committee presented on pp. 26 to 29. What are the characteristics of the variables that seem to have made this a highly productive, satisfying, and cohesive group that achieved a consensus end product? Compare your answers with those of classmates.

Bibliography

Andersen, Martin P., "A Model of Group Discussion," in Cathcart, Robert S., and Samovar, Larry A., eds. *Small Group Communication: A Reader,* 3d ed., Dubuque, IA.: Wm. C. Brown Company Publishers, 1979, pp. 43–54. A detailed model of the process of small group discussion.

Barker, Larry L., Cegala, Donald J., Kibler, Robert J., and Wahlers, Kathy J., *Groups in Process: An Introduction to Small Group,* Englewood Cliffs, N. J.: Prentice-Hall, 1979. See chapter 1, "A systems approach to small group communication."

Johnson, R. A., Kast, F. E., and Rosenzweig, J. E., *The Theory and Management of Systems,* 3d ed., New York: McGraw-Hill, 1973.

Tubbs, Stewart L., *A Systems Approach to Small Group Interaction,* Reading, Mass.: Addison-Wesley Publishing Co., 1978.

Von Bertalonffy, Ludwig; *General System Theory,* New York: George Braziller, 1968.

References

1. Bertram M. Gross, *Organizations and Their Managing* (New York: The Free Press, 1964), p. 113.

3

input variables: purposes and persons

Study Objectives

From your study of chapter 3 you should be able to:

1. Explain the concept "interdependent goal," and why this is vital to the success of a small group.

2. Detect the absence of a clear group objective, and help the group establish one.

3. Give examples of "parent" organizations and their committees, and describe the relationship between them.

4. List and describe the attitudes included in a positive "group orientation."

5. Assess your attitudes toward self as a discussant and small group leader, and describe ways to improve these.

6. Explain the ways in which authoritarian, dogmatic, and distrustful attitudes toward other persons are harmful to small group work.

7. Describe six characteristics of interactive behavior that are likely to evoke defensive reactions from group members.

8. Explain what is meant by an attitude of "inquiry," and rate the degree to which you and other group members manifest this attitude.

9. Describe how different degrees of communication apprehension and willingness to communicate will affect one's value to a discussion group, and at least two ways to reduce communication apprehension.

10. Explain how the size of a small group affects its processes and procedures, and explain the principle of "least-sized" groups.

Key Terms

Assertiveness behavior that manifests respect for both one's own rights and those of others, as opposed to aggressiveness and nonassertiveness.

Attitude a complex of beliefs and values held by a person toward some concept or class of objects, producing a tendency to react in a specific way toward the concept or an object of the class.

Authoritarianism tendency to accept uncritically the ideas, information and suggestions of high status persons or "authorities"; closely akin to autocratic attitudes and behaviors.

Communication apprehension anxiety or fear of speaking in any type of social situation, much like concepts of *reticence* and *shyness.*

Dogmatism a tendency to hold rigidly to personal beliefs; closedmindedness to evidence contrary to what is believed.

Encounter discussion group interaction in which members describe honestly and openly their reactions to each other.

Homophily a high degree of similarity among group members in such attributes as attitudes, values, and beliefs; "heterophily" is the opposite.

Interdependent goal (purpose) a group goal such that the achievement of it by one member is dependent upon achievement by all.

Inquiry, attitude of a seeking, searching attitude toward information and ideas, frequently called "openmindedness," characteristic of the discussant who shares ideas and information and is willing to change a point of view when acceptable new evidence or reasoning is adduced by others.

Objectivity an attitude characterized by freedom from dogmatism and prejudice, relatively impersonal in dealing with information and ideas.

Prejudice   a belief based on partial information about the object of the belief; an attitude toward a class of objects based on experience with one or few members of the class accompanied by a strong tendency to reject any contradictory evidence.

Principle of least-sized groups   formulated by H. Thelen, states that a group should be no larger than necessary to include among the members all needed information, skills and other resources necessary to achieve group goals.

Computer specialists have a saying, "garbage in, garbage out," that is equally applicable to small groups. No matter how skilled group members might be in communicating with each other during their discussions, the outputs will not be better than the quality of the resources available. The saying that "a committee is a group of people none of whom is capable of doing anything, deciding that nothing can be done" reflects this idea. Coaches recruit long and hard to get the best resources for a football or basketball team, for they know it takes players of exceptional potential to make a winning team. Likewise, no small group can be more effective than personnel and other resources permit. In this chapter I have emphasized the purpose and source of the group, the members' attitudes, and the number of members as input variables to the group process. In the next chapter we will consider the input variables of information resources and physical environments.

Purpose and Source of the Group

Unless there is some common purpose shared by the members, a small group cannot even be said to exist. The nature and clarity of the goals of the group are basic to how it will function.

When a purpose acceptable to all members has been identified, progress can be made and satisfaction achieved. While different members may have different personal objectives, these must contribute to the group's overall objective if the group is to be truly effective. Persons who place a high value on the purpose of the group will work diligently; persons who perceive that the group is making progress will remain satisfied, loyal, and diligent.

A committee assignment made me even more aware of the importance of clear goals that are seen as important by all members of a group. I was appointed to a special committee to evaluate and make recommendations to the administration of our university. At our first several meetings no one seemed to know what we were to accomplish or why *we* had been picked to serve on the committee. We met only because we felt we had to, but our meetings were apathetic in the extreme and we accomplished nothing. After several months we finally determined what we were expected to produce, and that it was very important. Some initial investigating showed us why each of us was needed on the committee, and then our meetings came to life. In a relatively short time we produced a well-documented report and set of recommendations, for which we have received much praise.

Sometimes a group will be ostensibly working toward one purpose, but actually working toward another. Many discussion groups (such as standing committees) lose sight of their original reason for being, yet go on discussing aimlessly. Such lack of purpose results in inefficiency, dissatisfaction, member loss, and decay of the group. Groups can be compared to other living organisms in this regard. All forms of life are formed of similar elements organized in some specific fashion. When the organism has begun to decay, it sooner or later must die. Then its elements break apart and are gradually incorporated into other organisms. In the same way that we keep our environment clean, satisfying, and productive by hastening recycling processes and not overloading the ecoconversion systems, so we need to help small groups that have served their purpose either adopt new objectives or end rapidly so they do not become a drain on society. How many "friendship" groups have you known that went stumbling along although most of the positive feelings for each other were gone? How many functionless committees, councils, etc., do you know that limp along, draining far more energy than their productivity warrants? Each of us can strike a blow for conservation of the social environment by helping such groups die quickly and with grace.

Even when there is something to be done by the group, little may be accomplished because the goal is not understood alike by all the members. I have frequently asked each member of a discussion group to write down the purpose(s) of the discussion, only to find that each person had a decidedly different idea about the group purpose. Lacking a common goal, progress is impossible. Goal clarity is essential for effective group discussion.

Many small groups are created by some "parent" organization. The U.S. Congress and most legislatures have a large number of committees, each of which is responsible for investigating and recommending or killing proposed laws. The constitution of almost every voluntary organization creates certain standing committees. Special committees are created by the membership, president, or executive committee to do specific things. For example, the chapter of the American Association of University Professors to which I belong has a Steering Committee to work out the general policy of the association and coordinate all its activities, an advisory committee to develop proposed language for a contract to be negotiated with the Board of Regents, a liaison committee for purposes of recruiting chapter members and carrying information between the steering committee and the members of the entire chapter, and a negotiating team that does the actual bargaining with the Board of Regents. Other committees are created as needs arise.

The *area of freedom* (scope of authority) of a committee, commission, board, or task force is defined and controlled by the parent organization. Often the area of freedom is defined in the form of a "charge" to a committee. If the area of freedom and its limits are not clearly described to the group, confusion is inevitable and much time is likely to be wasted. For example, many advisory committees express anger or generate needless conflict when an administrator or parent body does not follow their advice—they have lost sight of their area of freedom, which was only to recommend.

Concomitantly, no subordinate group should be created if there is not a real need for it, a clear and understandable purpose to be accomplished. Confusion, frustration, and waste are the inevitable results when the purpose is vague or unreal.

A graduate student in a seminar on small group communication conducted by me did an unusual and interesting paper on what she called "non-group meetings."[1] She had been able to observe a number of meetings of committees created by statute as part of the organization of a large public medical complex. Certain standing committees were required by the charter of the organization, and each had to meet at designated times. These committees had been given very general responsibility for dealing with certain problems that *might* arise in the management of the hospital complex, including such matters as violations of laws and unethical practices. However, more often than not when they met there was no business to attend to—no one had found anything wrong in their scope of responsibility. The result, she found, was considerable talking in very general and abstract terms, expressions of boredom, and expressions by the members that they were wasting valuable time of many highly paid professional persons. Yet they met, and said they must, because the charter of the organization required them to do so.

Very recently I was involved in a major conflict between a committee that heard faculty appeals to decisions made by a dean. We committee members thought the bylaws of our Board of Regents granted us the power to overturn the administrator's decisions, but the dean believed that we had no power but to *recommend* that he change his decisions. A great deal of professorial time was spent trying to resolve this conflict over our area of freedom. For a period of time we refused to consider any appeals. Finally, the dean agreed to abide by our decision on any appeal to his previous decision, and once again we began to function. In short, it is vital that a group be constantly aware of the limits on its authority.

Confusion of group purpose may also result from *hidden agendas*. This refers to an objective of an individual member (or a subgroup of members) that is different from the avowed group purpose. For example, one member may be seeking attention in order to get elected to an office. Another may need much response and affection, and may find ways to get it at the expense of the group as a whole. A member of an intercampus committee, which was assigned to develop a formula for equitable funding of all campuses of a state university system, found something wrong with every idea anyone presented. Finally, he admitted that his real purpose was to keep the present arrangement by which his campus received more money per student than did the other campuses. Hidden agendas like this one result from what is commonly called a "conflict of interest." Hidden agendas may or may not be at variance with the group purpose, but we must be on watch for evidence of them in behaviors that are detrimental to the group purpose. If detected, harmful hidden agendas can usually be dealt with by bringing them to the attention of the group.

The purpose of the group must be shared by all members; only to the extent that a member feels the purpose to be worthwhile is he or she likely to commit personal resources to it by attending meetings, doing preparatory work, etc. Competing demands will take priority, and the discussions will be unenlightened and unproductive if members are not committed.

Whatever a learning group discusses must be of special interest to its members—they must want to *learn* more about that subject, or to grow personally in the kinds of behaviors and skills the group is established to develop.

Of course individual members have many needs and individual purposes for belonging to a group: need for affiliation, need for sharing thoughts with others, need for affection, need for social esteem, need for self-development and actualization, and so on. Many of these personal needs can be met by belonging to a small group without interfering with the group's central purpose in any way. However, the group members must have some *interdependent* purpose: an interdependent goal means that achievement of it by any one person is dependent on achievement by all. Interdependence is the basis of the kind of decision we call *consensus*. A balanced tug of war illustrates interdependence. For any person to win, all on the team will win, and for a team to win, each member must want to win badly enough to exert the maximum effort he or she is capable of. It takes several persons to plan a successful luncheon dance or prom. If the members of the conflicting teams during labor negotiations really want to avoid a breakdown (with a possible strike), such a common interdependent purpose may be enough for them to overcome their conflicts in a spirit of compromise that produces an agreement both teams of negotiators can accept as "good." Thus in a strong group there is a clear sense and understanding that all are needed to succeed, and the members share a common fate of relative success or failure as a group. Any conflicts among the members are subordinate to the interdependent goal, which calls for the best possible collaborative and cooperative behavior.

Group members often have a hard time keeping their attention and statements focused on achievement of a shared goal. Whenever you are participating in a discussion among persons who do not seem to be working toward the same goal or talking about the same thing you can often help with goal-setting behavior such as asking one or more of the following questions:

"Why are we meeting here today?"

"What do we think we are trying to accomplish together?"

"What common goal(s) do we share?"

"What do we expect to accomplish through our discussion and work together?"

"Was our group assigned to produce a report of findings, a suggestion for a larger parent organization or administrator, or has it power to make final decisions and act?"

"Is this group seeking to understand a variety of ideas and points of view on a topic, or do we need to reach decisions to which all members are expected to subscribe?"

If the answer you get is unclear, action can be taken to change, clarify, or terminate group activity. Sometimes you can help with a simple restatement of the group's goal and asking how the discussion is related to it. If members are highly dissatisfied with their group, either the group purpose, individual purposes, or group membership must be changed. Persons working on what they feel is insignificant or against their individual objectives work poorly at best.

Member Attitudes

The most important resource to a small group is its members: their knowledge, attitudes, and skills. How well they can work together to achieve an interdependent goal depends on the attitudes they hold toward the purposes of the group, toward each other, and toward ideas and information.

An *attitude* can be defined as a complex of values and beliefs held by a person toward some concept that produces a tendency to respond in a specific way to that concept or perception. The more alike or *homophilus* members are in attitudes the more easily they will be able to understand each other and cooperate. *Homophily* refers to the degree of similarity among persons who interact on personal attributes, attitudes, beliefs, values, etc. Researchers have shown that a high degree of homophily leads to accuracy in message transmission, whereas a high degree of *heterophily* (difference) leads to inaccuracy or misunderstanding and conflicts.[2]

An attitude cannot be seen or measured directly. It can only be inferred from what a group member says and does. In this sense attitude is a "blackbox" term, or something that we presume to exist within a person based on what can be observed. We can measure beliefs with opinion scales (frequently called attitude scales) on which a person indicates a position of relative agreement or disagreement to some statement. We can hear what persons say during discussions, and observe how they behave as members of a group. How much value they give to an idea, concept, or thing can be determined by asking them to rank items and by observing what they do and what they don't do. From such observations we can infer if the attitude of a member toward some concept, action, or thing is positive or negative, and to what degree. Thus although "attitudes" remain somewhat vague in concept, they are vital to a group. I have described certain attitudes that are especially important to the dynamics and processes of a small group's discussions. Collectively these attitudes have been called a "group orientation."

Responsibility to the Group

A whole set of constructive attitudes can be summarized in the phrase *a sense of responsibility for the success of the group.* The constructive discussant feels a personal responsibility to see that the group achieves its goals, and will do what he or she reasonably can to help. Likewise, such a person will encourage others to manifest the same types of responsible behaviors. Such a person cannot "let George do it"; this participant is George.

The kind of group commitment that leads to consensus decisions has been related to the pronouns used by group members. Research has shown a significantly higher ratio of self-reference pronouns (I, me, my, mine, myself) to other or group referent pronouns (you, your, yours, we, us, our) in groups that failed to reach consensus than in groups that did. A discussant's use of pronouns will indicate the degree to which he or she is responsible to the group.

A responsible member can be depended upon to do an assignment that she has accepted and on which the group depends. If she agrees to bring certain information to the next meeting, it will be there. If she agrees to arrange a meeting place, she will do so without fail. If such a member cannot attend a meeting at which her participation is vital (and in a very small group it always is), she will let the group know of this in advance and as soon as possible.

This responsibility to the group continues after the discussion. The ideal discussant supports the group decisions. He speaks of "we" rather than "I" and "they." He accepts a full share of the blame for any group failure, and no more than his share of credit for group success. He carries out any task that he accepted as a representative of the group, never accepting any responsibility that he cannot or will not discharge. This discussant respects the confidence and trust of other group members, not revealing what they have stated in confidence during a discussion.

Persons who are responsible to the group are active participants, not the passives who fail to speak up or carry out work. Burgoon, Heston, and McCroskey describe such an attitude of commitment:

The good group member is willing to commit himself to the group process and product, whatever the outcome (assuming it doesn't violate his personal ethics). He is willing to devote time and energy to the group's activities. He gives as well as takes. This is basically a question of loyalty. Prior to any particular group meeting, each member should determine for himself if he is really committed to the group's membership and activities. The individual who has no initial commitment to a group, whose entering attitude is one of "wait and see," is not likely to be an asset. In times of stress, he is more likely to "abandon ship" than to address the problems seriously. If a person voluntarily chooses to be a member of a group, he has an obligation to maintain a commitment to it in return for the benefits he gains by membership.[3]

Shaw concluded from a number of studies that persons high on "dependability" are ". . . likely to emerge as leaders and to be successful in helping the group to be effective in accomplishing its task."[4]

In short, the valuable group member has an attitude of personal responsibility for the success of the group in achieving its goals, as manifested by commitments of time and energy, dependability in carrying out assignments, and loyalty in times of stress. If you lack such an attitude of commitment and responsibility to the group, it will be better for the group if you are not a member.

Attitudes toward Self

There is a consensus among writers about human relations that only persons who hold positive and objective self-concepts can relate openly, honestly, and objectively toward others. The self-attitudes essential to being a productive group member are summarized by Harris and others as "I'm okay."[5] One must like and trust self before it is possible to like and trust others. Although none of us can have a perfect and complete image of self, the more fully we understand our own motives and needs and accept them, the more openly we can communicate and work with others in a group. Members constantly worried about how their remarks and behaviors will be seen and reacted to by others will not likely speak up to test information and ideas advanced by others, no matter how poor those ideas may be. Thus they will withhold information and ideas the group needs to do a good job. Also, they will be more stinting in giving positive support and rewards to others, the kinds of statements and acts that make discussion rewarding and pleasant to participants.

Objectivity and acceptance of self can be enhanced in a number of ways. There are a number of scales and tests that you can take to gain a clearer picture of your self-attitudes. Your instructor may use some of these in your small group course, or they may be taken at almost any counseling and assessment center, such as most colleges and universities provide for students. You may want to take advantage of these if some private reflection and introspection indicate a problem.

Sharing feelings and experiences with others in an encounter discussion group can be helpful to many students with a low self-concept. Disclosing your doubts, fears, and attitudes about self in company with others can lead to greater self-acceptance and acceptance of others, provided the sharing is objective, honest, and reciprocated.[6]

Encounter means that the group members explore their reactions to each other and their personal feelings openly and honestly. When done in a supportive and positive way under the guidance of a skilled facilitator, encounter discussion can lead to much greater openness while participating in other small group discussions. As fellow group members give you feedback about how they are perceiving and responding to you, your self-images are greatly enriched. How we perceive ourselves is largely due to how we think other persons evaluate us, but often we do not know how others are responding and so cannot make adjustments in our behavior even if we want to. The feedback from other members in an encounter group can fill in many blind spots in self-concepts. Emphasis on the positive can greatly increase our level of self-acceptance and feelings of closeness to and trust of others. Negative feedback will let us know what to change and how, thus leading to more positive feedback and a more positive self-concept. As we discover that others have similar self-doubts and fears, self-acceptance grows and thus the positive self-image essential to being a fully functioning group member is developed.

Attitudes toward Others

As has already been indicated, attitudes toward self and attitudes toward others are inextricably interrelated; we can separate them only for emphasis and analysis.

Desire to Communicate

Various theorists have developed scales to measure related attitudes toward communicating with other persons that I have chosen to call collectively an attitude of a "desire to communicate." Reticence in speaking (Phillips), communication apprehension (McCroskey), and willingness to communicate (J. Burgoon) are the major concepts applicable to participating in group discussions. While the degree to which one desires to communicate with others in a group could be called a personality trait, it manifests itself only in potential interaction situations, and so reflects both an attitude of self-concern or doubt and of fear or defensiveness toward the reactions of others to what one says and how it is said.[7] The highly apprehensive communicator will typically avoid group interaction, and when such a person does speak the remark is likely to be irrelevant to preceding remarks and the purpose of the discussion. Such a person is unlikely to disagree, for disagreeing calls for explanation. The apprehensive member is unlikely to make his information and ideas available to the group, though intelligence and knowledge may be very high.

If you are currently enrolled in a small group course your instructor may choose to have you complete a scale for assessing your degree of apprehension about speaking in general or about participating in small groups. If you score high on such apprehensiveness, there are a number of courses of action that may be helpful to you. For one thing, a norm of accepting each other's different beliefs and opinions without ridicule or instant rejection can increase the security apprehensive members feel when expressing a belief or an opinion. Some small groups need a designated *leader* to enforce such a norm and encourage the more reticent or shy member(s). A simple appeal for fair play may help, such as: "When I said 'I don't think the evidence we have heard justifies that position' you cut me off and shouted I was wrong. All I want is an equal chance to have my ideas considered, and not have them interrupted by you. I don't think you even bothered to understand the implications of what I said." The more you speak up and are listened to, the more comfortable you are likely to be in a group, and the more active you are likely to become as a participant.

If you have a general tendency not to speak as indicated by a series of observations or a scale measuring your apprehensiveness about speaking out, your college or university may provide some training programs to assist you. They are often available from the department offering a course in small group discussion, or from a counseling center. They may include the technique known as "systematic desensitization" in which you learn to relax systematically and

Figure 3.1 The desire to communicate shows during group interaction.

control your tension level, or the technique of "cognitive modification" in which you learn to replace negative self-messages with positive ones. Do you often say something like this to yourself (silently, under your breath): "Nobody wants to hear what I have to say"; "I know I botched up how I said that"; "That's a dumb idea, so I won't say it"; "They'd just laugh if I offered that suggestion"; "That probably doesn't matter, so why say it"; "If it really is any good, someone else will suggest it." Training and practice in making positive self-statements can increase one's openness in communicating and value as a group member. If you do not have access to special training for communicative apprehensives, making a list of all such statements you make to yourself, then in actual discussions stopping yourself the instant you begin to think one of them (or say it) and replacing it with a positive message may be of real help: "They need to hear this"; "My ideas are as good as anyone's"; "If they laugh at this, they are missing the important point, for this could be a great idea for our group"; "I've got to get this out, for no one else may suggest it"; "The group needs this now, so I'll say it." The instant you find yourself thinking about how you are doing, and especially of what others may be thinking of you, try to refocus your attention on the issues being discussed and your apprehensiveness may drop greatly. Much apprehension about speaking up in discussions comes from thinking about how you are doing instead of what the group members are talking about, so changing your "internal talk" in this way can help much.

input variables: purposes and persons

Authoritarian Attitudes

There are many ways of knowing and of responding to persons who claim to know the truth and who "take over." What we are concerned with here is an attitude called authoritarianism. *Authoritarianism* is characterized by uncritical acceptance of ideas or information from a source identified as an authority and doing what an authority orders without examining the implications of such an action. High authoritarians tend to accept the opinions of persons in power in an unquestioning, unobjective way. The person low in authoritarianism asks for evidence, and makes an independent judgment of orders given by an authority figure.

The authoritarian characteristic overlaps the trait called *dogmatism,* which involves a high degree of rigidity in beliefs, or closedmindedness. The more dogmatic/authoritarian a person, the less willing he or she will be to listen in order to understand new ideas, to listen to and accept evidence that contradicts presently held beliefs, and to base conclusions on the total pool of evidence available to a discussion group.[8] Decisions of authoritarians will be more highly influenced by internal needs, feelings, and drives than by a desire to achieve a logically consistent outcome, or to reason among alternatives on the basis of probable outcomes. Since highly dogmatic persons listen poorly and are not likely to change their minds on the basis of evidence and reasoning, efforts to persuade them on such bases are likely to fail. Unless group members can persuade each other with such materials, when they hold different beliefs about a problem and what ought to be done to solve it, much time and effort will be spent in discussion but no consensus will emerge. The group is likely to suffer from much internal conflict and tension, and either a split may occur or others may finally give in to the dogmatists.

An attitude of authoritarianism is also characterized by a tendency to do what one is told. A group of high authoritarians will seek a dominating leader, one who will tell them what to do rather than accepting the responsibility for evaluating alternative courses of action and deciding as a group on the best evidence they can muster and reasoning from it to the course of action most likely to succeed. Such persons conform readily to the majority or to a high-status leader, even when the decision is clearly wrong. The dangerous results of authoritarian attitudes (which we are all likely to manifest in some situations) is demonstrated by Milgram, many of whose subjects were willing to give dangerous electrical shocks to other persons when told to do so by an authority (an experimenter in a lab coat).[9] Janis describes how acquiescing to the beliefs of high-status leaders or large majorities leads to poor decisions.[10] Haiman relates the authoritarianism trait to the functions and style of leadership seen as appropriate in small discussion groups.[11] The authoritarian tends to be preoccupied with power and dominant leader styles, to either take charge or follow someone who does so in an autocratic way. Haythorn and associates find that groups of authoritarians show less "positive affect" toward each other, do less asking for the opinions of others and make more "directive" remarks than do groups of egalitarians.[12] The high authoritarian, then, is more likely to be dogmatic or rigid in defense of ideas, unwilling to entertain the opinions of others, unconcerned for how others feel, and quite autocratic— all detrimental to teamwork in a group of peers.

Trust-Distrust

Cooperation depends on trusting others. Without trust, effective group discussion is literally impossible. Persons who are low in trustworthiness are likely to see others as untrustworthy, and so cannot work well in group discussions. Rotter and associates developed an Interpersonal Trust Scale, with which they have constructed a considerable body of knowledge of how trust affects interpersonal relations. Rotter defines trust as a general expectancy that ". . . the word, the promise, the verbal or written statement of another individual or group can be relied on."[13] Trust, he believes, results both from one's past experience with a type of person and situation in general, and from a specific relationship. Thus a man might develop a distrust of women in general, but still trust his own mother whom he believes is an exception to the rule that women can't be trusted. In general, though, Rotter believes persons display a stable attitude of generally trusting or distrusting others, with serious consequences for relationships among small group members. Persons who are trusting of others tend to be regarded by those others as more trustworthy and dependable. Persons who measure low in trust on the Interpersonal Trust Scale are not only perceived as less trustworthy and less trusting by others, but are also actually more likely to lie, cheat, and steal. High-trust college students have fewer personality conflicts and are better liked than low-trust students. Indeed, both high- and low-trusters liked high-trusters better than they liked low-trusters. Yet high-trusters are not more gullible or more likely to be taken in by deceptions than are low-trusters. In effect, the high-truster opts to trust a stranger until that person gives evidence that he cannot be trusted, whereas low-trusters opt to distrust a newcomer until there is clear evidence that he can be trusted. Many police studies have indicated that con artists are most successful with persons who are themselves dishonest and distrusting, rather than with honest and trusting persons. What seems to be called for in a small group—if discussions are to be productive of satisfaction, cohesiveness among members, and quality decisions—are persons who make positive assumptions about each other, trusting initially (at least until proven wrong), and who believe that the other participants want to arrive at a reasonable outcome in a reasonable way. Otherwise, the climate of the group is going to be one of distrust, suspicion, and little sharing of information and ideas, a competitive dog-eat-dog relationship.

Defensiveness

A whole cluster of attitudes is summed up in the one broader attitude of *defensiveness*. Discussants who perceive other group members as threatening expend much of their energy in defensive behavior, and are thus less able to give time and attention to the task of the group. Gibb describes this behavior:

Besides talking about the topic, he thinks about how he appears to others, how he may be seen more favorably, how he may win, dominate, impress, or escape punishment, and/or how he may avoid or mitigate a perceived or an anticipated attack.[14]

Any of us can and will feel defensive at times when we are attacked, but the person generally trusting of others can state that he or she is feeling defensive and describe what he or she is feeling defensive about, thus permitting the group to solve the distrust problem.

Gibb did an extensive study of the kinds of behaviors that evoke defensiveness among members of discussion groups. He found that as discussants became more defensive their understanding of each other became less and less accurate. He lists six categories of personal attitudes and concomitant behaviors that characterized defensive and supportive group climates. The defensive category is first in each of the six pairs of terms:

1. evaluation vs. description
2. control vs. problem orientation
3. strategy vs. spontaneity
4. neutrality vs. empathy
5. superiority vs. equality
6. certainty vs. provisionalism

We will examine each of these pairs of terms briefly so that you can compare your attitudes and statements to others in a discussion group, and in turn help others to be aware of their defensive behaviors that block productive small group communication.

Evaluation means that something in the words, voice, or actions of the sender seems *to the listener* to be judging him. *Descriptive* speaking behavior arouses a minimum of defensiveness; descriptions are expressions of feelings, events, beliefs, and so on, which do not in any way suggest that the listener change his behavior or attitude. They are limited to descriptions of the *speaker's* perceptions, beliefs, feelings, and values. It can be very difficult to even ask, "When did that happen?" so that it does not appear evaluative, unless the speaker sincerely desires only to understand, not to judge. *Evaluation* refers as much to too ready an agreeing or accepting as it does to negative judgments. We need to guard against the halo effect in which we support what another does or says because of some general acceptance of the person or the position he or she occupies.

Some examples of evaluative and descriptive expressions of opinion and feelings are compared below. Notice that in one case the speaker describes how she feels, whereas in the other way of speaking the feeling is only implied instead of being described, and the other person may be evaluated or blamed.

Descriptive	Evaluative
"I really like that idea."	"That's a wonderful idea."
"I'm angry at you, Joe, for blaming me for not getting out notices of the meeting. I mailed them over a week ago."	"Joe, you're awfully dumb to say that, for you just don't know what you're talking about."

Closely related to evaluation is the *control* orientation, which comes from a desire on the part of the speaker to dominate or change the listener. Most of us do not take kindly to orders from persons we perceive as our equals in authority. If attempts to control are expressed openly as the desires of the speaker rather than as orders, the likelihood of defensive responses is much less. Usually the would-be controller has a belief that the way to get work done in a group is for one person to take charge and to tell all the others what to do. Such a person may say something like: "Now here's our problem, and what we're going to do about it. Sandy, you get. . . ." The problem-oriented discussant would say something like: "We have a problem, as I see it, of raising enough money to buy a new church bus. How might we go about doing that?" The discussant with a "problem" orientation has no predetermined attitude, method, or solution. Rather, he or she is seeking to find the best alternative by cooperative thinking.

Strategy refers to attempts to manipulate another through a less than open statement of purpose. Feigned emotions, withholding information, or playing games are all seen as strategic ploys as opposed to completely open, trusting, and honest speaking. On the other hand, freedom from any deception, withholding, or game-playing produces acceptance, objectivity, and cooperation.

An attitude of *neutrality* is the very opposite of the sense of responsibility for the group and its members discussed earlier; it arouses defensiveness. A *neutral* person does not care about how others feel. Who can trust someone who does not care what happens to the group or other members? On the other hand, an open manner that conveys empathy and a belief that others have productive motives tends to produce nondefensive listening.

Any behavior by which one discussant indicates an attitude of *superiority* to another is likely to put that other on the defensive and so reduce objectivity and listening accuracy. The superiority shown may be based on education, power, wealth, status, intellectual ability, physical attributes, or anything—the resulting feelings of inadequacy on the part of a listener will reduce his or her openness and objectivity toward information and ideas. Competition is set up between a "top dog" and a "bottom dog." As Gibb says, ". . . differences in talent, ability, worth, appearance, status, and power . . . exist, but the low defense communicator seems to attach little importance to these distinctions."[15]

A particular danger of status differences is that high-status persons tend to ignore or reject ideas from persons of lower status. Low-status persons tend to accept or reject uncritically the ideas of high-status persons. In the one case, the low-status person accepts an authority figure uncritically; in the other, he acts defensively. To help assure that all discussants will be given an equitable hearing, it is helpful to have all addressed in a similar manner, for instance, by first names, titles, or Mr., Mrs., Miss, and Ms. Such equality in the way discussants are addressed can do much to reduce attitudes of superiority.

Certainty refers to the attitude of being right, dogmatism. Those who seem to have *the* answers and regard themselves as teachers rather than as coworkers put others on guard. Gibb found that persons perceived as dogmatic were seen as needing to win an argument rather than solve a problem, as needing to be right while the other's view must be wrong, or as seeing their ideas as immutable truth. Dogmatists do not accept disagreement graciously. The converse is the person who is willing to test his or her attitudes and ideas objectively, who holds provisional attitudes and beliefs, who investigates rather than affirms. Persons preferred as future fellow discussants were found to express their opinions much more provisionally than persons rejected as future fellow discussants.[16] No one really wants to be put down and on the defensive by fellow members. Not everyone's ideas are equally worthy, but everyone's ideas merit attention. Everyone deserves to have his or her questions answered without sarcasm or suspicion and to have his or her suggestions accorded respectful consideration.

Assertiveness

An assertive person is one who shows respect for both self and others. One must like and respect self to be assertive. Assertiveness is neither aggression nor passivity. The *aggressive person* is autocratic, dominating, demanding, pushy, attempting to force his or her ideas and practices on others. A passive or submissive person does not stand up for his or her rights in the face of aggressive behavior by another. The actions of assertive persons are described well by Cotler and Guerra:

Behaviorally speaking, an individual who is assertive can establish close, interpersonal relationships; can protect himself from being taken advantage of by others; can make decisions and free choices in life; can recognize and acquire more of his interpersonal needs; and can verbally and nonverbally express a wide range of feelings and thoughts. This is to be accomplished without experiencing undue amounts of anxiety or guilt and without violating the rights and dignity of others in the process.[17]

Aggressive discussants are likely to attack others as persons, engaging in name calling, innuendo, and other forms of personal attack and insult. Aggressiveness results in defensiveness, deflects thinking from the purpose of the group, and produces the kind of reciprocal dislike that leads to group disintegration. Aggressive discussants frequently interrupt others and, by talking more loudly and continuously, attempt to force their will on the group. Thus they show a lack of concern for the feelings and rights of other members. Such behavior cannot be tolerated in a group—it is the very antithesis of a *group orientation.* Either a small group must be willing to submit to the aggressive person, change the behavior to assertiveness, or get the aggressor out of the group.

The *passive or non-assertive person* will not speak up in defense of personal beliefs and values, and tends not to do a fair share of the work of the group. This pattern of behavior is sometimes called *passive-aggressive,* meaning that the person tends to "get even" with assertive colleagues not by speaking up but by failing to do a fair share of the work. When a passive discussant does disagree openly, it is usually without any explanation of why or argument for a different position.

The *assertive person,* a sort of golden mean between aggressive and passive, reflects the position "I'm OK—you're OK" by speaking up openly and directly and seeking compromise when there are competing views or when holding dogmatically to a position would lead to a stalemate. In a group formed for learning, the assertive member insists on others listening to understand, but likewise is an outstanding listener. In a problem-solving group he or she will not conform for the sake of unity, but will make a sincere effort to arrive at group consensus through a careful exploration of all points of view. Shaw summarized research concerning ascendant persons (who are assertive):

They attempt leadership, participate in group activities, are assertive, and are creative. They tend to emerge as leaders, promote group cohesiveness, influence group decisions, conform to group norms, and are popular.[18]

Attitudes toward Information and Ideas

Truth does not exist apart from the minds of persons who know and believe. We cannot transfer knowledge from person to person, but only signals from which each can create personal knowledge and meaning. There can be no meaningful problem solving or decision making by a group until the members have achieved a similar awareness of events and similar beliefs about these events and their implications. To achieve such perceptual congruity requires highly sensitive speaking and listening, and an attitude of *inquiry* toward information and ideas. *Dialectic,* the search for truth (in the sense of the best possible answer to a question), depends on the attitude of inquiry as opposed to certainty or a dogmatic stance on what is and should be. Small group discussion implies a form of dialectic by a group.

Persons who have made up their minds cannot honestly engage in a decision-making or problem-solving discussion. They can only seek to persuade others of the rightness of their prior positions by practicing persuasion; they cannot engage in dialectic. In discussion, attempting to persuade others is a very important process, but must be reciprocated—willingness to be persuaded by others, in a search for the best possible answers. Even learning discussions are blocked by the out-and-out persuader; the intent of discussants must be to share, to explore differing conceptions and to foster mutual understandings out of which common values, images, and actions can emerge among equals. In this regard, debate and persuasion are diametrically opposed to discussion. If one is not interested in understanding and exploring opinions, values, and ways of doing things different from one's own, one cannot engage in learning discussions, and if one has reached unalterable conclusions one cannot engage in decision-making discussions—only "pseudodiscussions." Such a participant will either subvert other participants, stymie group progress, or be excluded from the group after much friction and loss of time. To join a discussion group with one's mind closed on the issues facing the group, unable to suspend judgment and undergo the process of cognitive dissonance, is no less than a breach of morality. It demands of others what one is not willing or able to do oneself—change position.

This is not to say that argumentation has no place in discussions, that no one should take a strong stand, or that "giving in" is advised. Careful weighing of evidence, evaluation of all reasoning, detecting and testing assumptions, and constructive debating of different points of view can contribute greatly to the quality of group decisions. Open and honest conflict is a sign of cohesiveness and stability in a group; concealing differences of opinion and negative feelings indicates a lack of unity. Conflict over ideas and decisions reflects real concern and involvement. The best forge for testing ideas is to bring in all contrary evidence and arguments. Decisions based on avoidance of conflict or contrary evidence, or consisting of vague statements and platitudes, do not work; the details of solutions are not settled and the problem continues. Rigid adherence, conformity for its own sake, and dogmatic rejection of information or reasoning must be avoided.

The opposite of an attitude of inquiry toward information and ideas is *closedmindedness*. Closed-minded persons usually have formed their beliefs on the basis of some "authority" that they take to be unalterably true, so they will not inquire into any contradictory evidence or opinion. As one famous cartoon character put this, "It ain't what people don't know hurts 'em so much as what they know that ain't so." Lee calls this attitude the "mood of allness" in which a person indicates "he wishes to go no farther, to talk no more about something which is to him impossible, unthinkable, wrong, unnecessary, or just plain out of the question. He has spoken and there is little use in trying to make him see otherwise."[19] He may declare, "We've done it another way and we just aren't going to try something new and dangerous,

I refuse to listen to such nonsense." "How naive can you be?," or "Let's not waste time with that one." Such comments indicate what Phillips calls the game of "It Can't Be Done," in which a speaker may even give a tightly reasoned argument to show the apparent impossibility of solving a problem ("the best minds have failed to solve it") or of implementing a proposal.[20]

Perhaps you have had the experience of talking with persons whose minds are made up. I recently discussed the relative merits of collective bargaining with a number of highly educated persons, and was dismayed to have some of them manifest extreme closedmindedness with such statements as "I'm just against unions in principle. They're wrong. I wouldn't even consider joining one." Others said something like this: "Unionism is good. Management just doesn't care about us who do the real work." No evidence, no reasoning, no exceptions allowed for—just an extreme position, unqualified, with in one case even the statement: "There is no sense in discussing it. There is no place for a union here or in any university."

Often dogmatic persons conclude the very opposite of what others conclude from the same evidence. For example, Dwight Eisenhower was almost universally regarded as highly patriotic and loyal. To reactionaries, this was strong evidence that he was a Communist dupe. Most of us like to think that we are open-minded, but careful analysis of many statements from discussions indicates that many discussants' minds are more closed than open. Your mind is closed to the degree that you (1) consistently and absolutely reject ideas that you disbelieve; (2) you cannot distinguish among beliefs different from your own but see them as the same; and (3) you can see no similarity between your own beliefs and disbeliefs.[21]

A special type of closedmindedness is called *prejudice*. The term prejudice indicates a judgment that is unreasonable, without bothering to gain sufficient knowledge on which to base the judgment, hence an opinion that is formed without full and sufficient inquiry. In a very real sense we can never know all that could be known about anything, so we need constantly to be open to new and different evidence. How this matters in discussions is stated quite pointedly by a leading researcher into the mechanisms of prejudice, Gordon Allport: "Attitudes become prejudices only if they are not reversible when exposed to new knowledge."[22] It would be nice if we humans were always rational and open to new ideas and information. But such is not the case—all of us hold prejudices.

If you have this problem, what can be done to replace closed-minded behavior and prejudice with an attitude of inquiry? First, accept your own tendency to act dogmatically and prejudicially as normal, and then be on guard for any tendency in yourself to reject information that contradicts personal belief, regardless of where you got the belief. Try to give such new information or reasoning special attention, no matter how hard that may be. Try stating it aloud to the satisfaction of the person who uttered it. To do so will not be easy, but it will make it possible for you to offset your own prejudices with an attitude of inquiry, and thus your group may find agreement on the basis of evidence rather than remain deadlocked due to unalterable beliefs. Second, you might try asking for points of view other than your own. In a continuing group it would be well to tackle the problem head-on by discussing the attitude itself with the group. An effective way to do this is to discuss specific cases of persons acting with a mood of dismissal. Few persons will persist in making allness statements if they are aware that other group members perceive them to be closed-minded. Taking the short form of the Dogmatism Test and discussing the results may have a positive effect on the members of a group inclined to dismissal and dogmatic statements.[23] It may help to keep reminding the group that mutual respect must be given if group cooperation is to be possible.

Group Size

The **number** of persons comprising a small group has a major impact on the group's resources, processes, and discussions. The abilities, knowledge, and skills available to the group increases somewhat for each added member, increasing the potential for problem-solving effectiveness. But this apparent gain is offset at some point by the increased complexity of the organization required to coordinate behaviors of the members and the increased likelihood of internal conflicts.

As group size increases, the complexity of interpersonal relationships increases geometrically. For example, if we consider only the two-person relationships possible, the rate of increase is indicated by this formula: Number of 2-person relationships $= N(N-1)/2$, in which N is the number of members. Thus in a two-person group there is only one two-person relationship possible, in a group of three members there can be three such relationships, in a group of five members there can be 10 dyadic relationships, and in a group of 10 members there can be 45. The complexities of who interacts with whom are much greater than even the simple formula above indicates. Consider a four-person group with members A, B, C, and D. Each can speak to each other, to each possible combination of two persons, or to all three other members—a total of twenty-eight initiating interactions. For an eight-person group the possibilities are 1,056! In a group of four members the expected ratio of one-to-one messages as compared to one-to-group would be 3/1. However the interactive behaviors Bostrom found in his experimental groups of different sizes were not distributed at all like this:

Most comments in groups of four or five members were addressed to either one person or the group as a whole (roughly 95%). As group size increased from three to four to five, the percentage of one-to-one comments increased steadily from 46.8 to 58.2 to 64.7. Conversely, the percentage of messages addressed to the rest of the group as a whole decreased.[24]

Figure 3.2 Large groups tend to be more formal, structured, and frustrating than small ones.

As the size of a group increases, the opportunity for each member to participate in discussion decreases, but the effect tends to be something different from a simple reduction in average number of minutes available per member. There is some evidence that the total amount of talking tends to be less as group size increases.[25] More importantly, the distribution of participation gets more and more uneven as the number of members increases. A few members tend to dominate the discussion, with others participating relatively less. The amount of participation in groups of three or four members was found to be relatively equal, but as groups increased in size up to eight members the difference in the percentage of remarks by the most and least active members became greater and greater.[26] There is a tendency for one central person to do relatively more and more of the talking.[27] Thus, size increases the degree of structure and centralization of leadership in one person. Speeches tend to become longer, often including several points not pertinent to the issue at the moment.

Lower individual rates of participation are closely associated with lower satisfaction with a group. In student learning groups, increased size resulted in lower satisfaction with the discussions.[28] Such increased frustration is associated with decreased cohesiveness, hence less power of the group to influence its members and to maintain their loyalty. I have repeatedly had students participate in learning discussions in groups of from fifteen to eighteen members, in groups of five or six members, and in groups of two or three members.

Afterward they are asked to rate how satisfied they are with the discussions. Every time the average rating has been much higher for groups of five or six. Although the size of two or three permits more opportunity to speak, it is also rather stifling to divergence and the amount of information and ideas is so limited that the students tend to find these groups less than ideal.

As group size increases, more centralized control of procedures is both expected and needed. Leadership roles become more specialized and formal. Great demands are made on designated leaders to keep order, to keep the discussion organized, and to control the flow of ideas. Large groups usually rely on formal rules of parliamentary procedure, with the general rule being that the larger the group the more the "rules of order" need to be detailed and followed rigorously. It is easier for an autocrat to dominate a large group than a small one.

Other effects commonly occurring when group size increases include greater difficulty in establishing criteria or values, more time reaching a decision, lowering of cohesiveness (attraction to the group), and a tendency for cliques to develop within the group.[29] Small wonder, then, that students who have become proficient in discussing in groups of five to seven persons often flounder in confusion when the class as a whole tries to engage in discussion with the same sort of informality and loose structure used in smaller groups.

How large should a discussion group be? The answer depends in a large part on the purpose of the group and its organizational setting. As early as 1927, Smith demonstrated that groups of three were more efficient in solving problems with "easy" solutions than groups of six members, but groups of six were more efficient with problems requiring that a number of solutions be considered and poor ones promptly rejected.[30] Slater found that experimental problem-solving discussion groups of four to six members were most satisfying to the participants, whereas groups larger than six were felt to encourage too much personal aggressiveness, inconsiderateness, competitiveness, centralization, or disorganization into cliques. Participants in groups of less than four reported being too tense and too constrained to express their attitudes and feelings openly.[31] Groups with even numbers of members tend to have more trouble reaching agreement than do odd-numbered groups. Studies of committees have shown the most *common* sizes to be five, seven, and nine.[32]

Keeping the results of such studies in mind, and that maximum personal involvement is essential for high productivity and efficient use of human beings, the group should be large enough to accomplish its goals and at the same time insure members of satisfaction through opportunity for frequent participation. Thelen's "principle of individual challenge in the least-sized groups" is applicable. Thelen declared that to secure maximum motivation and quality performance, we should establish the *"smallest groups in which it is possible to have represented at a functional level all the social and achievement skills required for the particular required activity."*[33]

Other factors being taken care of, the ideal task-oriented discussion group seems to be five, which is small enough to promote an all-channel network and to permit informality and ease in reaching decisions, yet large enough to bring the many types of information and varied points of view needed for wise decisions. For learning groups, the size may range from as few as three to as many as fifteen or more. If the purpose is to encourage individual questioning and thinking, choose a small group. If the purpose is to expose participants to as many points of view as possible, a larger group is better.

Summary

In this chapter we have considered three major input variables: group purpose and authority, member attitudes, and the number of persons in a group. Only to the extent that group members share a sense of purpose to which all are committed can small group discussions be effective. The area of freedom must be clear to all members, or frustration and failure are inevitable. A strong sense of interdependence among members for goal achievement lies at the base of cooperative effort.

Positive member attitudes toward the group, self, and others are major resources from which group goal achievement can be launched. A high degree of responsibility and dependability to do what one can and agrees to do, positive self-regard, willingness to communicate openly and honestly, egalitarian attitudes free from dogmatism and closedmindedness, an initial attitude of trust in other persons with a low level of personal defensiveness, and personal assertiveness without aggressive attitudes are basic personal resources needed for successful discussion in small groups. Finally, an attitude of *inquiry* toward information and ideas (as opposed to advocacy, closedmindedness and prejudice) is vital to group discussion whether the goal is to reach a decision or for members' personal learning.

To function well, a discussion group should have enough members to encompass all the skills and knowledge needed to accomplish group objectives, yet be small enough to keep the level of interpersonal and organizational formality low. As a guideline I have suggested Thelen's principle of "least-sized groups." If all other factors are taken care of, an ideal size for discussion groups seems to be about five. Serious changes in group process occur in connection with increases in the number of members, decreasing equality of opportunity to participate, satisfaction, cohesiveness, and sharing in the leadership of the group.

Members with such positive attitudes as have been described in this chapter are essential, but they must also have a fund of information, ideas, and skills relevant to the purpose of the group. In the next chapter we will consider these input resources that must be available if the group process is to be an effective system.

Exercises

1. Either in writing (1–2 paragraphs) or orally, describe a committee with which you are personally familiar that had trouble because the members ignored or forgot their area of freedom in relation to a parent organization. Share your example with several classmates, then discuss what principles or guidelines for small group work you can deduce from the examples.

2. How much do you agree that an interdependent purpose is essential to any small group? Share your answers with several classmates, being careful to explain the reasons and any evidence to support your answer.

3. Observe a small discussion group. When you finish observing, rate each discussant on the scale below.

10		0
very responsible and committed		totally irresponsible and uncommitted

   Then write a brief paragraph describing the basis for your judgment of each member. Compare your ratings and observations with those of two or three classmates who independently observed the same group. How well do you agree? What seem to be the behavioral differences on which you judge a group member to be relatively responsible and committed?

4. Discuss the following in a large group of classmates: "How much can we trust each other to tell the truth and to carry a fair share of the work in small groups we form in this class?"

5. See how well you understand the kinds of statements and behaviors that foster defensiveness and openness-trust in a group, and how these relate to a cooperative vs. competitive climate by matching the following:

   _____ certainty   A. cooperative relationships
   _____ control   B. competitive relationships
   _____ description
   _____ empathy
   _____ evaluation
   _____ neutrality
   _____ problem solving
   _____ provisionalism
   _____ spontaneity
   _____ strategies

6. Clip three or four examples of dogmatic or closed-minded statements about some issue, object, or class of people. You can often find these in letters to the editor of a daily newspaper. Next, revise each statement so that the writer manifests an attitude of *inquiry* while still expressing an opinion.

7. List three or four prejudices you once held, but have now abandoned. Describe how you changed each. Then see if you can identify two or three prejudices you still hold, and describe how you will have to behave differently to manifest an attitude of inquiry in each of these cases.

Bibliography

Adler, Ronald B., *Confidence in Communication: A Guide to Assertive and Social Skills,* New York: Holt, Rinehart and Winston, 1977. An excellent book to help you develop effective attitudes and skills.

Burgoon, Michael; Heston, Judee K.; and McCroskey, James, *Small Group Communication: A Functional Approach,* New York: Holt, Rinehart and Winston, 1974.

Egan, Gerard, *Face to Face: The Small Group Experience and Interpersonal Growth,* Monterey, Cal.: Brooks/Cole Publishing Company, 1973.

Lee, Irving J., *How to Talk with People,* New York: Harper & Row, Publishers, 1952.

Nixon, Howard L., II, *The Small Group,* Englewood Cliffs, N.J.: Prentice-Hall, 1979, pp. 208–13.

Rogers, Carl R., *Carl Rogers on Encounter Groups,* New York: Harper & Row, Publishers, 1970.

Rokeach, Milton, *The Open and Closed Mind,* New York: Basic Books, 1960.

Shaw, Marvin E., *Group Dynamics: The Psychology of Small Group Behavior,* 2nd ed., New York: McGraw-Hill, 1976, chapter 6.

References

1. Mary Ann Strider, "The Non-Group Meeting," unpublished paper, 1974.
2. E. M. Rogers and K. K. Bhowmik, "Homophily-Heterophily: Relational Concepts for Communication Research," *Public Opinion Quarterly* 34 (1972), pp. 194–213.
3. Michael Burgoon, Judee K. Heston, and James C. McCroskey, *Small Group Communication: A Functional Approach* (New York: Holt, Rinehart and Winston, 1974), p. 159.

4. Marvin E. Shaw, *Group Dynamics: The Psychology of Small Group Behavior* 2nd ed. (New York: McGraw-Hill Book Company, 1976), p. 182.

5. Thomas A. Harris, *I'm OK—You're OK* (New York: Harper and Row, Publishers, 1969).

6. For more detail on this subject and an explanation of how such reciprocal self-disclosure can help, see Gerard Egan, *Face to Face: The Small Group Experience and Interpersonal Growth* (Monterey, Cal.: Brook/Cole Publishing Company, 1973); and David W. Johnson, *Reaching Out: Interpersonal Effectiveness and Self-Actualization* (Englewood Cliffs, N.J.: Prentice-Hall, 1972).

7. James C. McCroskey, "Oral Communication Apprehension," *Human Communication Research* 4 (1977), pp. 78–96.

8. Milton Rokeach, *The Open and Closed Mind* (New York: Basic Books, 1960).

9. Stanley Milgram, "Some Conditions of Obedience and Disobedience to Authority," *Human Relations* 18 (1965), pp. 57–76.

10. Irving L. Janis, *Victims of Group Think* (Boston: Houghton Mifflin Company, 1973).

11. Franklyn S. Haiman, "A Measurement of Authoritarian Attitudes toward Discussion Leadership," *Quarterly Journal of Speech* 41 (1955), pp. 140–44.

12. William W. Haythorn, Arthur Couch, D. Haefner, P. Langham, and L. F. Carter, "The Behavior of Authoritarian and Equalitive Personalities in Groups," *Human Relations* (1956), pp. 54–74.

13. A concise summary of this research is provided in Julian B. Rotter, "Trust and Gullibility," *Psychology Today* 14 (October 1980), pp. 35–42, 102.

14. Jack R. Gibb, "Defensive Communication," *Journal of Communication* 11 (1961), pp. 141–48.

15. Ibid., p. 146.

16. John K. Brilhart, "An Exploratory Study of Relationships between the Evaluating Process and Associated Behaviors of Participants in Six Study-Groups," (Ph.D. dissertation, Pennsylvania State University, 1962), pp. 180–85.

17. Sherwin B. Cotler and Julio J. Guerra, *Assertion Training* (Champaign, Ill.: Research Press, 1976), p. 3.

18. Marvin E. Shaw, *Group Dynamics,* 2nd ed. (New York: McGraw-Hill Book Company, 1976), p. 180.

19. Irving J. Lee, *How to Talk with People* (New York: Harper & Row, Publishers, 1952), p. 46.

20. Gerald M. Philips, *Communication and the Small Group,* 2nd ed. (Indianapolis: The Bobbs-Merrill Company, 1973), p. 145.

21. Dale G. Leathers, "Belief-Disbelief Systems: The Communicative Vacuum of the Radical Right," in C. J. Stewart, D. J. Ochs, and G. P. Mohrman, eds., *Explorations in Rhetorical Criticism* (University Park, Pa.: The Pennsylvania State University Press, 1973), pp. 127–31.

22. Gordon Allport, *The Nature of Prejudice* (Garden City, New York: Doubleday, 1958), p. 9.

23. V. C. Troldahl and F. A. Powell, "A Short Form Dogmatism Scale for Use in Field Studies," *Social Forces* 44 (1965), pp. 211–14.

24. Robert N. Bostrom, "Patterns of Communicative Interaction in Small Groups," *Speech Monographs* 37 (1970), pp. 257–63.

25. R. M. Williams and M. L. Mattson, "The Effects of Social Groupings upon the Language of Pre-School Children," *Child Development* 13 (1942), pp. 233–45; B. P. Indik, "Organization Size and Member Participation: Some Empirical Tests of Alternatives," *Human Relations* 18 (1965), pp. 339–50.

26. Robert F. Bales et al., "Channels of Communication in Small Groups," *American Sociological Review* 16 (1951), pp. 461–68.

27. E. F. Stephan and E. G. Mishler, "The Distribution of Participation in Small Groups," *American Sociological Review* 17 (1952), pp. 598–608.

28. James A. Schellenberg, "Group Size As a Factor in Success of Academic Discussion Groups," *Journal of Educational Psychology* 33 (1959), pp. 73–79.

29. See bibliography for research sources that support these generalizations.

30. E. B. Smith, "Some Psychological Aspects of Committee Work," *Journal of Abnormal and Social Psychology* 11 (1927), pp. 348–68, 437–64.

31. Philip E. Slater, "Contrasting Correlates of Group Size," *Sociometry* 21 (1958), pp. 129–39.

32. Clovis R. Shepherd, *Small Groups* (San Francisco: Chandler Publishing Company, 1964), p. 4.

33. Herbert A. Thelen, *Dynamics of Groups at Work* (Chicago: University of Chicago Press, 1954), p. 187.

4 input variables: physical environment and informational resources

Study Objectives

As a result of studying chapter 4, you should be able to:

1. Explain the impact of room size and decorations, seating arrangements, furnishings, and other environmental factors on small group members and communication among them.

2. Make appropriate physical arrangements for a small group meeting.

3. List and explain a procedure for locating, gathering, evaluating, and organizing information needed for a small group discussion.

4. Distinguish between statements of fact and statements of inference.

5. Evaluate the importance, validity, and probability of information and opinions bearing on the subject of a discussion.

6. Understand the importance of organizing your stock of information prior to engaging in discussion, and how to do so.

Key Terms

Assumption a belief that is taken for granted, and used in reasoning *as if* it were a statement of fact without checking for evidence of its truthfulness.

Bibliography a list of readings or print sources, including books, journals, magazines, research papers, pamphlets, newspapers, etc., bearing on a given topic, problem, or issue.

Fact, statement of a description of a specific event that was observed by some person, often including in the statement when, how, and by whom the observation was made; may be either true or false.

Implication a statement that is a logical derivative, extension, or conclusion of a belief or opinion.

Inference, statement of any statement that includes more than a description of some event, involving some degree of uncertainty and probability; cannot be checked for truth or falsity by observation.

The physical environment in which a small group finds itself and the information and ideas available for processing by the group make a vast difference in the process of discussion and the outcomes of it. Although the most ideal of settings and facilities cannot produce effective and satisfying discussions, inadequate settings can greatly interfere with group processes. If adequate physical arrangements have been made, the group can accomplish a great deal if the members are adequately armed with informational resources.

The Physical Environment

For many years researchers have investigated the general hypothesis that the characteristics of a room influences individual behavior and group interaction. An ugly room with stark gray walls, a bare light bulb, junk lying around, and hard floors evoked such responses as fatigue, headaches, irritability, and hostility. A room with warm beige walls, draperies, windows, comfortable furniture, and adequate lighting evoked feelings of pleasure, importance, comfort, and a desire to remain in the room.[1]

The size of a room has an effect on how closely group members will sit to each other. Sommer found an inverse relationship between room size and distance between conversants: as the size of the room is increased, the distance people choose to have between them decreases.[2] It seems likely from this finding that a small group can meet just as well in a fairly large room as in a small one if the room is attractive, comfortable, and free of distractions. My personal experience indicates that this is so.

It is very important that group meeting rooms be free from distractions and provide privacy. Listening to fellow discussants is taxing enough, without the competing stimuli of a television set in the background, non-members moving in and out of a room, pets, and similar distractions. Numerous students have reported that meeting in each others homes is often unproductive, for babies, spouses, and pets frequently interrupt their work. Sometimes overstuffed furniture is so relaxing that tired members doze off. Most groups report that meeting in a quiet room on campus or a simple apartment seems to work best for them.

Seating arrangements are especially important to productive discussions. Hare and Bales found that the way chairs are placed in a room influences the pattern of interaction.[3] When seated in a circle, members tend to talk most often to those opposite them rather than to those sitting on either side. If the group has a very dominant leader, persons will tend to get into side-bar conversations with those seated next to them. At a rectangular table, such as is frequently found in a meeting room, persons at the corners contribute least to the discussion, whereas members of the group at the ends and central positions on the sides speak more often. Many groups expect a designated leader to sit at one end of a rectangular table. In my role as chairman of a small group I once tried sitting in a corner spot, only to discover that almost everyone showed signs of discomfort. I asked if the group wanted me to move to the end of the table; all said "yes," so I did move with an obvious improvement in the discussion. It seems to be a widely accepted norm that leaders should sit at the end of a long table. I once was asked what might facilitate more responses from members of a group of store managers who met periodically with top management to discuss corporate policies and problems they were encountering. They had a meeting room with two long tables arranged in a T, with the top managers sitting at the head table. I suggested putting the tables side by side to form a large square, and removing all corner chairs. Simple and obvious, but the president reported that this made a big improvement in subsequent meetings. One academic department I observed met in a typing room, with small tables in rows. I suggested arranging the tables in a rough circle. Again, the result was a great increase in participation and much more lively discussion from member to member without the chairperson seeming to be expected to remark after each member comment.

What guidelines can we derive from such research and observations? The optimum for private discussion is a circular seating arrangement with members seated close together. In most discussions, each member should also have a writing surface. If the group meets in a classroom with flexible seating, have the participants push chairs into a circle (or a semicircle where everyone can see the chalkboard). In a room with fixed seating, a few portable chairs can be brought in or some participants can sit sideways in their chairs in order to form a rough circle. If you have a long rectangular table, get the persons at the middle of each side to push their chairs out from the table, thus allowing for some eye contact between all members. If possible, do not seat anyone at the very corners of a square or rectangular table. A few small tables can be arranged to approximate a circle. See figure 4.1.

If group members are not well acquainted, each should be given a tag or "tent" on which to write or print his or her name. Satisfactory name tags can be made from 3″ by 5″ file cards, with the name printed with crayon or felt-tip pen, and held in place with a straight pin. A plain 5″ by 8″ file card makes a good name tent when folded lengthwise. It is printed on both sides and set in front of the discussant so all members of the group can readily read the name.

Adequate lighting, comfortable temperature, and ventilation should be provided in any meeting room. If smoking is permitted, each discussant should have easy access to an ashtray. However, before smoking begins it is important to determine if anyone is adversely affected by smoke, and if so there should be no smoking. Many persons will not participate in groups where smoking is allowed. A few will not attend meetings where smoking occurs. This issue should be settled when a group gets underway, at its first meeting.

Although it is not always possible, any problem-solving group can make good use of a chalkboard or easel with a pad of large plain paper for recording information, ideas, and questions. Other necessary equipment or supplies should be all ready to operate before a meeting begins so that getting it set up or distributed does not break in on the interaction: tape recorder, charts, projector and slides, pencils and note pads, etc.

Figure 4.1 Seating arrangements for discussion groups.

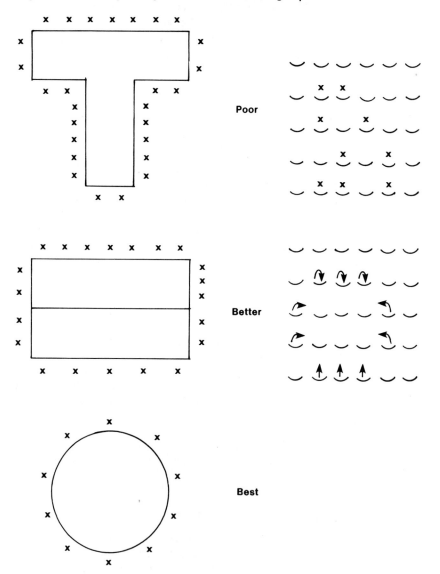

Poor

Better

Best

Figure 4.2   All ready for the committee to gather.

Informational Resources

Perhaps because we converse so readily in chance meetings with others, many persons look upon a forthcoming discussion as something for which no one (except possibly a designated leader) would prepare. This is a most counter-productive attitude. For most discussions, as in many ventures, to fail to prepare is to prepare to fail.

Effective discussion, like effective public speaking, grows out of depend-able knowledge and clear thinking, which can come only from preparation. Of course there are productive discussions for which nobody seems to have made specific preparations. But appearances here, as in many situations, are deceiving. Participating in such discussions are persons who by nature of their work, life and study are well prepared: a group of speech communication teachers discussing how to help students overcome reticence, graduate students in public administration talking about reforms needed in the city charter, or a group of dog fanciers talking about how to train their animals. Even the experts can do a better job if they prepare specifically.

Effective group discussion is never a pooling of ignorance. Every depend-able conclusion, solution, interpretation, or belief rests on dependable evidence and valid reasoning from the evidence. Half-informed participants can reach only half-informed decisions. The valuable participant has plumbed his subject deeply. Think for a moment of a group of college students trying to intelli-gently discuss such topics as capital punishment or the control of atomic arms without having first done extensive reading on the subject. Would you place credence in the conclusions of such a group?

How highly group members value the prepared, informed participant was shown in research on emergent leadership in leaderless discussion groups. Geier found that being perceived as uninformed was the greatest single reason why members of leaderless discussion groups were quickly eliminated from any bid for major influence in the group.[4] You simply can't bluff for long in a group that is at all informed and critical of information and ideas. Group members are well advised to make serious individual efforts to be well informed.

Groups are frequently plagued by playboys who keep telling irrelevant jokes or pulling the group off the topic. Such nuisances are almost always poorly informed. One promotor of study-discussion programs advocated this policy: "If anyone has not read the materials, he is not permitted to speak unless to ask a question." Needless to say, this policy produced prepared participants and satisfying discussions. Many study-discussion leaders report that when the participants have not prepared, the ensuing discussion is listless, disorganized, shallow, and frustrating. Many students in my small group communication courses have reported in case studies of their project groups that little progress was made until finally everyone did the research needed. Then a lot was accomplished in a short time with the needed information now available.

Not only do discussants need information if their groups are to be effective, but it must be relevant, accurate, valid, and as complete as possible. This means that tests of the quality of information must be applied both while preparing for and participating in discussions. The evidence on which decisions are reached may include such nonverbal materials as maps, photos, and objects (e.g., sample products, weapons, tools), and such verbal materials as statements of fact, opinion, and policy. How reliable and valid the information may be is crucial in deciding whether or not to use it—an out-of-date map, a "salted" ore sample, a biased set of statistics, an uninformed opinion, an untested bit of advice, or an outdated concept (e.g., "women belong in the home") can lead to very poor group decisions indeed!

The contrast between being uninformed and informed was discovered by a group of students at a large university. They began attacking the university food service, with a host of complaints about what was wrong and what should be done to improve it. Fortunately, they soon realized that they knew very little about the facts of the subject except for what they had seen and heard as students and customers. Thus, they decided to conduct a careful investigation. The labor was divided among the group members, some studying menu planning, others studying food preparation, others looking into costs, and others investigating food service at other schools. Information was gathered from home economists, dieticians, food service employees, journals, and books. At the next meeting this group of informed students pooled their knowledge, and came to the conclusion that they had the finest food service of any university in their section of the country, that meals were reasonably priced, that menus were better planned than most family diets, and that many of the complaints were due to ignorance or to misuse of the food service by students.

The problem soon changed to, "How can we get the students at our university to appreciate the excellence of our food service, and to take better advantage of it?" They also made a few recommendations for minor improvements in the food service, all based on the facts of the case. These suggestions were well received by the man in charge of the service, who expressed his appreciation and put several of the group's suggestions into effect.

Since valid information is so important to productive small group discussion, the question now becomes "What can we do to gather the information we need as a group?" The answer will depend in part on the purpose of the group and the knowledge already in possession of the members. A general procedure for locating information, evaluating and organizing it is presented next. The steps are presented in the order in which they should be taken for a minimum of wasted effort and time. This procedure may be modified somewhat if you are well versed in the problem area, but none of these steps can be omitted without a possible loss in group effectiveness: (1) review and organize your present stock of information and ideas on the subject; (2) gather needed information; (3) evaluate the information and ideas you have now collected; and (4) organize the information and ideas into a tentative outline.

1. Review and Organize Your Present Stock of Information and Ideas

Undoubtedly you already have some information and experience on the subject, or you would not be discussing it. Taking a systematic inventory of this knowledge can save you much time in preparation, and will enable you to recall what you need when you need to. To begin reading at this point would be wasteful and inefficient.

a. Place the problem or subject in perspective. To what is it related? What will it affect, or by what is it affected? For example, in trying to plan a scholarship program for a corporation, one should consider the corporation's financial condition, long-range plans, obligations to the community, public relations, types of employees, and the like.

b. Make an inventory of what you know about the subject. An approach that may help you recall is to list courses taken, jobs held, reports, firsthand experiences, articles read, books, ideas, and so forth. Additional headings will suggest themselves as you proceed. These headings can be put on sheets of scratch paper. Then jot down in brief form everything that comes to mind. Let your mind be "freewheeling," without being concerned with the degree of importance, relevance, or even validity.

c. Organize your information into a problem-solving outline. This can be in a rough pencil draft. Look over your notes for main issues, topics, or questions about the problem, being guided by a model outline suggested in chapter 8.

d. Look for deficiencies. Your outline of information will reveal what you do *not* know, where specific information is needed, and which ideas or opinions are unsupported.

2. *Gather Needed Information*

You are now ready to plan research to correct deficiencies in your knowledge and thinking.

Some group members I have observed acted as if once the question or problem had been announced they could just begin looking for evidence in any way and place, and expect to gain the resources needed for effective group work. Whatever the members happened to find in recent magazines, newspapers, and encyclopedias was taken as if it were necessarily valid and sufficient. Further, the group had no system for obtaining needed information and ideas; its "research" was very haphazard. The result of such a haphazard preparation is "garbage in" informational resources and "garbage out" types of conclusions and learnings. A systematic procedure for gaining informational inputs will usually prevent such an undersirable outcome.

A group cannot deal with a major problem or assignment in one meeting. Even if the members have known about the topic or problem in advance, their individual stocks of information and ideas are likely to be very uneven, and their research to date quite full of gaps. Some areas of relevant knowledge will have been looked into by everyone but others totally overlooked. Complicated problems and topics require at least two meetings, and usually several. Recall the example presented in chapter 2 of the committee of professors charged with drafting a college constitution. In addition to clarifying the area of freedom and overall goals of a small group, part of the initial meeting should be devoted to planning how to obtain needed information in the most efficient way possible likely to produce a comprehensive picture of what is known on the subject at this time.

First, the group should indentify *and list* as many as possible of the issues and topics they will need to explore. Second, the group should assess the adequacy of their collective knowledge and then determine what is needed, thus preparing a list of topics for research. As Harnack, Fest, and Jones say, "Groups more often err on the side of too little evidence; but it is also important to remember that it is never possible to gather all the evidence there is.[5]" Third, the group should assign research responsibilities to members. This step is frequently overlooked as a way of preventing inefficiency and gaps in knowledge acquisition. Individual assignments will also increase individual responsibility and commitment.[6] The best way to make assignments is to let members choose from the list of topics and sources, with the group's secretary keeping a list of who has undertaken each task. A definite date should be established for each person or sub-group to have their findings ready to report.

As a general rule, all members should do some common background study and two or more persons should examine every major article, book, or other source. This will help to offset individual perceptual biases. If each member is a specialist with no one to check his or her findings and interpretations, many errors could creep into the group's understanding of the available information. If a member does not do a competent job of investigating and reporting, the group will suffer greatly from incorrect or inadequate information. Group "experts" also tend to dampen interaction on a topic when they are the only member with detailed knowledge on it. Of course, while you are looking up the source you have been assigned you may run across other relevant items, and would record these and bring them to the attention of the group.

Once you have a list of topics or sources, you are ready to begin your detailed personal preparation. We will review only briefly the means for getting information and recording it, for this topic has probably been covered previously in your speech and composition classes.

Information and ideas slip from memory or twist themselves in recall unless we make *accurate* and *complete* notes. Carrying books, magazines, and recordings to a discussion would at best be clumsy, and you might get so lost in the mess that you distract your group.

The best system of note-taking is to record each bit of information or idea on a separate 3″ by 5″ note card. Put a topic heading on the card, followed by the specific subject. Then list exact details of the source, just as you would for a bibliography. Finally, record the information, idea, or quotation. Figure 4.3 shows how to do this.

The note cards provide both accuracy and flexibility. One can arrange them in various groups as one synthesizes and interprets the evidence collected. They can be consulted with ease during discussion without having to leaf through a disorganized notebook. Full reference data permit others to evaluate the credibility of the evidence. It is virtually useless to say something appeared in *The New York Times* or *Newsweek* or "a book by some psychologist." Information may come from many sources, of which three types are most likely to be important in preparing for group discussion: (1) direct observation, (2) reading, and (3) interviews.

Figure 4.3 Note card example.

PREPARING TO DISCUSS   Get General Understanding First

    Harnack, R. Victor, and Fest, Thorrel B., *Group Discussion: Theory and Technique.* New York: Appleton-Century-Crofts, 1964, pp. 118-19.
    "Unless the member is already rather thoroughly acquainted with the nature of the problem to be solved, he ought to spend some time investigating the nature of the overall problem before he begins looking for the specific evidence that is his assignment. . . . Looking at the whole problem will help the individual in three ways. First, he will be better able to fit his specific assignment into the total picture. Second, he will be prepared to understand and evaluate the contributions made by others with different assignments. Third, he may discover some evidence or ideas that may have escaped the notice of those investigating the other aspects of the problem."

input variables: physical environment
and informational resources
    75

Direct Observation

Many times information that is needed can come only from some first-hand observation by members of a group, and often first-hand observation is needed to give a sense of realism to the symbolic information available in surveys, tables of statistics, and other print sources. For example, a group that had the goal of developing a plan for making decent housing available to low-income persons might find a plethora of information in print, but still would benefit from direct observation of the actual residences of such persons in the slums and ghettos of a city, and of the kinds of housing available at different prices. In Omaha a commission to look at potential sites for government subsidized housing found it necessary to visit proposed building sites even though they had available maps and reports of what was available. Before discussing how to reduce parking problems on a campus you might need to observe the parking lots over a period of time. A group of students desiring to improve conditions in a self-service coffee shop of a student union spent some time observing what was happening there at various times throughout the day. They recorded the number of persons who did and did not bus their waste materials, the kinds and amount of litter on the floor and tables, the placement and condition of waste containers, and the signs encouraging users to keep the room clean. Another group could get information on how uncut weeds and trees were obscuring traffic control signs only by systematically observing a large number of intersections. A small group can decide if first-hand observation is called for, then assign the task to members most interested in doing this work of information gathering.

Reading

For many topics and problems the major pool of informational resources will be found in books, journals, newspapers, government documents, and other printed pages. Before an individual or small group begins reading and taking notes, it is important to get a perspective on what print resources are likely to yield information on an issue: the number, type, and quality of the sources. To do that, you will need to compile a *bibliography,* which is a list of published works relevant to a particular topic, problem, or issue. Ideally, you would locate and evaluate all the recent printed information that was relevant before making any final decision about the nature and extent of a problem. That is not always possible, but most certainly you should not limit reading to only one or two sources. Likewise, you would want to read from sources that espoused all points of view, not just one side of a controversial issue. To do so will produce a strong bias in your information, with no way to cross-check the truth and validity of what you read.

To be as efficient as possible in compiling a bibliography, first prepare a list of key terms—"descriptors"—bearing on the topic to guide your search for print items. A reference librarian can often be of considerable help in doing this. A number of major bibliographies, indexes, and compilations of abstracts are now in computer programs, each of which has an entire thesaurus of key term descriptors. You may have access to such a service to help your group gain material on a subject. If not, your group or individual list of terms will provide a fine starting point, and as you proceed to gather items from the library other key terms will be discovered. For example, in preparing to discuss "What type of lottery, if any, should our state conduct?" the key words you first used might include: lottery, sweepstakes, gambling, crime, revenue, tax, and betting. As you began to search specialized bibliographies and read articles you might locate other terms to help your search, such as "victimless" and "wagering."

A good library manual, available at virtually every college or university library, is a great help in building a bibliography and locating materials. You may find help in bibliographies of bibliographies, which list special published bibliographies by topic, such as: *A World Bibliography of Bibliographies and of Bibliographic Catalogues . . . , Bibliographical Index,* and *Bulletin of Bibliography and Magazine Notes.* Bibliographies will be found at the end of many books, doctoral dissertations (see *Dissertation Abstracts* to locate these), and research articles. The subject section of the card catalog of the library may reveal books not previously located. You can locate materials in magazines, journals, and newspapers with such special indexes as: *The Reader's Guide to Periodical Literature, Applied Science and Technology Index, The Education Index,* and *The New York Times Index.* Do not overlook publications by federal and state governments. Most libraries have special sections of such material. Most helpful in locating relevant information in these publications in the *Monthly Catalog of U.S. Government Publications,* followed by the *Monthly Checklist of State Publications.*

Even while you are compiling a bibliography you can begin reading, and all members of the group should read some of the same things in order to provide a common background. As we shall see in the final section of the book, learning discussion depends on all having read or otherwise shared the same sources. It is especially important when reading for information bearing on a "fact-finding" or "policy" problem that you read efficiently. Often you can read an abstract or summary of an article, thus determining whether or not you need to read the entire thing for details. Instead of reading an entire book, look in the index and table of contents for clues to what is pertinent. Skim rapidly until you find something of value to your group's special purpose. Then read carefully, taking notes of the most important ideas and facts. You may even want to make copies of certain passages or articles to share with other members of your group.

While reading in preparation for a learning discussion of a controversial issue you should read from as many contrasting interpretations or points of view as possible. Before discussing the relative merits of capital punishment, for example, you should study the writings of both those who favor and those who oppose it. *To learn, we must consider that which does not conform to our present beliefs.* We must perceive, accept, and adapt to new information and thinking. This is very difficult to do. We tend to listen to persons who believe as we do and to read only that which supports our present beliefs and values. We tend to be undercritical of such sources, and to be overly critical of sources that contradict us. It has been shown that we tend to forget evidence or beliefs inconsistent with our own.[7]

When a learning discussion is planned to explore poetry, try reading it aloud to yourself. See how much of it you can interpret, and notice any feelings you experience while reading. Notice how it is constructed. Make notes of questions you have and of stanzas that puzzle you. Then go to the meeting in a mood of inquiry, ready to discover and share.

Interviews

When you can observe only a small part of an entire operation (for example, a nuclear reactor or the operation of a farm) or when you are not sufficiently knowledgeable to observe meaningfully, you may need to interview persons who are trained observers, highly experienced, and have firsthand contact with your subject. Members of the group that observed the operation of the campus coffee shop also interviewed a number of users to determine how they felt about its condition and to ask their reasons for busing or not busing their cups, waste paper, and leftover food. They also interviewed the manager to determine why certain materials that were sources of litter were being used. Members of the faculty constitution committee asked friends at other universities about how they thought their constitutions had worked in practice. Members of the bargaining team to which I belong have interviewed several highly experienced experts for advice not available in print about specific tactics and strategies. However, remember that busy persons who have written down their knowledge and ideas would prefer that you read first, then interview them to clarify or gather only information and ideas not yet publicly available.

If only a few persons need to be consulted, members of a group may want to conduct an in-depth interview with several open-ended questions designed to obtain responses bearing on the problem or topic. Open-ended questions will often elicit unexpected information that the interviewer would not have obtained in response to limited questions. If several group members will be interviewing a larger number of persons, each interviewer should have the same set of questions to ask, with forms on which to record the answers. If the questions have been properly planned the results can be tabulated and easily interpreted. For example, study the questions asked and the summary of answers reported in a newspaper carrying one of the national polls (such as those conducted by Gallup or Harris). One group of discussion students did a project to discover differences between first dates of approximately thirty years ago and today. They selected a sample of interviewees from two age groups, then asked all these persons the same set of questions:

1. Do you remember your first date? Yes _____ No _____

2. How old were you at the time of your first date? _____

3. How did you first become acquainted with the person you dated?

4. Was this a solo or double date?

5. If you remember, what did you do on this date?

6. Did you get a kiss on this date? Yes _____ No _____

Other Sources of Information

Useful information may crop up anywhere, anytime. You may hear something important to your forthcoming discussion while listening to a radio or television program. Quite frequently lectures or speeches will be a source of information. An idea may occur to you when you are not consciously thinking about the problem—for example, while riding to work or school. You may be able to direct a conversation with friends to the problem your group is working on and thus get some surprising and helpful information and ideas. Most of us find it helpful to carry some sort of note-taking materials so we can jot down these things when they occur, lest we forget or distort them. The important thing is to be alert for unexpected and serendipitous information, and to record it promptly.

3. Evaluate the Information and Ideas You Have Collected

You will need to evaluate the information and ideas you have gathered in the light of all you have learned through individual research of the problem or subject for discussion. Many of your ideas may collapse in the presence of contradictory evidence. Some of your information may be spurious, from suspect sources, or in direct contradiction to other information. Some will be irrelevant to the problem facing the group. Now is the time to cull the misleading, false, suspect, unsubstantiated, or irrelevant so you will not misinform, confuse, or delay your group.

Distinguish between Statements of Fact and Inferences

It is especially important, both in gathering data and evaluating it during discussion, to distinguish between statements of fact and statements of inference, opinion, advice, preference, or definition.

The major difference between statements of fact and all other types of statements is that factual statements are *true* or *false* in a special sense of these terms. *A statement of fact* is a declarative sentence that refers to an *observation* of some event in the world. The event is described, and the statement includes or implies a method of observing by which the statement could be tested for truth or accuracy. It is a *true* statement of fact if accurate to the observed events, and can only refer to a *past* event actually observed. Facts either exist or do not exist; they are not discussable as such. The truth or validity of such a statement may or may not be directly verifiable. If the statement refers to a presently ongoing situation accessible to the group, it can be verified. If not, only the presence of the statement can be verified (that is, if the statement refers to something that is not continuing or is not accessible to the group). For example, we could not verify that George III occupied the throne of England in 1773—only that records indicate he was king. However, if several independent sources report the same information as fact, you can be more confident than if it comes from only one unverified source. You might not be able to directly verify the population of Australia, but only what the census report at a given date revealed. As benchmarks to help you recognize them, statements of fact:

are limited to description;

can be made only *after* observation;

are limited in the number that can be made;

if primary, can be made only by a direct observer;

are as close to certain as humans can get.

On the other hand, statements of opinion and inference:

go *beyond* what was directly observed;

can be made at any time without regard to observation;

are unlimited in the number that can be made about anything;

can be made by anyone, observer or not;

entail some degree of probability, of inferential risk, or uncertainty.

Statements of advice, taste, or preference do not refer to direct observation, but report a personal liking, choice, value, or taste of someone.

A few examples may help to clarify these differences:

Statements of Fact:
The population of Omaha recorded in the 1970 census was 363,421.
On June 3, 1976, Jack Egrat owned two cats.
Three men with guns held up the Bank of Ralston on May 20, 1970, and escaped with $5,200.

Statements of Opinion and Inference:

Omaha is growing rapidly.

Jack Egart likes cats.

The heart of a good university is its (library, faculty, standards).

We should legalize gambling to reduce the state tax.

You will get to New York from Cleveland by following I-80 (not if you have a wreck!).

Evaluating Survey and Statistical Data

Factual-type statements including statistics or the results of surveys need to be evaluated with special care for dependability. Surveying is a highly sophisticated operation, and must be done correctly or the results can be very misleading. If the results are not based on a random or other scientific sample, the results of a survey are quite likely to be misleading. How questions are asked, and by whom, can make a very large difference in the results.[8]

Pay careful attention to statistics. Is the method explained by which the data used in computing the statistics were gathered? Is the method of computing averages or trends described and appropriate? Unless one of your group members is trained in statistical methods, before you accept statistical data as the basis for an important conclusion you should try to get a researcher/statistician to interpret and evaluate such information to avoid drawing erroneous conclusions. Unfortunately, persons sometimes lie when they write up "information," and some writers are not capable of evaluating their own reasoning from limited information.

Evaluating the Sources and Implications of Opinions

Occasionally a student, when first introduced to the differences between statements of fact and of opinion, tends to act as if statements of opinion are unwise or unnecessary in a discussion. Hardly so! As was said before, facts as such are not even discussable, but provide the basis for our discussions of what to do, what values to accept, etc. A group must not only deal with the world as it has been observed, but also determine priorities of value, ethics, goals, and procedures acceptable to all. Inference must be made as to what will probably happen *if* we adopt each possible course of action. The facts regarding combustion pollution as they affect the environment and the use of resources must be examined, but what to do depends on values, opinions, and judgments acceptable to all if a rational law is to be adopted.

Unexamined opinions are poor guides to belief or action. Statements of inference and opinion cannot be tested for truth or falsity by direct observation as can statements of fact, but they can be evaluated for the degree of probability that they are valid and useful. First, you will want to consider the source of the opinion.

1. Is this person (or other source) a recognized expert on the subject? How do other experts in the field regard the person who expressed the opinion? If they hold differing opinions, how might these be explained?
2. Does the source have a vested interest that might have influenced this opinion? For example, think of the different opinions about whether or not the government should supply special funds to help a large corporation avoid bankruptcy that might be reached by an executive of the corporation, a labor leader of a union whose members work in the plants of the company, a politician trying to impress his constituents with how much he is reducing government spending, and an independent economist.
3. How well does the source support his or her opinion with documented evidence? Is the evidence well organized, with supporting statistics, tables, and clear reasoning?
4. How consistent is this opinion with others expressed by the source? If the statement is not consistent with other opinions and predictions from the same person, is there an acceptable explanation for the change?

Second, consider the *implications* of the opinion. To what further inferences or conclusions does it logically lead, and are these acceptable to the group? For example, a writer may argue that outlawing private ownership of handguns would protect us from accidents and murderers. What are the implications of this opinion? That dangerous devices should not be allowed in the hands of citizens at large? That only unessential dangerous tools that could be used as murder weapons should be restricted? That eventually all potential weapons of murder should be removed from citizens? That less innocent persons would be killed if handguns were taken from the public? Another writer may argue that anyone should be allowed to own a handgun after demonstrating competence in handling it safely and correctly and if the person has no felony record. What are the implications of that opinion? That only convicted felons will use handguns to kill other persons? That most accidents would be prevented if persons knew how to handle guns safely? That handguns are useful to many persons? Still another may argue that legislation controlling handgun ownership is not needed, but that stringent and certain punishment should be meted out to anyone using a handgun in the commission of a crime; that this would solve the "real problem" without creating new problems. What are the assumptions of this position? That the threat of certain punishment is an effective deterrent? That killings by handguns are acts of only criminal "types"? Probably you can detect many implications of each of the above opinions. The point is this—when a group decision depends on opinions, it is most important to *test* these opinions, especially for what they assume and imply. To do so is the essence of discussion. Not to do so is to assure very poor group decisions and policies.

4. *Organize Your Information and Ideas*

The most efficient and useful way to organize your knowledge is to write a tentative outline, using either a sequence for problem solving (see chapter 8) or one of the patterns for organizing a learning discussion (chapter 11). Ask yourself "What are the questions that must be answered by our group to arrive at a full understanding of the problem or subject?" The answers you are able to give to that question will serve as tentative main issues or points in your preparation outline.

With some tentative major issues you can now arrange your notes into piles, one per issue or possible outline heading. You may be able to further sub-divide some of the piles of notes into sub-headings. For example, information bearing on the nature of a problem might be arranged under the broad topics of "who is affected," "seriousness of the problem," "where the problem exists," "contributing causes," and so on. Organizing your information in such a way will give you a good idea of what is more or less important, suggest how to write your preparation outline, make it easier for you to locate pertinent notes when a topic comes up during the discussion, help you in preparing to ask questions that the group needs to consider, and generally assist you and your group in maintaining an orderly and comprehensive discussion of a complex subject.

When you are preparing for a problem-solving discussion your outline may contain some possible solutions you have found or thought of; doubtless it should. You may have some evidence and reasoning that shows how similar solutions were tried on similar problems. You may even have some suggestions on how to put a plan into effect, how to check to see if it works, and how to make adjustments. However, such thinking and planning is tentative. The worst sort of preparation is to go to a group discussion prepared to advocate a particular solution against all comers. Just as bad is to feel that one's personal definition and understanding of the problem is the complete problem. If researching and outlining make a participant closed-minded, it is better to remain ignorant. At least an ignorant person will not deadlock the group, and perhaps will listen and learn from others. Remember that the experts in almost any field, the persons at the very frontier of knowledge, are the least dogmatic and sure of themselves. From these persons the discussant who has read widely, thought long, and made a detailed outline should take heed. At the best he or she will now be prepared to contribute some reliable information, some ideas for testing in the forge of the group's collective knowledge and thinking, and perhaps most important, to listen with more understanding, to ask knowing questions, and thus to help shape an image of and a solution to the problem.

When preparing for learning discussion you may or may not need to prepare an outline. Sometimes a study outline is supplied by a teacher or discussion moderator. For most academic discussions an outline will be quite helpful as a means to pre-sorting and clarifying your knowledge and thinking. Regardless, you will get much more from the discussion as well as be prepared to give more to your fellow learners-through-discussion if you write down the following kinds of items as they occur to you while doing any reading or other preparation:

Significant issues for the group to discuss;
Controversial points of view or policies that the group should examine;
Passages that are unclear, and any questions you want to raise;
How a proposition of a writer relates to his or her personal life and
    experience;
Any other related information or experience that comes to mind.

Summary

In this chapter we have examined two major types of input variables to the process of effective small group discussion—the physical setting and informational resources. A setting conducive to discussion is free from distractions, is comfortable, provides discussants with a clear view of each other, reflects the egalitarian relationship among participants, and includes facilities that might be needed for group recording and individual notes.

But the most ideal physical facilities can only set the stage for a discussion. Adequate informational resources are the grist for the mill of discussion, and the end products can be no better than the information and ideas put into the discussion. Such resources come from discussants who have made the effort to be well armed with information, ideas, and questions. Groups dealing with extensive problems need to devote initial planning to how they will obtain such materials and assign responsibility for their acquisition. Members can begin by reviewing and organizing what they already know. Then they will need to compile a bibliography of sources and to do the observing, reading, interviewing, note-taking, and outlining required to obtain, evaluate, and organize information. A preparation outline will usually make it possible to gain perspective on a large mass of information, raise needed questions, and help locate notes when they are relevant to the issues being discussed. To fail to prepare thoroughly for discussions is to prepare to fail in achieving the objectives for which they are held.

Exercises

1. Plan how to arrange your regular classroom (or other meeting room) for a problem-solving discussion by the entire class. Then make a diagram for seating members of your class for three or four simultaneous small group discussions in the same room.

2. Your instructor may give you an essay or a segment of a discussion to analyze for statements of fact, inference, and taste or value. Classify each statement as to type; ignore statements that do not fit into any of

these three categories. If you classify a statement as one of fact, indicate whether or not it could be verified, and how such verification could be accomplished.

3. In class, select a topic or problem of interest to all. Then:
    a. Prepare a bibliography of references on the topic, keeping a record of all the bibliographic sources you used;
    b. Prepare yourself to discuss the subject, including a detailed outline and the note cards from all the sources you consulted. These may be submitted to your instructor following the discussion. Be sure your outline contains all the questions you can think of that must be answered by the group to fully understand the problem, arrive at common goals and values, and reach a decision.

4. Observe and evaluate a discussion (perhaps in fishbowl fashion in your classroom) for the amount of information, the quality of the information, the consistency of the statements of opinion expressed by each participant, and the implications of the values expressed.

5. Take several statements of opinion and value, and for each write out any (1) assumptions on which it rests and (2) any implications of the statement. Compare the assumptions you detected and the implications you drew from each statement with the lists of these prepared by several classmates in a small group discussion. What conclusions can your group make as guidelines for testing statements of opinion and value?

    Your instructor may choose to take the statements from a recording of your actual discussions at an earlier date, from the list below, or some other source.
    "Country-western music is better than rock."
    "Natural wood makes better paneling than does fiberboard."
    "X-rated films should not be shown on television."
    "Physical assaults and killings are more obscene than any sex practices of consenting adults."
    "Religion is essential to a wholesome life."
    "Any person who is conscious should have the right to die when he or she chooses."
    "No more nuclear power plants should be built in the United States."

6. The same discussion group should meet in three very different settings over a short time span (one or two days), with different seating, room size, lighting, etc. Then report your observations of the effects of the environment in a short paper or as a journal entry; summarize findings in each small group of your class, and have a member of each group report the group's findings to the entire class. This may also be done for different seating arrangements and distances among discussants in the regular classroom.

Bibliography

Babbie, Earl R., *The Practice of Social Research,* 2nd ed., Belmont, Cal.: Wadsworth Publishing Company, 1979, chapter 12.

Huff, Darrel C., *How to Lie with Statistics*, New York: W. W. Norton & Company, 1954.

References

1. J. Bilodeau and H. Schlosberg, "Similarity in Simulating Conditions As a Variable in Retroactive Inhibition," *Journal of Experimental Psychology* 41 (1959), pp. 199–204; A. Maslow and N. L. Mintz, "Effects of Esthetic Surroundings: I. Initial Effects of Three Esthetic Conditions upon Perceived 'Energy' and 'Well-Being' in Faces," *Journal of Psychology* 41 (1956), pp. 247–54; N. L. Mintz, "Effects of Esthetic Surroundings: II. Prolonged and Repeated Experience in a 'Beautiful' and an 'Ugly' Room," *Journal of Psychology* 41 (1956), pp. 459–66.
2. Robert Sommer, "The Distance for Comfortable Conversation: A Further Study," *Sociometry* 25 (1962), pp. 111–16.
3. A. Paul Hare and R. F. Bales, "Seating Position and Small Group Interaction," *Sociometry* 26 (1963), pp. 480–86.
4. John G. Geier, "A Trait Approach to the Study of Leadership in Small Groups," in Robert S. Cathcart and Larry A. Samovar, eds., *Small Group Communication: A Reader* (Dubuque: Wm. C. Brown Company Publishers, 1970), p. 414.
5. R. Victor Harnack, T. B. Fest, and B. S. Jones, *Group Discussion: Theory and Technique*, 2nd ed. (Englewood Cliffs, N.J.: Prentice-Hall, 1977), p. 119.
6. David M. Shaw, "Size of Share in Task and Motivation in Work Groups," *Sociometry* 23 (1960), pp. 203–8.
7. Sir Frederic Bartlett, *Thinking: An Experimental and Social Study* (New York: Basic Books, 1958).
8. If you are interested in reading about scientific sampling and survey procedures likely to produce results representative of a large population (such as the Gallup poll usually achieves), see Earl R. Babbie, *The Practice of Social Research*, 2nd ed. (Belmont, CA: Wadsworth Publishing Company, 1979), chapter 12.

5 process variables of the small group

Study Objectives

As a result of your study of chapter 5 you should become familiar with seven process variables that are major group dynamics, and be able to:

1. List and explain the phases that most small groups pass through, describe the kinds of behaviors and activities most prevalent at each phase, and be able to identify the phase of development of any group of which you are a member or observer.

2. Identify the sources of both primary and secondary tension, and suggest at least a few ways to control and reduce each type of tension.

3. Explain what is meant by the phrase "a group's role structure," and list and describe the types of behavioral functions that contribute to group achievement and those that are purely self-oriented.

4. Describe three communication networks common in small group discussion and the impact of each on output variables.

5. Explain some of the effects of status differences on group processes and outputs.

6. Identify and write the norms of a small group and the evidence of these, describe how norms are developed, and know how to change a detrimental norm.

7. Explain *cohesiveness*, list several ways of measuring the degree of cohesiveness among members of a small group, and be able to apply six techniques for enhancing the level of cohesiveness.

Key Terms

Behavioral function (behavior)   how an act or behavior of a small group member affects the group.

Cohesiveness   the degree of attraction members feel for the group; unity.

Fantasy chain   a series of statements by members of a discussion group in which they dramatize a story about other persons in other places and times, in order to create a social reality, norms, and shared values.

Network of communication   the interpersonal channels open to the flow of messages within a small group; collectively, who in the group may (or does) talk to whom.

Norm   a rule of conduct or guideline for behavior of members of a group.

Phase   stage in the development and history of a small group.

Primary tension   social unease that occurs when members of a new group first meet or at beginning of meetings of a long-term group.

Role   a pattern of behavior displayed by and expected of a member of a small group; a composite of the behavioral functions performed relatively frequently by a member.

Secondary tension   tension and discomfort experienced by members of a group from conflict over values, points of view, and alternative solutions.

Self-oriented behavior   any act of a small group member that is motivated by personal needs rather than the needs of the group.

Social or maintenance behaviors   member acts that primarily serve to reduce tensions, increase solidarity, and facilitate teamwork rather than accomplishing the work of the group.

Status   position of a member in the hierarchy of influence and power within a small group, a corollary of prestige; may be attributed on basis of personal characteristics, but must be earned on basis of performance in a continuing group.

Task behavior   any act of a member that primarily contributes to accomplishing the goal of that group.

Thus far we have considered some of the major input variables, the "raw materials" of the small group. In this chapter we begin to examine the process or "throughput" variables, i.e., characteristics of the functioning of the system. In a very real sense these are both process and output variables, for the development of functional processes is one of the major outputs of small group interaction. The focus in this chapter will be on the system level rather than on characteristics of the individual member. Member behaviors will be considered from the perspective of their meaning or effects on the processes of the small group as a whole.

In subsequent chapters some of the most important group process variables are dealt with in detail: communication, conflict management, decision making, problem solving, and leadership. In this chapter we will attempt to gain a more general understanding of the dynamics of small group interaction by looking at phase changes through time, status and roles of members, norms, and cohesiveness.

Phases Through Time

Researchers have studied how small human groups develop and change through time. As a general rule there are gradual changes in the way the group system functions, but some very abrupt changes can also be observed. Any demarcation into distinct phases is somewhat arbitrary: the decision of when a group has moved from one phase to another, and even of how many phases there may be, depends on the person doing the observing and classifying of phases or stages. However, all small groups do pass through several stages or phases in their life history, the exact sequence depending on the primary purpose of the group's interaction and other variables. Time is certainly an important variable for understanding any group.

Single-meeting groups differ from most committees and other types of groups that meet for several or more discussions. The one-meeting group has no chance to develop a history, regular procedures and rituals, or extensive norms and values. Except for previous contacts with other participants in different group contexts, there is little basis on which to predict each other's behavior. There is no future for the group, no need to build cohesiveness. Models of group emergence have little relevance. An assigned leader will usually be accepted willingly unless he or she is totally incompetent. With little time to spare, members usually accept the designated discussion leader's statements about the purpose and procedures for the meeting. If the leader has an agenda or outline to follow, the group will likely do so with gratitude.

When members know that they will be meeting numerous times, they will take much more time to get organized and will move through a series of phases in the life history of the group. First comes a *period of orientation* during which the group will not readily follow any outline for problem solving. Even though it may appear that the discussion is about facts of a problem, objectives, and possible alternatives, the real agenda item will be the development of a group structure: roles for members (especially, who will be our primary leader), norms to govern behavior, shared values, general procedures for decision making and problem solving, who will interact with whom and in what ways, shared objectives, and so forth. This period of time may seem like aimless milling around to an untrained observer. But after such relational issues have been resolved to some degree, the group will go into a *work* phase characterized by much compiling of information, suggesting of courses of action, and more or less open conflict until decisions emerge. Depending on the degree to which the group achieved a stable structure of roles, norms, and procedures, there may be continual cycling between serious work and problems of interpersonal relations, with the group seeming to have to begin anew at many meetings. Or it may move forward from problem to problem with great dispatch, spending little time on matters of value, procedure, roles, and interpersonal relations.

Invariably there will be some cycling through time between matters of work to be done and group maintenance (socioemotional relationships). Every problem-solving group has both task and social dimensions to be dealt with through discussion; these are virtually the same in an encounter group. By 1950 Bales had factored all group member behaviors as being primarily concerned with either task or socioemotional matters.[1] Tuckman found issues of group task and structure both continuing to occupy the group during its period of development. These are not totally separable, but the emphasis will shift from social relations to task as a group becomes more clearly organized through time.[2]

Tuckman reviewed a large number of studies of phases in the development of several types of small groups. From a wide variety of different phases described by observers of therapy, encounter, learning and problem-solving groups he synthesized a four-phase theory of group development applicable to all small groups. He chose rhyming words to stand for these four stages:[3]

Phase 1: **Forming**—During the initial stage a collection of people attempts to develop into a group with a sense of interdependence of purpose and membership; also called the "orientation" phase by several writers.
While "forming" is going on the discussants are sizing each other up, trying to decide how each will act and react, what the attitudes, skills and competencies of other members may be, and whether or not to make a personal commitment to the group. Collectively, there is likely to be much talking about goals, "where we are going." A structure of norms and roles (including leadership) begins to emerge.

Phase 2: **Storming**—During this phase the interaction is likely to be marked by a great deal of conflict about information, the nature of the task facing the group, and how to achieve it. At a different level this phase involves a struggle for power, influence and leadership roles. There will be considerable open resistance to influence by other members and what appear to be majorities, with few or no members appearing willing to accept and support the suggestions of others. It may seem that nothing is being accomplished with so much open conflict, but the groundwork for later cooperation and coordination is being laid.

Phase 3: **Norming**—In this phase the group works out definite ways of proceeding, guidelines or rules for member conduct, and standards for evaluating their decisions. There is likely to be much open expression of opinions, now marked by considerably more agreeing with each other than in phase 2. In place of strong positions of individuality common in phase 2 are efforts to reduce conflict. If the group is going to be productive, a structure of roles and statuses emerges, along with a high degree of cohesiveness.

Phase 4: **Performing**—Discussion will now be centered on the task of the group. A solution to the problem (if any) may emerge fairly quickly with consensus or majority support. There is likely to be a lot of rephrasing of the solution by various members of the group. If needed, plans for putting the solution into effect are worked out.

Tuckman's interests as a social psychologist and his objective of finding similar phases in the life histories of groups with divergent major purposes may have led him to label three of the four phases with words concerning social relations. Actually, productive task work, producing the groundwork for a final group solution, may be going on in these phases. In that sense "performing" is occurring to some degree in all phases of the group's life. The important thing for the beginning student of small group dynamics is to be aware that it is *typical* for groups to move through various stages, as it is for all human relationships, from a phase in which identification of common interests and a basis for cooperation and trust is laid down, to an exploration of various alternatives, to a period of time in which there is rapid goal achievement. Long-term groups will tend to spiral somewhat through these phases, going back over the periods of forming, storming, and norming from meeting to meeting, as new problems and members are introduced into the group system, and as other components of the small group system change through time. Such a spiralling through growth and work stages should be no surprise, for it is characteristic of all living systems as the cycles of the seasons, growth phases, and repeated environmental problems arise. Scheidel and Crowell showed that there is even a spiral-like progression during the time when many groups consider and evaluate each possible course of action as a solution to their problem.[4] This spiralling through phases is illustrated in figure 5.1, showing progressively shorter orientation phases (forming, storming, and norming) and relatively longer performing (task) stages as the group develops. The arrows intersecting the loops of the spiral represent the introduction of something new into the small group system.

Figure 5.1   The process of group development.

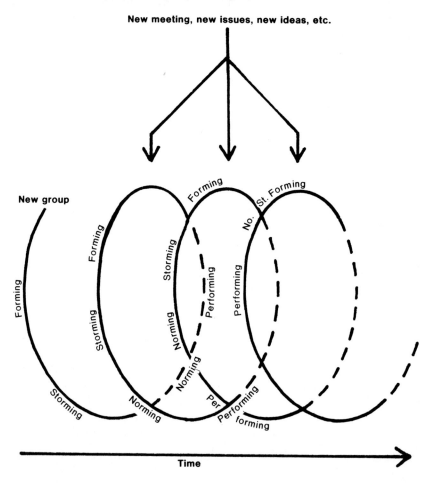

The tension experienced by members also varies through time, dependent upon handling of both social and task issues. When one feels tense, one may be irritable, ill at ease, and generally uncomfortable. Muscles are tightened in the face, neck, abdomen, hands, and even in the feet and legs. Headaches may develop if tension is not dealt with. Depending on the source, Bormann has labelled the two types of tension as *primary* and *secondary*.

Primary tension is his name for

the social unease and stiffness that accompanies getting acquainted. . . . The earmarks of primary tension are extreme politeness, apparent boredness or tiredness, and considerable sighing and yawning. When members show primary tension, they speak softly and tentatively. Frequently they can think of nothing to say, and many long pauses result.[5]

Members who are extremely affected by primary tension may pull back from the circle of others, look away from the group, or even read. Most such persons are apprehensive about meeting new persons, afraid of not being accepted, and have a negative self-concept.

Members of one-meeting groups cannot afford the time needed to get well acquainted with each other, but groups that will meet often may be wise to do so. Groups failing to do so, talking only about their work and the problems confronting them, often continue to be plagued by shyness, reticence, apparent apathy, absenteeism, and inability to reach decisions based on open and honest confrontation of ideas and beliefs. Very early in the life of a continuing group it pays to deal directly with primary tensions: take time to talk about who each person is, ask each other questions, air differences in feelings and backgrounds, chat about hobbies and interests, maybe even have a social hour or party. Don't expect members of a continuing group to get to work on the agenda at the very start of each new meeting, either. Even groups with considerable history experience some amount of primary tension at the start of each meeting. Members need to confirm where they stand with each other, to reaffirm their relationships, and that each is accepted as a unique individual. Thus a brief period of "ventilation," chitchat, or small talk is needed before getting down to work, often before the meeting is "called to order" by a designated leader.

Secondary tension results from differences among members as they try to accomplish their goals. Persons in a small group differ over their perception of a problem, over procedures for working as a group, over values of relative importance and goodness, over alternative means for achieving goals, and over who should do what for the group. The signs of tension from such conflicts are quite different from those of primary tension. Voices get loud and strained. There may be long pauses, followed by two or more persons trying to talk at once. Members twist and fidget in their seats, bang on the table, wave their arms, or even get up and pace around the room.

Every group must develop norms and procedures for reducing secondary tension. Once it is under control, a decision will usually emerge quickly, be confirmed by the group, and details of implementation will be worked out rapidly. Throughout its history a group will cycle from periods of high to low tension among members, and periods of high to low harmony and productivity in accomplishing the work of the group. Figure 5.2 represents such cycling in a hypothetical group. Above the dotted line are the periods of high tension, while periods of high productivity are below the dotted line. Some groups try to ignore secondary tensions because dealing with them is often very difficult, uncomfortable, or even painful. A group may dodge the issue of a clash over values or means to a goal.

They leave the touchy area of human relations and return to the safe area of doing the job. The problem, however, never goes away, and if ignored or dodged will continue to . . . impede their progress. Facing up to secondary tensions realistically is the best way to release them.[6]

Figure 5.2 The tension cycle in a hypothetical problem-solving group.

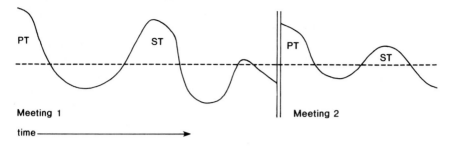

Meeting 1

time ⟶

Key: PT—primary tension
ST—secondary tension
- - - - level of tension, above which group is inefficient

This may mean discussing how members feel about each other, joking, and openly discussing each other's behavior, roles, and norms. It may take conciliating, compromising, or other techniques for resolving conflicts and disagreements. Some degree of tension is helpful, of course. Just as the individual is not productive when totally relaxed or hypertense, so with the group. Learning to maintain a productive level of tension, developing tension-reliever roles, and procedures for handling tension are keys to effective group discussion.

Role Structure

In a mature, fully-organized small group each member has a definite position or *role*. The concept of positions or roles in a small group is most clearly seen in an athletic group such as a basketball or baseball team. Each member has a set of definite responsibilities, plus more general ones to assist other members of the team as needed. All share to some degree in shooting or batting, and in the event one member is not able to perform optimally, members can often substitute for each other. Who plays each position is determined largely by the relative performance skills of all the members of the group. A discussion group with the task of problem solving or learning will in time develop almost as definite a structure of member roles as does an athletic team. This is accomplished through a sort of trial-and-comparison basis. Although certain socioemotional and procedural roles are needed in every small group, many of these and most of the task roles depend on the purpose and environment of the group. While a new group is forming, much effort will be spent in determining who can best perform the kinds of behaviors needed to unify and coordinate the activities of the members, and to accomplish the group's tasks. Some of the roles may change considerably in later phases of the group's life as new demands are made on the members from the environment, different stages of the problem-solving process, and partial changes in membership.

Some discussion groups have certain appointed or elected posts. For example, most committees have a designated chairperson who is responsible for such duties as calling meetings, planning agendas, coordinating the work of other committee members, and making reports to the parent organization. A committee may also have a designated secretary or recorder. Study-discussion groups invariably have a designated leader (or leaders) responsible for initiating and organizing the discussions; such groups may also have a host who supplies light refreshments. A board of directors will usually consist of the president, the treasurer, the secretary, and other officers of the parent organization, each of whom has certain definite functions to perform for the board as well as for the parent body.

For a small group to be effective, a stable set of roles (or division of labor) *must* emerge and be accepted by all members. Then each member can be expected to perform certain types of actions or tasks for the group. This is not to say that everyone plays a role totally different from everyone else, or that two or more members may not perform the same types of functions. Indeed, some behaviors—such as supplying needed information—may be widely shared among the members. But in the mature small group each person has a unique *set* of functions to perform, which combined with those of the other members provide for all the group's needs in discussing and doing its work. Any effective long-term group has specialists who can be counted on to act when their skills are needed for summarizing, testing ideas, managing conflicts, and so on. However, the group must not depend too much on these specialists, or else when they are absent no one else will be able to step in to perform those behaviors vital to the progress of the group.

Ideally, group members have considerable flexibility, and each can provide a wide variety of the behaviors useful to the group. Perhaps the ideal all-around discussants would be those who are so sensitive and versatile that they could diagnose what each group to which they belong needs from them, and perform those things. But no human being can be all things, so we tend to seek role profiles suited both to our skills and limitations and to the needs of each group. In a course concerned with small group communication you have an excellent laboratory for developing new behaviors to achieve greater flexibility in the roles you can perform in small groups.

The role a person has varies from group to group. For a minute think of several different small groups to which you have belonged—I bet you behaved very differently in some of these groups. You probably have noticed, also, that in some groups your role changed considerably through time as you changed, as new persons joined the group, and as the problems facing the group changed. A major principle of small group theory is this: *the role of each member of a group is worked out by interaction between the member and the rest of the group.* Hence the role structure is unique to each group—I have never seen any two groups in which the roles were even close to the same, anymore than they are in any two plays (it is from dramatic theory that we borrow the concept of role). What seems to happen is this: a member of a discussion group does something. If others respond favorably, that member is likely to do this sort of thing again, a response to previous positive reinforcement. Soon that type of behavior is a part of his or her role. If other members reject the behavior or do not respond favorably (negative reinforcement), the person will not be likely to act that way again. Gradually, from this pattern of selective reinforcement, a fairly stable set of roles emerges in the group, and members come to expect each other to behave in some ways and not in others. Of course a member who has been reinforced for proposing new ideas may not always be able to do so as the problems change, and members who have not previously been initiators of ideas may suddenly have experience leading them to try idea initiating. If positively reinforced, a new facet has been added to their roles. Roles do change somewhat.

In the study of member behaviors and roles, group researchers and theorists have developed numerous classification systems, all of them oversimplified. Each such set of roles or behaviors has some limited uses and inadequacies. For example, the most commonly cited is the *task* and *socioemotional* categories already referred to. But every communicative act in a group discussion has both content (task) and relationship (social) implications. If a member says, "Betty, why don't you get us some coffee?" she is both suggesting a task for Betty to perform *and* that she has a right to expect Betty to do what she asks (relationship). If I suggest that two members who are talking past each other in an excited argument about two different solutions (secondary tension being manifested) should listen more carefully, my statement although focused on their way of relating to each other, may also have a direct bearing on the task achievement of the group. And it not only implies a procedure for them to follow, but also that my role in relation to them is such that I have a right to suggest changes in their behavior. Every act in a discussion, then, can be viewed as having both a *task* and a *relational* aspect, probably with greater impact in one area than in the other. As shown in Figure 5.3, an act could have much impact on both dimensions, much on one and little on the other, much on both, or little on either.

A person's role in a small group is made up of many behaviors of various types. The complete role of an individual is a sort of summary of these types of behavior, reflective of the relative proportions of each. In the next section of this chapter I have presented a list of types of behavioral functions that members of small groups perform during discussions. During a single speech a person may perform more than one of these behaviors, such as both giving information and asking for more information from others. We tend to name a person's role on the basis of the kinds of behaviors he or she most often performs as a group member, but in reality the role consists of an amalgam of those kinds of behaviors that he or she provides most often and in relatively high proportions compared to other group members. Figure 5.4 illustrates roles of two members of a small group.

Figure 5.3 Two major dimensions of the impact of discussant behaviors.

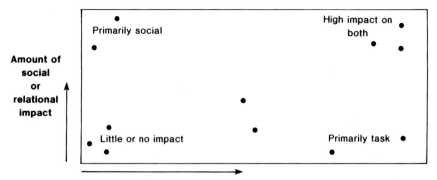

Amount of
social
or
relational
impact

Primarily social

High impact on
both

Little or no impact

Primarily task

Amount of impact on group task achievement

● Specific act or behavior

Figure 5.4 Roles of two hypothetical group members as composites of behavioral functions.

Idea Leader	Procedural Leader
Initiating and orienting	Initiating and orienting
	Information giving
Information giving	Information seeking
	Opinion seeking
Information seeking	Norming
Opinion giving	Coordinating
	Consensus testing
Evaluating	Suggesting procedure
Dramatizing	Harmonizing

Types of Behavioral Functions

Initiating and orienting—proposing goals, plans of action, or activities; prodding group to greater activity; defining position of group in relation to external structure or goal.

Information giving—offering facts and information, evidence, personal experience, and knowledge pertinent to the group task.

Information seeking—asking other members for information; requesting relevant evidence.

Opinion giving—stating beliefs, values, interpretations judgments; drawing conclusions from evidence.

Opinion seeking—asking other members for their opinions.

Evaluating—expressing judgments about the relative worth of information or ideas; proposing or applying criteria.

Clarifying and elaborating—interpreting issues; clarifying ambiguous statements; developing an idea previously expressed by giving examples, illustrations, and explanations.

Dramatizing—nontask (sometimes even deviant to the group purpose) comments that evoke fantasies about persons and places other than the present group and time, including joking, storytelling, and fantasizing; often the theme of the drama is a tentative value or norm being tested as a possible group norm or position.

Coordinating—showing relationships between or among ideas; integrating two or more solutions into one; summarizing or reviewing what has previously been said in bits and pieces; suggesting teamwork and cooperation.

Consensus testing—asking if group has reached a decision acceptable to all; suggesting that agreement may have been reached.

Suggesting procedure—suggesting an agenda of issues, outline, problem-solving pattern, or special technique; proposing some procedure or sequence to follow.

Recording—keeping group records on chalkboard or paper, preparing reports and minutes; serving as group secretary and memory.

Harmonizing—reducing secondary tension by reconciling disagreements; pointing out common ground of values and beliefs; suggesting compromises; conciliating or placating an angry person.

Tension relieving—introducing strangers, and helping them to feel at ease; reducing status differences; encouraging informality.

Norming—suggesting standards of behavior for members; challenging unproductive ways of behaving in group; giving negative response when another violates a group norm.

These are the major types of behavior that are needed to develop a collection of persons into a group, coordinate their efforts, provide and use resources, and thus achieve interdependent goals.

Other types of behaviors that spring from purely personal needs work at odds with the best interests of the group as a whole. Among these self-centered types of acts are the following:

Withdrawing—avoiding important differences; refusing to cope with conflicts; refusing to take a stand; covering up feelings; giving no response to comments of others.

Blocking—preventing progress toward group goals by constantly raising objections, repeatedly bringing up the same topic or issue after the group has considered it and rejected it. (It is not blocking to keep raising an idea or topic the group has not really listened to or considered.)

Recognition seeking—boasting, calling attention to one's own expertise or experience when it is not necessary to establish credibility or relevant to group task; relating irrelevant experiences; game-playing to elicit sympathy or pity.

Horseplaying—making tangential jokes; engaging in horseplay that takes the group away from serious work or maintenance behavior.

Advocating—playing the advocate for the interests of a different group, thus acting as its representative, apologist, or advocate counter to the best interests or consensus of the current group.

Dominating—giving orders; interrupting and cutting off; flattering to get own way; insisting on own way.

Attacking—attacking the competence of another, name-calling, impugning the motive of another instead of describing own feelings; joking at expense of another; attempting to destroy "face" of another.

This list of self-oriented behaviors could be expanded considerably. The important thing is for you to be aware of whether a member is trying to contribute to the interdependent group goal, or manipulating and using other members for selfish goals at odds with the best interests of the group as a whole.

Networks of Communication

Concomitant with the development of somewhat specialized roles in a group is the development of a communication network. The phrase *communication network* refers to a pattern of message flow or *linkages* of who actually speaks to whom in discussions. A member who opens a meeting may find the others expecting him to initiate discussion on a new topic or at subsequent meetings. A person who speaks frequently will find others looking (literally) to him or her for some comment on each new issue or when there is a lag in conversation. Infrequent verbal participants will themselves be more and more overlooked, and the comments they do make ignored.

Figure 5.5 Communication networks.

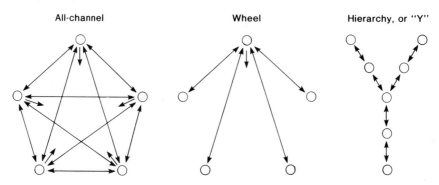

All-channel   Wheel   Hierarchy, or "Y"

Most of the so-called *network* studies of communication in task groups seem to be largely irrelevant to discussion groups in natural (as opposed to laboratory) settings. Persons passing notes through holes in plywood partitions (typical in the network studies) to solve contrived problems imposed on them do not interact any more like persons in discussion groups than do baboons in a zoo interact like baboons in natural clans in a forest or veldt.

Many types of networks have been identified, but the *permissible* as well as the actually used channels must be looked at in any group to fully understand its structure. Hopefully, the democratic group has an *all-channel* network in which all participants are free to comment on a one-to-one basis with all others, and to the group as a whole (see Figure 5.5). A *wheel* network is to be avoided in which all comments are directed toward one central person (*leader*) who alone may speak to the group as a whole or to any individual in it. A *Y*, or *hierarchical network,* occurs when an autocratic leader has *lieutenants* with whom he or she interacts directly, and who in turn talk to subordinates. The persons at the ends of the Y rarely if ever interact directly with the leader. In both wheel and Y networks the central person is usually very satisfied with his participation and status, but the peripheral members tend to find little satisfaction in participation in the group. Sometimes, however, the central person (*leader*) becomes overloaded with more messages from other group members than he or she can handle, and then becomes frustrated and dissatisfied. The central person is then said to be suffering *information overload.* A wheel or Y network forces some members into a position of low sending, and hence low satisfaction. Interaction in such restricted networks sometimes breaks down into two or more *private* conversations going on at the same time between pairs of individuals during a group meeting. The all-channel network permits rapid communication without having to get clearance from a central gatekeeping authority; everyone is free to say what he or she wants while it is pertinent and fresh in mind. Communication flows freely from person to person. At least half of the comments are addressed to the group as a whole, and all group members can hear and attend to all one-to-one or one-to-few comments. Free feedback of questions and responses is thus encouraged. Many studies have shown morale to be highest when all channels are open, and some have indicated superior problem solving on complex tasks by groups with such networks compared to more restricted networks of flow of communication. To have a functional all-channel network will take some conscious effort on the part of group members, but you are well advised to see that departures from such a completely open net are very brief.

Status

Status refers to the relative importance of each member and his or her prestige. As group roles emerge, each person is placed on a sort of *ladder* or *pecking order* within the group. Thus, status is closely associated with position in a communication network. Researchers have found that high-status members talk more often than do low-status members, that highs communicate more often with each other than with lows, and that lows tend to address their comments to persons higher in status than themselves rather than to members of equal or lower status.[7] Discussants tend to interrupt and ignore the comments of low-status persons far more often than those of highs. However, the status heirarchy of a small group is not inflexible; it may change through time as members make contributions to the group's goals, and roles change. Most persons find satisfaction in the psychological rewards that come from high status: being admired, responded to, supported, and liked. We spend much time and effort acquiring the symbols of high status—fine automobiles, tailored clothing, houses in exclusive neighborhoods, trophies, and titles.

When a small group is first developing, status will often be ascribed on the basis of each member's position in the society external to the small group, guided by such benchmarks as wealth, education, work, personal fame, or position in the parent organization of a committee. For example, a committee comprised of a college dean, a professor of biology, an English instructor, two seniors, and two sophomores would initially have that order of ascribed status. But status is *earned* or achieved in the small working group based on each member's perceived contributions to the group's goals, so that order would likely change drastically as functional roles emerged.

Sex has an unpredictable impact on status and roles in a group today, depending on the beliefs and values of the members. A decade ago one could predict that in a mixed sex group a male would almost always emerge as leader, and that the status of females would on the average be lower than the status of males. As Bormann and Bormann say, some men " . . . tend to resist the leadership of a woman, no matter how capable . . ." and some women will refuse " . . . as a matter of principle to follow any plans suggested by a man."[8] When the discussion group mirrors the struggle between the sexes for position in society at large, this hidden agenda item will interfere with productive work. Further complications arise when sexual attraction occurs between members of a small group, as many case studies by my students attest.

Most small groups establish two or three levels of status in their hierarchy. This does not mean that lower status members are not judged to be of value, or that they are unhappy in the group. Cohesive groups value the contributions of each member, and every member knows it. High is not necessarily better, just more influential. Case studies of student groups often contain such comments as this: "Every member of our group played a vital role. Jim, our leader, was most important in the success of our project, but even quiet Norman made a vital contribution with his careful research and by arranging a place where we could meet. He could always be counted on to do his part. I would not change a member of this group even if I could."

Norms

Every group develops *norms*. These are rules of conduct, standards of participation, or expectations of how members should behave. They are not regulations imposed by a head person with power to punish, but guidelines that all or most members accept implicitly. Norms both guide and regulate behavior of group members. They determine how and to whom members speak, how they dress, where and how they sit, what they talk about, what language may be used, and so on.

During the developmental stage of a new small group, norms are developed rapidly, often without the members realizing what is occurring. The first meeting is quite important in establishing norms, especially the first few minutes. At that time, behaviors that are typical of primary tension can become norms if the tension is not released early—speaking softly, being extremely polite, avoiding questioning the sources of another's information, or even opinionated and dogmatic ways of stating beliefs can become norms if not challenged.

Perhaps a few examples of norms will help you to understand them better. These are stated as "dos" and "don'ts." Taking the trouble to formulate norms in this way often helps to clarify their nature and function. Evidence that these norms were in force in many groups has been observed by this writer.

Group norms may or may not be stated openly, but they can be detected by a keen observer. In many cases the observer must infer a norm from behaviors of group members. If all members manifest a particular type of act that is strong evidence that a norm encouraging or requiring such behavior exists. The best evidence of all comes when someone acts contrary to a norm and is then punished in some way by the group. For example, others may frown, fail to respond, comment negatively about the behavior, or even scold

effective group discussion

the violator: "Let's stick to the issues and not go blaming one another." Every norm has some impact on a group's productivity and member satisfaction. The norms that are counterproductive or reduce satisfaction need to be changed.

Two general types of norms develop as a group culture emerges: (1) those governing the specialized role of each member and (2) those that apply to all members. Members share in the expectation that both types of norms will be complied with.

Some examples of role-specific norms are:

"The leader should prepare and distribute an agenda in advance of each meeting."

"The leader should summarize from time to time, but other members may do so if the leader does not when a summary is needed."

"Mary may play the critical tester of all ideas, asking for evidence, pointing out logical fallacies, and otherwise evaluating."

"Mike should tell a joke to relieve secondary tension when the climate gets stressful from an argument over different points of view."

Some examples of typical norms that would apply to every member of a small group are:

"Each speaker should relate his or her comment to what has been said previously during the discussion."(productive)

"Discussants should avoid challenging the President's opinions." (counter-productive)

Conformity to procedural norms is essential if members are to work together. Discussants are usually inclined to conform to the procedural norms of the group. Any violation of the norms may mean that the norm is not understood by the violater or he or she disagrees with it. If procedural norms are clearly understood but still violated by one or more members, this should be called to the attention of the group and some action should be taken. Continued violation means the member feels the norm is somehow detrimental. Here are two examples of procedural norms typical of effective discussion groups: "Members should stick to the agenda, unless all agree to change it." "While brainstorming, no one should criticize any idea suggested."

In order to clarify and possibly change the norms of a discussion group, first study their effects. Group awareness of harmful effects can lead to change. A participant should try to discover answers to the following questions if he or she senses that something is wrong that may be due to a counterproductive norm:

1. What regularities of behavior can be seen? (For example, who talks to whom? How do the persons talk? Where do they sit? To what degree do they ask for evidence supporting a position? How are ideas evaluated?)

2. What seem to be the practical effects of each of these modes of behaving? (For example, are ideas going untested? Are some members' ideas accepted uncritically while others' ideas are ignored or rejected? Do members always sit in the same positions? Is there much evidence of frustration?)
3. What happens when a member deviates from a norm? Is this deviant behavior punished in some way?

Once you have formulated the norm you believe to be detrimental to the group, state it to the members, describe the evidence of its existence, and suggest that it be replaced by a different norm or pattern of behavior. The group will likely discuss this problem for a few minutes, and decide to make the change. Even if this is done by consensus, members may still need reminders of the new norm for some time to come until it has become largely habituated.

Norms are based on the shared values—beliefs of what is relatively good or bad, productive or unproductive. Values are often explored and developed in what appear to be tangents to a group's discussion topic, in sequences of comments that are called *fantasy chains*. The process of group dramatizing or fantasy chaining was first described by Bales in 1970.[9] Bales claimed that all fantasy chaining relates to *unconscious meanings* or needs of one or more participants. Hence such fantasies have great power to motivate discussants. Usually several persons participate in a group fantasy chain, but not necessarily all members. Consider how this process occurs. Quite often the group seems at a loss for what to say or do. Talking peters out, or perhaps there is an awkward tenseness due to conflict among members. Suddenly someone says something that appears to be off the subject, a tangent about persons in some other time and place.

Interaction speeds up, a pitch of excitement is heard in the voices; often there is some conflict or an edge of hostility. The volume of sound often goes up as the group begins the chain association. Many signs of interest are seen among those who do not participate verbally. Restless . . . movements increase as people try to find a way to get into the conversation. New images and reported events may be rapidly injected, but apparently somehow on the same theme, psychologically . . . for some period—a minute or two, sometimes much longer.[10]

The fantasy is manifestly about persons and events outside the group, that could have occurred in another time (past or future) and another place. At the same time, on a different level, the talk mirrors indirectly the problems of the group at the moment, such as fears, dislikes, loves, jealousies, tense relations between members, relations with other groups, unverbalized hidden agendas, etc.

Fantasy chains can easily be detected by an observer watching for them by noting sudden changes of pace, levels of excitement, and a sort of electric tension in the air. To interpret the fantasy, Bales suggested that the observer look for a sudden insight into what is going on in the group that has not been

effective group discussion

openly discussed. Systematic analysis will not work. Through fantasy chains a group establishes a new realm of social reality for its members, a myth that becomes the truth, a sense of unity in a group involved in some dramatic conflict, with shared values and interests.

Cohesiveness

The term *cohesiveness* is used by social psychologists to refer to the common bonds and sentiments that hold a group together.

To say that a group is high in cohesiveness is to say that the relationships among members, on the average, are highly attractive to them; they have a high degree of "stick togetherness" and unity. Defining cohesiveness operationally has not been easy, for we cannot measure the concept directly. How would you observe and measure "the resultant of all the forces acting on the members to remain in the group," a widely accepted definition?[11] Obviously you cannot, but must observe selected behaviors that can be considered an index of how cohesive a small group may be: members' individual assessments of how closely knit they are as a group; how strongly members feel a sense of belonging or affiliation to the group as expressed on a scale; attendance at meetings; favorable remarks about the group to outsiders; degree of conformity to group norms that call for behaviors different from those the members manifest in other social situations; achievement of consensus or lack thereof, especially in expressions of value.

Researchers have shown that groups high in cohesiveness have greater rates of interaction than less cohesive groups, express more positive feelings for each other, and have more satisfaction with the group and its products. The higher the cohesiveness of the group, the greater control over member behaviors the group as a whole will be able to exert.[12]

A high degree of cohesiveness is associated with a high degree of ability to cope effectively with unusual problems, and to work as a team in meeting emergencies. Production groups, if highly cohesive, *can* produce more than low cohesive groups, but may not do so if the members are being influenced by intragroup norms for less production. High cohesiveness is associated with the group's ability to get members to conform to the majority or high-status members' desires. Janis has pointed out that conformity in many problem-solving groups contributes to very low-quality decisions, the result of "groupthink" that allows for no disagreement with beliefs of high-status members.[13] Deviance from the beliefs of high-status members or the majority may be put down so powerfully that a person holding valid information that negates those beliefs even begins to doubt his own information. As such groups continue through time they become very predictable, less creative, less able to use novel ideas—the "nuts" are silenced or even put out. The very persons who could contribute most to the quality of solutions by pointing out fallacious thinking find the group less and less attractive while the cohesiveness among the majority is growing. Thus we have a dilemma of how to maintain a productive degree of creativity and critical thinking while at the same time maintaining a high degree of cohesiveness essential to high potential, personal satisfaction, and loyalty. Specific techniques will be presented later, especially for designated leaders. *Awareness of the problem* is the point here.

However, we do know that a group that accomplishes its objectives, provides members with satisfaction in their participation, offers prestige in belonging, and is successful in competing with other groups, has high attractiveness to its members. This knowledge can be used to offset the strains produced by uncertainty, risk, and deferment of judgment necessary to achieve high-quality work. We also know that cohesiveness is fostered by the degree to which members know and like each other as persons, their frequency of interaction, and the amount of influence exerted by each on the group. Interestingly, open disagreeing has been shown to be more frequent in high-cohesive groups than in low-cohesive groups. A climate of trust in which each member feels secure permits expressions of disagreement on issues, facts, and ideas— provided the disagreement is aimed at arriving at high-quality solutions. But if high-status members resist disagreement as a personal affront, then whatever cohesiveness is achieved by other means will be at the expense of low-quality decision making—*groupthink*. Highly successful and cohesive groups tend to first get well acquainted and interested in each other as persons. They accept the need for secondary tension generated by disagreements, and find ways to reduce these tensions by giving priority to evidence, rational thinking, and compromise. After decisions have been reached, such groups restate the value of the group and of each of its members. Members can be heard saying such things as: "I'm proud of our group, we really thresh out ideas until we arrive at the best, and then we team up." "Even if I disagreed with you, Joe, I'm glad you spoke up. We disagreed openly and honestly, and I learned a lot from you. I like that."

In order to enhance cohesiveness, Bormann and Bormann suggest that a group should consciously do the following:

1. Develop a strong identity as a group and a group tradition or history. This can be done by developing nicknames for the group, insignia of membership, referring to past events with pride and pleasure, ceremonies and rituals, and emphasizing the high quality of accomplishments.
2. Stress teamwork, and give credit to the group. Avoid talking about what you did personally for the group, especially if you are the designated leader. Volunteering to do things for the group, and emphasizing how important the group is to you will help get members feeling closer to each other.
3. Recognize contributions to the group goal by members, thus rewarding individual members from *within* the group. Low-status members especially need reward and praise from other group members, and *not* criticism, if they are to develop the loyalty that will make them more productive and dependable.

4. Show human concern for the persons who make up the group, providing warmth, affection, and direct attention to personal tensions and problems that members indicate. As soon as personal needs are dealt with, however, the group should get back to the group task.

5. Support both disagreement and agreement, which basically means working for a norm of open expression of disagreement or support for ideas. Highly cohesive groups show more disagreement; open conflict needs to be encouraged, not repressed. When the conflicts are settled, signs of solidarity such as joking, laughing together, compliments to persons who supported rejected ideas that helped build a better group solution, and comments such as "Let's get behind this" are needed.

6. Help the group set clear and attainable goals, which also provide enough of a challenge to yield a sense of pride in group achievement. Continuing groups that fail to reach their objectives tend to display lowered cohesiveness and may even break up. On the other hand, beating a high school team would not enhance the cohesiveness of a college soccer squad.[14]

Summary

In chapter 5 we have examined seven major process variables: phase movements through time, interpersonal tensions, a role structure developed from individual behavioral functions, a communication network, status levels, norms, and cohesiveness. Every group moves through at least four major phases of development: forming, storming, norming, and performing, with constant fluctuations in both primary and secondary tension levels among members. From their personal behaviors and responses to them, group members carve out individual roles as composites of their typical behaviors in the group, which should be task and maintenance oriented rather than self-oriented. A communication network develops among the members, ideally an all-channel network rather than a wheel or Y. Roles in the communication network are accompanied by different levels of status and power among the members. A set of norms governing behaviors of all members emerges as the group matures, which can be changed as needed if brought to a level of consciousness. A high level of cohesiveness among members is both a product and a process variable in the effective discussion group.

In the next chapter we will consider in depth the process of communication by which interaction occurs, and how it can be made as productive as possible.

Exercises

1. You and two or three classmates should observe the same group discussion and *independently* write out all the norms you could observe at work in the group. Make brief notes of what you noticed as evidence of each norm. Indicate if you think the norm was goal productive with

a $(+)$, had no effect on productivity with a (0), or was counterproductive with a $(-)$. Write the norms as rules of conduct using the following form:

General norm—"Members of this group (should, should not, or may) _____ ."
Role-specific norm— "(The leader, the secretary, Mary, etc.) should (or should not) _____ ."

In the evidence column put descriptions of behavior you actually observed, such as what was done regularly and accepted, or behavior that was given negative reinforcement.

Norm	Evidence of the Norm	Impact

2. Observe a group with one or more classmates, each observing independently. Using a list of behavioral functions as a guide (see p. 100) classify the acts of each member. This will give you a tally of how often each person performs each function. Then write a name for and description of the role taken by each member. Compare your findings with those of your fellow observer(s).

3. Rank the members of the group you observed in number 2, above, according to the status of each in the group. Your ranked list will show the relative amount of power and influence you think each exerts in the group.

4. First, make a list of at least ten small groups in which you have been an active member during the past year (your instructor may wish to change this time span). Then, in a single sentence, describe the role you had in each group. Compare your list with the lists of three to five classmates. What do you discover about a person's roles in different groups?

5. Diagram the flow of communication in a discussion group you observe, using the form shown on page 268. Be sure to record how many times each person speaks and to whom. What is the proportion of the total statements made by each member? What sort of communication network exists in the group?

Bibliography

Bormann, Earnest G., *Discussion and Group Methods: Theory and Practice*, 2nd ed., New York: Harper & Row, 1975, chapters 8 & 9.

Nixon, Howard L. II, *The Small Group*, Englewood Cliffs, N.J.: Prentice-Hall, 1979, chapters 4 & 6.

Tuckman, Bruce W., "Developmental Sequences in Small Groups," *Psychological Bulletin* 63 (1965): 384–99.

References

1. Robert F. Bales, *Interaction Process Analysis* (Reading, Mass.: Addison-Wesley Publishing Company, 1950).
2. Bruce W. Tuckman, "Developmental Sequences in Small Groups," *Psychological Bulletin* 63 (1965), pp. 384–99.
3. *Ibid.*
4. Thomas M. Scheidel and Laura Crowell, "Idea Development in Small Discussion Groups," *Quarterly Journal of Speech* 50 (1964), pp. 140–45.
5. Earnest G. Bormann, *Discussion and Group Methods: Theory and Practice,* 2nd ed. (New York: Harper & Row, Publishers, 1975), pp. 181–82.
6. *Ibid.,* p. 190.
7. J. I. Hurwitz, A. F. Zander, and B. Hymovitch, "Some Effects of Power on the Relations among Group Members," in *Group Dynamics: Research and Theory*, 3rd ed., D. Cartwright and A. Zander, eds. (New York: Harper & Row, Publishers, 1968), pp. 291–97.
8. Earnest G. Bormann and Nancy C. Bormann, *Effective Small Group Communication*, 2nd ed. (Minneapolis: Burgess Publishing Company, 1976), p. 52.
9. Robert F. Bales, *Personality and Interpersonal Behavior* (New York: Holt, Rinehart and Winston, Inc., 1970), pp. 105–8, 136–55.
10. *Ibid.,* p. 138.
11. Leon Festinger, "Informal Social Communication," *Psychological Review* 57 (1950), p. 274.
12. Howard L. Nixon II, *The Small Group* (Englewood Cliffs, N.J.: Prentice-Hall, 1979), pp. 74–76.
13. Irving L. Janis, *Victims of Groupthink* (Boston: Houghton Mifflin Company, 1973).
14. Adapted from Earnest G. Bormann and Nancy C. Bormann, *Effective Small Group Communication*, 2nd ed. (Minneapolis: Burgess Publishing Company, 1976), pp. 70–76.

6

communication within the small group

Study Objectives

As a result of studying chapter 6 you should be able to:

1. Describe how signals are encoded, transmitted, received, transformed, interpreted, and responded to in both intrapersonal and small group communication systems.

2. Differentiate between the content, affective, and relational components of interpersonal messages.

3. Understand the symbolic nature of language, and how to prevent many misunderstandings by how you select and arrange your words and how you respond to verbal messages from others.

4. Formulate general questions for group discussions that measure up to seven criteria.

5. Understand the benefit to discussion groups of members who are rhetorically sensitive, and become more so yourself.

6. Distinguish among the six major functions of questions raised during discussions, and be able to ask clear questions of all six types.

7. Know the functions and types of nonverbal signals in small group communication.

8. Describe the behavioral characteristics of active listeners.

9. Write reports and minutes of small group meetings that will be acceptable to all members.

Key Terms

Bypassing   misunderstanding resulting from two persons not realizing they have different referents / meanings for the same words.

Complete communication circuit   open interchange system in which both persons send and receive signals, so that a signal from one is responded to by the other, and the response is acknowledged.

Concrete words   low-level abstractions, referring to a specific object, experience, relationship, etc.

Defensive listening   interpretation and response of other's statement characterized by evaluation, control, strategy, neutrality, superiority, or certainty in the listener.

Defense-evoking words   words with such negative connotations that the listener reacts defensively; "trigger" words.

Doublespeak or gobbledygook   lengthy abstruse statements designed to avoid a clear answer to a question, yet give the impression that the question has been answered.

Feedback   perception of one's own behavior or response of another, which perception modifies further communicative output.

High-level abstraction   word or phrase commonly used to refer to a broad category of objects, relationships, concepts, etc.

Interpersonal communication   transactional process in which one person's verbal and nonverbal behavior evokes meaning in another.

Intrapersonal communication   process of signal generation, transmission, interpretation and response within the nervous system of an individual.

Listening actively   consciously attending to signals from others in an effort to understand as precisely as possible the intended meaning of a speaker.

Minutes   written sequential report of every item included in the agenda actually followed in a group meeting, with complete record of all motions and votes.

Nonverbal cues   signals other than words to which discussants react.

Paraverbal cues   nonverbal cues of voice and utterance other than words themselves.

Question   verbal request for a response; interrogational statement.

Answerable   one for which an answer can be provided from some sort of observation or interpretation of observations.

Group goal   a question that concerns the general objective of a group discussion.

Information   seeks specific statements of fact.

Interpretation   seeks judgments or opinions about the meaning of a body of facts.

Orientation   seeks answer that will help define context or external structure and goals.

Policy   asks for solutions or general plan of action.

Procedural   seeks guidelines, procedure to follow, method of discussion.

Socio-emotional   seeks feelings, concerns, tensions, interpersonal attitudes of members toward each other and group.

Value   special type of question of interpretation seeking judgment of goodness, merit, or worth.

Referent   that which is referred to by a symbol; the object of denotation by a word, sentence, or statement.

Rhetorical sensitivity   an attitude toward encoding verbal messages that includes thinking about what could be said and how to say it *before* speaking.

Symbol   anything used to represent something else with which it has no necessary or inherent relationship; all words are symbols.

Syntax   arrangement of words in a statement; rules of grammar concerning word arrangement.

Communication, a process with many subvariables, is the means of creating similar perceptions among members, sharing values, developing interdependence, coordinating effort, sharing information and ideas, and forging a newly-formed group into a unified social system.

You may have studied the process of human communication in a previous speech communication course. If so, much of this chapter may be review for you. Even if that is the case, be careful to notice how the key terms and concepts concerning communicating are defined and used in this book. There have been scores of definitions of communication, from very simple to highly complex. Mutual understanding requires that all of us attempting to communicate use words in similar ways. Before proceeding further in the chapter, read the following article by King, "The Nature of Communication"; it presents an outstanding and clear definition and description of interpersonal communication among group members.

The Nature of Communication[1]
Stephen W. King

Three weeks into a course entitled "Small Group Communication" an earnest student raised her hand and asked, "Now that we know what a 'small group' is, Professor, what is 'communication'?" Many students snickered, thinking the question tremendously naive and trivial.

However, I was apprehensive. Was this student going to force me to deal with the difficult but essential question of definition? I tried to get out of the tense moment by flippantly saying, "What is *not* communication?"

Undaunted, the student pressed her question, "You didn't answer the question; you merely circumvented it."

Trapped! So I said, "Well, Stevens defined it as 'the discriminatory response of an organism to a stimulus,' Miller and Steinberg asserted that communication 'involves an intentional, transactional, symbolic process,' and Samovar and Mills concluded that communication 'includes all methods of conveying any kind of thought or feeling between persons.' "*

Gaining confidence the student looked at me and said, "Professor, that was simply a smorgasbord of definitions offering me a great deal of choice but not much clarification."

I prayed for the bell to ring indicating the end of the period. No bell, so I said, "O.K., Miller and Steinberg's definition is the right one. Now, do you understand?"

"No," said the student, "that's the point. You gave me a definition but I don't understand why that definition captures the essence of 'communication' while the others do not. I guess I want to understand 'communication' not define it."

*S. S. Stevens, "A Definition of Communication," *Journal of the Acoustical Society of America*, 22 (1950), p. 689; G. Miller and M. Steinberg, *Between People: A New Analysis of Interpersonal Communication*, Chicago: Science Research Associates, 1975, p. 34; L. Samovar and J. Mills, *Oral Communication: Message and Response*, 3rd ed. Dubuque, Iowa: Wm. C. Brown Company Publishers, 1976, p. 4.

Of course, she was right. Thus, I begrudgingly began a dialogue aimed at understanding communication, its fundamental nature and conceptual boundaries. I invite you to join us on this expedition in search of understanding.

We can begin our expedition with a brief story:

(1) Professor Samuel Withit left the library one morning and saw one of his students across the quad wave to him. He waved back. (2) A few moments later Professor Withit walked by another of his students who gave a friendly "hello" smile. (3) Professor Withit did not see the student and continued to walk to his office without acknowledging the smile. The student, miffed by the rebuff, cut class for the rest of the week. (4) Upon entering the departmental offices, Professor Withit overheard one of his ex-students telling another student, "Professor Withit's class is one of the toughest in this department." (5) Later, Professor Withit dictated a letter to his secretary and requested that the letter be mailed that day. Two days later the letter left the office.

How many of these five incidents would you classify as examples of communication? All five? Two? None of them? Very probably other people would disagree with whatever answer you decided upon. Such difference of opinion is more than just an interesting disagreement; we must ask the question, "Why?" Quite simply, the answer centers on the fact that to decide to call something by a name, in this case "communication," reflects your understanding and, at this point in your study of communication, you *all* probably have different ideas about what is or is not "communication." Let's look at each of these five incidents and try to discover the points at which some of your understandings might differ.

In incident number one (1) no words are exchanged. Because of this, did you exclude this as an example of communication? In incident two (2), a signal—a smile—was sent but not received. Is reception necessary for communication? Professor Withit's behavior in incident number three (3) unintentionally affected his student. Are such accidental effects communication? In incident four (4), Professor Withit was not the intended receiver of the signal sent by one of his ex-students. Did the student communicate anyway? Finally, in incident five (5), the professor's instruction to the secretary was apparently received but not effective. Is the study of communication limited to effective communication?

Possibly your concept of communication allows you to include all the incidents as examples of communication. However, if another person conceived of communication as only those exchanges of ideas through words, incidents one, two, and three would be dropped because words were not uttered. If another individual thought communication dealt only with messages intentionally sent, incidents three and four would not qualify. If success was a prerequisite for yet a third person, incidents two, four, and five would not be included. It is apparent that if we are going to go much further in this study of communication, we must come to a shared understanding of the term.

One way to understand a phenomenon is to identify its parts or components. Accordingly, let's try to decide what the fundamental ingredients of communication are. First, nonverbal communication, which does not rely on words, is a reality. If it is not, why do people get so upset over various hand gestures? Why did Professor Withit's student skip class for a week? Second, to concern ourselves only with successful idea exchange is like calling "teaching" only that which results in the student getting an "A." The result would be that neither education nor communication would ever be improved since no one would have investigated the causes of failure. We must look at both successful and unsuccessful communication. Finally, if we limit ourselves to only those messages intentionally sent, two problems become apparent. First, we have to make some very questionable decisions about what is going on inside a sender's head. Second, and more importantly, we must ignore many messages that do, in fact, have impact, such as Professor Withit's unintentional slight of his student. With these distinctions in mind, let me suggest a description of communication that reflects our understanding of communication to this point: *Communication is a process whereby symbols generated by people are received and responded to by other people.*

Understood in this way we would include all the incidents of Professor Withit's morning except number two (2). In that case the student sent a message, a smile, but it was not received and responded to. Communication was attempted but not achieved. All the other incidents, however, were examples of communication.

Characteristics of Communication

Another way to test the adequacy of our understanding of communication is to see if our concept can accommodate basic truths about communication. Accordingly, let's see if our description of communication fits with five commonly accepted characteristics of communication:

(1) Communication is a process.
(2) Communication is complex.
(3) Communication is symbolic.
(4) Communication is a receiver phenomenon.
(5) Communication is transitory.

Communication is a process. This statement implies that communication "does not have *a* beginning, *an* end, *a* fixed sequence of events. It is not static, at rest. It is moving. The ingredients within a process interact; each affects all of the others."† Viewed in this way, communication is both dynamic—that is, constantly changing—and interactive—at least two actively participating individuals are involved. We can separate the ingredients only if we stop the process to look at it. For example, in an argument between an employer and employee many things are happening simultaneously, each one affecting the others—e.g., the employee thinks his boss hates him, the rebuke confirms that impression, the employee's reaction is seen as a challenge to the boss's authority, other employees giggle at the exchange, increasing the employer's determination to reassert authority, etc. To sum up, the idea of process means that many ingredients—variables—are interacting at the same time to produce results.

Communication is complex. The complexity of communication is reflected in two important observations. First, being a process, it is not as direct and one-way as an injection into the arm administered by a physician. Rather, communication proceeds on verbal and nonverbal levels, in both directions.

†D. Berlo, *The Process of Communication,* New York: Holt, Rinehart and Winston, 1960, p. 24.

Second, communication is complex because it involves so many variables, or ingredients. Consider, for example, how many variables are operative during a simple converation between you and a friend. It is more than just a matter of exchanging ideas with another person; "whenever there is communication there are at least six 'people' involved: the person you think yourself to be; the man your partner thinks you are; the person you believe your partner thinks you are; plus the three equivalent 'persons' at the other end of the circuit."‡ To these six "people" we must add the topic, the communication setting, the goal of communication, and the many other variables that affect any communication event. In addition, everyone has an individual personality, a set of needs, a past history, important personal relationships, and a unique way of seeing the world.

Communication is symbolic. One obvious but important characteristic of communication is that it involves the use of symbols of some kind. Symbols are arbitrary, man-made signs that represent thought. Two important implications of symbol use concern us here. First, a given symbol means something different to everyone. Symbols such as "beauty," "intelligence," and "democracy" illustrate well the many meanings invoked by single symbols. Therefore, communication is not the simple transfer of thought from one person to another. Rather, it is a process in which one individual encodes—translates—his thoughts into a symbol and sends that message via some medium to a receiver. The receiver then translates the message into thought—decodes the symbols. Thought and meaning are not transferred: messages are. Once the student of communication sheds the idea that communication is the transfer of meaning and adopts the view that *communication is an exchange of symbols,* a more realistic conception of the communication process is achieved.

The second important consequence of the fact that communication is symbolic is that not all symbols are words. The peace symbol, "thumbs down," long hair, and sarcastic voice inflection are all symbols that communicate ideas or sets of ideas. Indeed, many researchers contend that more than half of the meaning we gain in face-to-face communication is achieved through these nonverbal cues. The recognition and study of the importance of these nonverbal symbols is a critical aspect of understanding human communication.

Communication is a receiver phenomenon. Remember the second student that Professor Withit met earlier in this essay? That student smiled (an attempt to communicate nonverbally) but the professor did not see the smile. According to the description of communication we developed, the student did not communicate because the professor did not receive and respond to the symbol. This example illustrates an important aspect of communication: "Communication always occurs *in* the receiver."§ Notice how the concept of communication differs from a concept like "love." It is possible to love someone and not have the person aware of it. Even though the object of one's love is unaware of the existence of the feeling, the feeling nevertheless is real.

‡D. Barnlund, "Toward a Meaning-Centered Philosophy of Communication," *Journal of Communication,* 2 (1962), p. 40.

§L. Thayer, *Communication and Communication Systems,* Homewood, Illinois: Richard D. Irwin, Inc., 1968, p. 113.

Communication, on the other hand, requires that the receiver be just that—a receiver. Communication attempts that do not reach the receiver, like the attempts of our hapless smiling student, are merely attempts at communication, not communication.

There is another implication we must keep in mind. If communication occurs within the receiver, the intention of the sender is largely unimportant. For example, whether or not Professor Withit intended to slight his student, he did. Whether or not the student whose discussion Professor Withit overheard intended it, his message was nevertheless picked up. Communication occurred because an individual received and responded to a set of symbols.

Third, if communication is identified by receiver response, we ought to examine the types of responses that occur. Let's again examine the episodes with which this essay began. Clearly, one result of the communication was a change in attitudes: the first student probably likes his professor a little more and the second student a little less, or maybe a lot less. Additionally, the professor probably did not think much of his secretary when he found out that the letter was mailed late. Apparently, then, one general effect of communication is that our attitudes toward people and things change. Another type of response was illustrated by the student who skipped class for a week. Obviously, the student's behavior was changed by the communication. By reading this essay, your knowledge of communication will be affected. Clearly, change in knowledge is another general type of response to communication. At this point, we should understand that communication occurs in the receiver and that its potential effects on the receiver are numerous.

Finally, being a receiver phenomenon means that communication occurs when the receiver attaches meaning to others' behavior. As a consequence of the dominant role of the receiver, some researchers have concluded that it is impossible to not communicate. Simply, "one cannot not communicate."// All behavior, when perceived by another, has potential message value or communicative significance. That is, people assign meaning to other people's behavior or nonbehavior. For example, Professor Withit's failure to respond to one of his students angered the student. Therefore, if *all* behavior can have message value or meaning, it is impossible to not communicate, since you can't stop behaving. Anything you do or do not do *may* have meaning for one who perceives it. A few examples may illustrate this important characteristic of communication.

If you were to ask your roommate a question, is there anything he/she could do that would not mean something to you? What if he/she ignored your question? What if he/she answered sarcastically? What if he/she responded in a very cheery way? What if he/she left the room? No matter what he/she did, you would interpret the behavior as meaning something to you.

When you sit next to a person in the campus coffee shop and he says "hello," he is obviously communicating. Is not the same person communicating when he just looks at his food and ignores your presence? Of course he is! He

//P. Watzlawick, J. Beavin, and D. Jackson, *The Pragmatics of Human Communication*, New York: W. W. Norton, 1967, p. 48.

is saying, "I'm here to eat and not to carry on idle chatter with a person I don't know." Is there anything that person could do to which you would not attach meaning? Probably not.

The fact that "one cannot *not* communicate" is important. It means that the study of communication must focus on all your behavior and not just on that part of the time when your mouth is open. Furthermore, it increases your responsibility to recognize that what you say and do influences other people.

Communication is transitory. This principle has two parts. First, communication is irreversible. It can only go onward: it cannot back up and try again. This characteristic of communication is best illustrated by the absurdity of the judge's admonition, "The jury will disregard the testimony just given." Impossible! Second, communication is unrepeatable. Even if the message is repeated word for word, the audience has been changed by the first attempt. Therefore, they are different receivers attaching a different meaning to the same message. This principle of communication is well illustrated by the common experience of either telling or hearing a joke the second time; it just is not the same.

So far it works! If we conceive of communication as a "process whereby symbols generated by people are received and responded to by other people" we can account for the observations that communication is a process, is complex, is symbolic, is a receiver phenomenon, and that communication is transitory. Let's test our understanding in yet another way.

Myths of Communication
Another test of the adequacy of our concept of communication is whether it helps us reject myths or misconceptions about communication. Using our description of communication see how it allows us to avoid five of the most common mistaken conclusions about communication.

1. "I understand communication. I've done it for years." Because of this false assumption, people have communicated poorly for centuries. You have breathed for years, driven cars for years, listened to radios for years, and thought for years, and yet you probably realize that knowing more about physiology, engineering, electronics, and psychology could improve your own performance. Many successful salespersons do not understand persuasion. Doing something does not necessarily imply that one understands what he or she is doing.

2. "Communication can be improved simply by improving communication skills." This myth is based on two fallacies. First, it assumes that there are "certain unequivocal laws which, if followed, lead to success, and, if not, to failure."# That simply is not the case. Communication is far too complex a process and our investigation (so far) too unsophisticated for such rules to exist. If such rules were available, they could be printed and distributed at freshman orientation, and all departments of English and Speech Communication could be disbanded.

#Thayer, p. 8.

effective group discussion

Second, this myth focuses attention on the speaker, which, according to our description of communication, is stressing the wrong person. Remember, communication is a receiver phenomenon. The study of communication, therefore, should not focus on what the speaker *does to* a receiver (which treats the receiver as a passive, mindless blob), but should focus on what happens within the receiver as the result of the speaker's behavior.

Communication is not necessarily improved merely by improving communication skills. Indeed, communication is improved "first, by the communicator's understanding of the communication process, then by the communicator's attitudes and orientations; and only then by the techniques the communicator employs."**

3. "I didn't misunderstand him, he misunderstood me." Because of human nature, we are always convinced that we are right and the other person is wrong. For example, I have heard students say things like, "It was John's fault, his speech was so confusing nobody could have understood it." Then, two minutes later, the same student remarked, "It wasn't my fault, what I said could not have been clearer. John must be stupid." Poor John! He was blamed when he was the sender *and* when he was the receiver. John's problem was that he was the *other* person, and that's who is always at fault.

To understand and to improve communication, you have to be willing to accept the idea that communication is a two-way process with at least two active participants and "fault" must be divided between them.

4. "Most problems, from interpersonal to international, are caused by communication breakdowns. These breakdowns are abnormal and easily correctable." Let's look at the first sentence of this most common of myths. In recent years a number of widely discussed, little understood, and generally ambiguous terms and phrases, such as "communication breakdown," "communication gap," and "credibility gap," have been introduced into our everyday vocabulary. These terms have become the dumping ground for many phenomena we can't explain in an easier or more direct way. The fact that college administrators and students disagree is not a communication breakdown. The fact that teenagers frequently argue with parents is not a communication gap. The fact that minorities demonstrate for a greater share of the economic "action" in this country is not a communication breakdown. Calling these problems gaps or breakdowns ignores the psychological, economic, political, and physical realities which caused the symptom of poor or infrequent communication.

The second part of this myth is equally erroneous. Ineffective communication is not abnormal. Communication is complex and poorly understood; is it any wonder that without much knowledge or training in communication we are not very good at it? Further, since communication is so complex, can we expect it to be easily corrected when it is found to be inefficient?

**Thayer, p. 8.

5. "All communication is attempting to achieve perfect understanding between participants." This myth is dangerous on two counts. First, it assumes that "perfect understanding" is possible. Second, it denies an important reality: sometimes the goal of communication is to be misunderstood.

To achieve "perfect understanding" through communication limited to a humanly-devised symbol system is impossible. Our symbols frequently do not come close to fitting the ideas they are supposed to represent; at best, they are approximations. There is always a very real possibility, indeed probability, that the idea you try to communicate will not be the idea your communication partner decodes from the symbols you have chosen to represent the idea. Recognizing that symbols are inexact, we should try to make our communication as efficient as possible. This, rather than "perfection," is a realistic and attainable goal.

Do you always want to be perfectly understood? Probably not. Have you never answered a test question vaguely to avoid demonstrating ignorance? Have you never sidestepped giving an opinion about a friend's new car or clothing? Often we intentionally garble our messages so as to avoid embarrassment or hide our true feelings. The following selection from an Oscar Wilde play illustrates this use of communication well.

> THE DUCHESS: "Do, as a concession to my poor wits, Lord
> Darlington, just explain to me what you really mean."
> LORD DARLINGTON: "I think I had better not. Nowadays to be
> intelligible is to be found out."††

What Is Not Communication

One final test of our understanding of communication is whether we can use such understanding to identify what is not communication. That is, we should be able to answer the question, "What isn't communication?"

We have said that communication takes place whenever someone attaches meaning to another's behavior. It is clear that unless one's behavior is perceived by someone, communication has not occurred. That is, what one does or says in isolation is not communication.‡‡ Furthermore, we must exclude those behaviors which, though perceived, have no meaning or significance for the perceiver. Perceived behavior to which the perceiver does not attach meaning is not communication. Every day we interact with others in ways that result in no significant interpretation or meaning being attached to the perceived behavior. For example, when you jostle your way in or out of a crowded lecture hall, your behavior and that of many others are mutually perceived, but only in the rare circumstances of inordinate rudeness does anyone attach meaning to that type of perceived behavior. Note that this argument retains the focus of our study on the receiver: Does the receiver attach meaning to that which is perceived? Obviously, what is meaningful for

††O. Wilde, *Lady Windermeir's Fan,* cited by Thayer, p. 306.
‡‡Of course, communication with ourselves can be considered communication—intrapersonal communication. However, this essay has focused on the social or interpersonal nature of communication.

effective group discussion

one person might be inconsequential for another. For example, you would probably ignore the fact that your friend does not wear a watch, but a psychiatrist may take that to mean something significant about your friend's psyche.

Thus, to answer the original question, behavior that is not perceived by another or to which no significant meaning is attached is not communication. Behavior that is both perceived and meaningful is communication.

You may now argue, "O.K., but earlier you said that communication can't be turned off, and now you say some perceived behavior is not communication. Isn't that contradictory?" Not at all. Not all behavior communicates, but it has the *potential* for communication. The important distinction is that you cannot *avoid* communicating. It is impossible for you to turn communication off as you do a radio. When this point was presented earlier in the essay, I was looking at the sender and forcing him or her to recognize all the ways he or she is constantly giving off communicative behavior. When I say that all behavior need not be communication, I am focusing on the receiver and asking the question— does the receiver actually assign meaning to perceived behavior? Not all behavior actually communicates, but it does have communication potential.

Summary

Are you now ready for a definition? We described communication and then tested our understanding of the thing described in many ways. We found that our understanding of communication helped us identify what is and isn't communication, it assisted in rejecting fallacious myths about communication, and it can accommodate several basic truths about communication. Accordingly, we can now define communication in a way that *reflects* our understanding, rather than merely assert a definition that is separate from our understanding. Simply, we understand communication to be "a process whereby symbols generated by people are received and responded to by other people."

Levels of Communication Systems

The communication process can be studied at any level of human behavior, intrapersonal or social. *Intrapersonal* communicating occurs within the individual human being as electro-chemical signals course throughout the nervous system carrying incoming and outgoing messages. These messages contain information from the world outside the person and the internal world of body functions. Intrapersonal includes cognitive processes we call *thinking* and *perception. Social* levels of communication involve two or more persons exchanging signals. At the *interpersonal* level the communication process occurs between two persons as they exchange verbal and nonverbal signals in an interactive process. When signals from another person are received, they are processed in each person's intrapersonal communication system. *Small group communication* refers to interpersonal communication when three or more persons are simultaneously sending, receiving, and internally processing and reacting to signals from each other. The upper limit of the small group is the point at which during such interactive signal exchange participants lose awareness of some other group members as individuals. At that point *public communication* is said to have commenced, involving at any moment a primary source of signals to other persons not perceived for the most part as distinct and unique by the source, but as *social units* who are members of an *audience*. The most common forms of public communication are public speeches and written messages in a signal-carrying medium available to a defined audience. Public communication becomes *mass communication* when the signals are carried by some medium potentially available to an indeterminately large number of persons—television, radio, newspaper, pamphlet, book, magazine, film, recording, etc. Regardless of the extent of the signal-carrying system or network, intrapersonal communication occurs in all persons receiving and reacting to the signals.

It follows logically from the preceeding description of the levels at which communication can be studied that in the small group intrapersonal, interpersonal, and small group communicating are all involved and important to the outputs of the small group. Much of what we have previously considered in this book has a very direct bearing on the communication among members, and is frequently included in books and articles treating "small group communication" attitudes, habits, personal skills, and so forth. Indeed, the concept of the small group as a system implies the interactivity and interdependence of *all* variables and components that comprise the group.

The Intrapersonal Communication System

In the past two decades scientists have greatly expanded our knowledge of intrapersonal communication, especially knowledge about the nature of the sensors, signals, brain and other central nervous system (CNS) operations, and how we interpret signals. The science of intrapersonal communication is highly complex and includes far too much for inclusion in this book. For our purposes as students of discussion within small groups of persons, I will describe only in the general way needed to appreciate what is likely to go wrong when members of a group interact.

As illustrated in figure 6.1, any given intrapersonal communication episode begins with a signal from some source that impacts on a sensor of a person, in this case "Ev" (for Everyone). The signal can come from inside or outside the body: a rise in heart rate, pressure on a toe, a gas bubble in the stomach, a flashing light, a sudden roar from a steam valve, a voice. The moment a sensor reacts to a signal an episode of intrapersonal communication has begun in Ev. Assume that Ev's entire information processing system is intact. The sensor(s) emits signals into an afferent nerve that carries it into the central nervous system (spinal cord and brain), where various switching operations occur, sending signals to one or more divisions of this great central information processor of the person. Based on Ev's physical and psychosocial needs, the condition of Ev's systems, past experiences and knowledge, values,

Figure 6.1 An intrapersonal communication system.

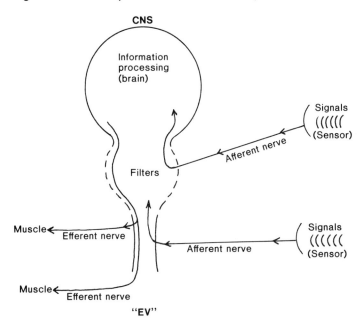

beliefs, expectations, and other variables that cannot all be enumerated, the CNS will respond in some way—a decision is made and action taken. The "decision" may or may not be at a level of consciousness. For example, the filters of the CNS may decide that no action is appropriate at the time, and "kill" the signal—thus the response is no *overt* response. This happens often when you are sleeping and do not waken to a voice that has impinged on the ears and energized the auditory nerve so that signals are carried to the brain. Sometimes the response to such a signal is to weave it into a dream. If the signal to the ears is interpreted at a level below consciousness as being especially important, or is of sufficient power, you will waken, consciously try to interpret the sound, and respond in some overt way. Thus a mother of a very young infant may waken at its slightest cry, rise from bed and go to the baby, but she may sleep through a much louder sound from adults talking nearby, or an auto horn. In the small group, a person who has previously had very little to say, or is considered a marginal member of the group, may not even be perceived at a conscious level by the more active members when he or she does finally speak up, unless he or she does so forcefully.

Of all the multitude of signals constantly coming into Ev's CNS, only one at a time can be the focus of attention, while the rest are either below a level of consciousness dealt with by the autonomic nervous system, a background to the signals focussed on, or for all practical purposes ignored. To reach the threshold of awareness, a signal must be of a particular strength and duration, varying somewhat from sensor to sensor, time to time, and person to person. The receptors of some persons will respond to signals too weak for the sensors of other persons. Thus Ev may not hear what Bev hears, but be aware of sights and sounds that Lev cannot respond to. Often one must participate both vocally and nonvocally with considerable energy to have his or her signals become the center of attention by other members of the group.

The Small Group Communication System

Small group communication occurs whenever three or more persons simultaneously emit and respond to signals from each other. Figure 6.2 represents communication among three members of a small group, A, B, and C. The process by which they interact is called *transactional,* for each is both sender and receiver, influencer and influenced, and each creates a personal meaning for the signals to which he or she responds. Of course signals from other members are selectively received by the sensors and transformed into nerve messages, then interpreted in the CNS. The *response* signals must be converted from electro-chemical signals in the nervous system of each to some form that can be conveyed in the media that link the discussants. The most important signals in discussions are carried by air and light waves. Each person reflects light waves that then carry the reflected visual signals to the eyes of other members who are looking. When these light waves impinge upon the retinas of the other discussants, they are transformed by a chemical process into afferent nerve signals (electrochemical) that are carried to the CNS for processing as described at the intrapersonal level. Movement, dress, gesture, body form, facial expression, eye focus and pupil opening size, and distance are among the many types of important light messages received by discussants that can be interpreted and responded to as meaningful signals. At the same time, air molecules are moving in waves in response to the actions of each discussant's speech mechanism (vocal folds, lips, jaw, palate, etc.). These air waves may be encoded words, or such nonverbal signals as coughs, wheezes, sighs, and whistles. Thus what originated as a *meaning* in one person has been converted (transformed) into signals in efferent nerves, then into muscle actions, then into air and/or light waves, then into some sensor activity, then transformed again into electrochemical signals in the receiver's afferent nerves, processed in the CNS, and given meaning as a *perception,* thought, or mental image. The only characteristics of a message that can remain unchanged during all these transformations is the arrangement or structure of bits of energy.

In the preceeding article, King stated that the process of communication was highly complex. Now you can understand a little more clearly just how complex it is, and can readily understand that in any discussion involving this process much can go wrong that will evoke misunderstanding.

effective group discussion

Figure 6.2 A small group communication system.

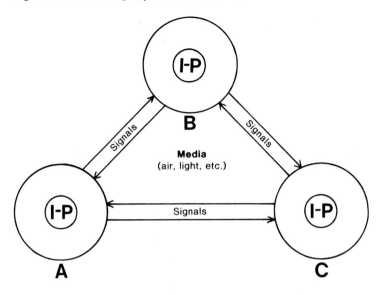

It will require great attention and effort if we are not to have many serious misunderstandings among members of a small group, leading to perceptual dissimilarity, low cohesiveness, dissatisfaction, and poor solutions to problems.

The Complete Communicative Transaction

The idea of a complete transaction has already been touched upon. For a complete and validated interpersonal transaction to occur there must be a response to an initial message and an acknowledgement of that response so that both parties to the interchange know that they have communicated as desired. Thus if member A says, "What happened in the student center that everyone is talking about?" (Initiation), B might say, "A big fight broke out between members of two fraternities" (Response), to which A would possibly nod or say "Oh, I see" (Acknowledgement). In the case of a small group, each speaker addressing the group as a whole needs a response of some perceivable sort from each other member (maybe only a nod or a frown), and needs, in turn, to acknowledge that response. The speaker may find that he or she has to correct or revise the original message because the response indicates he or she was not understood as intended. Or the response may be the lack of response—in which case the speaker has two choices: to drop it or to restate in a more forceful or different way. Nothing is more dampening to cohesiveness, interest, and enthusiasm than a lack of perceivable response—*feedback*—denying the speaker's very existence by indicating "you matter not at all; you are not worth responding to." To be passive during group interaction is to be a very negative force. Passivity displays an attitude of rejection of others, and of noninvolvement in the group.

Notice if there is a difference in the amount of response to each other by members of groups in which you participate. With which do you find yourself most comfortable—those who react openly and clearly, or those who give little response? I suggest that you monitor your own response behavior, and change it if you find that you are a discussant who fails to respond actively to speakers; in short, don't break the communication circuit. Many student journals have had statements like this: "Even though Jean didn't say much, I was able to tell where she stood. You could tell from her face and movements that she was involved. Ed was another story. It was hard to tell how he felt, and I never could trust him."

Message Components

Messages are composed of sets of signals from which discussants derive meanings. Thus a message might consist of a short speech by one member, including both words and nonverbal elements. Another message might be limited to nonverbal signals, such as a blend of facial expressions, gestures, and a change in posture interpreted by receivers as meaning that the signaller was not interested in what was being said by others. There is no such thing as an entirely nonverbal (signals other than words) or verbal (words) human transaction. Every statement has its nonverbal elements, and responses to nonverbal messages always include words, at least at the intrapersonal level of communication within the receiver. To illustrate this, look at another person who is saying nothing, and see if you can keep from *thinking* words while you interpret what you see.

In addition to its verbal and nonverbal elements, every verbal message has direct and indirect implications of at least three types: content, affective, and relational. The *content* level is what is often called the *denotative* aspect of words, or what the speaker is talking about. Thus someone might say "Eighty-four persons were murdered in Central City last year according to the police department's annual crime report," denoting the statistic and what it represents in criminal behavior. The *affective* level of the message is how the speaker feels about what has been denoted; his or her manner while speaking might be interpreted as showing great concern, or being rather neutral to all these deaths. The *relational* implication of the statement concerns how the speaker sees his or her relationship to the listeners, usually conveyed in nonverbal signals. Thus the speaker's manner while speaking may indicate to the other participants that he or she wants to be taken as an unchallengeable authority, sees the other participants as equals, or feels very subservient to them. Attitudes of arrogance, dominance, submissiveness, distrust, superiority, neutrality, or concern are not often stated directly as such, but listeners interpret them from nonverbal cues—such are the *relational* aspects of interpersonal messages among small group members.

In the following section of this chapter, I will first focus attention on verbal, then on nonverbal signals. In actual discussions these are emitted and interpreted as inseparable components of messages.

Verbal Codes

It is generally easy to perceive most of the verbal messages exchanged by group members as they speak and occasionally pass written statements to each other. Ideally, the verbal messages are encoded so that the maximum perceptual similarity possible among members is evoked by them. Understanding the symbolic nature of words and some of the ways in which misunderstanding can be reduced when verbal messages are exchanged can do much to improve your participation in discussions.

Language gives us humans great advantages over other animals in communicating, but at the same time its very nature can lead to misunderstanding. A language consists of a code of words, paralinguistic (or paraverbal) nonverbal signals (such as pauses, pitch changes, changes in intensity of word utterance, and changes in lengths of sounds), and rules of syntax and grammar for arranging and modifying the words of the code. As a reader of this book you are a member of the community of English-speaking people, but there are many subdivisions of that community. You are doubtless familiar with several of these, sometimes called *dialects*. Every organization and every small group through time develops its own specialized version of the more general language code that its members share. Thus professors of geology use a special version of English different from that used by scholars of education, and car salespersons develop their own dialect or jargon. One's membership in a continuing group is contingent upon learning and using the special language accepted by and used among the members of the group.

All words are symbolic. They have no meanings in and of themselves, but are used in some conventional ways by a community of users to represent specified items and classes of experience. *There is no meaning to a word apart from the persons using and responding to it.* Different languages use different words to refer to the same objects, further demonstrating the principle that *meanings are not in words, but in the users of the words.* Figure 6.3 shows some of the different words used by persons to refer to the same object. The object or experience referred to by a symbol is called the *referent*. Only if speaker and listeners have approximately the same referent for a word will they have perceptual similarity. In figure 6.4, Joe says "I have a lot of junk in my room." His referent includes two balls, magazines, a fishing rod, an old trophy, a broken tennis racket, and a box of things left over from a party piled in one corner of the room. Herbie is thinking of some marijuana and other dope, and he is wondering if Joe is a pothead or a pusher. Mary envisions the litter on top of her dresser, and she suspects Joe is as careless as she is' about cleaning up after preparing for a date. Obviously Joe's words had very different meanings to these three persons. By social agreement we may communicate

Figure 6.3 Many words, one referent.

Referent

Words (symbols)

Chair (English)
Chaise (French)
Stuhl (German)
Sedia (Italian)
Silla (Spanish)
Stol (Swedish)

effectively with symbols only when we have similar referents for them, and similar symbols for the same referents. If you say "There is a frog on the floor" what might you mean? My dictionary lists many different uses of the word *frog* discovered by the persons who compiled the dictionary: some of them are an amphibious animal, a decoration around a button hole, a railroad track crossover, shoulder braid on a dress uniform, a throat irritation, and an object to hold flowers in a vase.

The understanding that symbols (including all words) have no necessary referents, as do signs such as rabbit tracks in snow or droppings from a horse, can help you to prevent a variety of misunderstandings common in small group discussions. You will want to be on guard for these: bypassing, ambiguity and vagueness, and defense-inducing terms.

Combat Bypassing

Two discussants bypass each other when they have different referents for the same word or phrase, but think they have the same meanings. Each hears the same words, but the images each creates are so different as to represent a serious misunderstanding. They are "talking past each other." For example, I once listened to a group discussing religious beliefs argue for about half an hour (wasted time!) about whether or not man had free will. The group formed sides, led by an atheist and an avowed Methodist. After listening to a tape recording of the discussion and getting to specific cases they realized that they were actually in agreement! Each side had been using the term "free will" to refer to a very different phenomenon. They were able to see that all believed man had free will (Type 1, some ability to make conscious choices among alternatives), but did not have a free will (Type 2, much of what happens in

Figure 6.4 One statement, different referents.

life is beyond our control and is determined by the converging of forces within and without). In a very simple case of bypassing, a young nurse reported this: "I left a pan of water, soap, washcloth, and towel with a new patient, telling him it was time for his bed bath. When I returned in half an hour I found him scrubbing his bed with the cloth, but personally unwashed. He was not supposed to get out of bed!" In another instance a man whose car battery was too low to turn over the engine told a helpful motorist who had stopped that because he had an automatic transmission she would have to push him about thirty-five miles per hour. You guessed it—she backed up and rammed into his rear bumper at thirty-five miles per hour, doing $300 damage![2] I have watched members of many groups go on talking blithely as if they understood each other when any careful observer could tell that members had very different meanings for some key term. This usually results in conflict at a later date, especially if the misunderstanding is over some course of action to be taken by the group. Tempers flare, individuals go on the defensive, and time is wasted—and sometimes serious damage is done—as a result of bypassing.

Bypassing results from acting as if words have meanings in and of themselves, or "right" meanings. We can communicate effectively with words only if we are in agreement on the referent at a given time (just as when playing poker we must agree on the value of each chip color before the game). As listeners, we can often determine what a speaker means from the context, from what we know about the speaker's background, and from nonverbal cues. Even then our meanings may be considerably different from the speaker's, and will always differ slightly in the fullest sense of the word *meaning*. For example, we may use the word *dog* to refer to animals-that-wag-tails-when-happy, but in our culture we might also refer to a used car, an unattractive person, or a clamp as a dog. Persons attempting to communicate with symbols must discover whether or not they are using the symbols for the same (or very similar) referents.

Reduce Ambiguity and Vagueness

In discussions of ideas, many of the statements are necessarily highly abstract, with vague or ambiguous referents. A vague or ambiguous statement could have any of several meanings. As one moves away from terms referring to specific and unique items, the degree of abstractness and ambiguity increases. Consider the following set of terms, each of which is higher in level of abstraction and thus more vague than the ones preceeding it:

Jantha Whitman, freshman at Booker College

freshman students at Booker College

college students

students

women

humans

mammals

living things

When the first term is used between persons both acquainted with Jantha, the picture in the speaker's head is likely to be similar to the picture in the head of the listener, and the listener could pick out Jantha from a group if asked to do so. But when we talk of "students," "politicians," "democracy," or "environmental problems" the pictures and feelings speakers and listeners experience will often differ greatly. Only terms that name unique objects are likely to be free of any vagueness or ambiguity. For example, one discussant said: "Lecturing is a poor method of teaching." Another responded: "Oh, no it isn't." An argument ensued until a third discussant asked for some examples (lower order abstractions). The speakers were then able to agree on specific instances of effective and ineffective lecturing, especially when some quantitative research data were introduced. The vagueness reduced, the group reached agreement on a less abstract statement: "Lecturing, if well organized, filled with concrete instances, and done by a skilled speaker, can be an effective means of presenting factual information and theoretical concepts. It is usually less effective than discussion for changing attitudes or developing thinking skills."

Leathers studied the impact of abstract statements on a series of laboratory discussions. He found that the abstract statements consistently had a disruptive effect on subsequent discussion, and that the degree of disruption increased as the statements became more highly abstract. His groups contained "plant" discussants who were trained to say things like "Don't you think this is a matter of historical dialectism?" After such a statement, most of the naive discussants became confused and tense, and some just withdrew from further participation.[3]

Ambiguity results from phrases that could readily have either of two types of meaning to the listeners. For example, "I just can't say enough that is good about his effort for the company." What does the speaker mean? That the employee being discussed made such extensive contributions that it is impossible to describe them all, or that he did so little that the speaker cannot give the kind of recommendation the listeners want for a possible candidate for a new position? In such a case, even vocal cues may not clear up the ambiguity.

Ambiguity can also result from a "mixed" message, one in which the words seem to imply one meaning but the vocal cues indicate something different. For example a speaker might say "That seems like a great idea" in a flat pitch with little emphasis, thus implying with her voice that she does not really care about the idea. Or a speaker might say "Take as long as you like to think this through" while glancing at his watch. Such ambiguous actions are highly disruptive to a discussion.

What to do? Spotting vague or ambiguous statements and asking the speaker to clarify can do much to prevent misunderstanding. Ask for specific examples. Paraphrase in less abstract terms and ask for confirmation. Use concrete examples to illustrate your own abstract statements. Use synonyms. Instead of beginning a discussion with a vague or ambiguous question, you can often prevent confusion by introducing a specific case problem including details of what happened.

Occasionally a speaker does not want to be understood or has nothing specific to say, but wants to give the impression of having said something profound. Then he or she may employ a form of abstract language called *doublespeak* or *gobbledygook*. Doublespeak refers to the use of language to confuse or deceive by speaking in affectively neutral circumlocutions even though the subject is one about which the discussants have strong feelings. Doublespeak is often used to give the impression of having answered a direct question while actually evading it. The listener is confused by the lengthy, vague utterance but gets the general impression that he was answered in sophisticated language beyond his ken. Rather than appear "dumb" by insisting on a clear answer, he lets the diversion pass. A vivid example of doublespeak was provided by Ron Ziegler, press secretary to President Nixon, when he was asked if certain tape recordings of presidential conversations were complete or edited. His reply:

I would feel that most of the conversations that took place in those areas of the White House that did have the recording system would in almost their entirety be in existence but the special prosecutor, the court, and I think, the American people are sufficiently familiar with the recording system to know where the recording devices existed and to know the situation in terms of the recording process but I feel, although the process has not been undertaken yet in the preparation of material to abide by the court decision, really, what the answer to the question is.

Bureaucrats, diplomats, and military spokesmen seem especially prone to use doublespeak. Consider such examples as calling a shovel a "combat emplacement evacuator," a parachute "an aerodynamic personnel accelerator," or illegal wiretapping "intelligence gathering."[4] When someone answers your question with doublespeak, insist on an answer you are sure you understand or the discussion will all too often go awry.

Clichés are widely used but highly vague statements that frequently stop objective thinking and realistic consideration of an issue. It is easy to say "A stitch in time saves nine," or "A penny saved is a penny earned, you know." These sayings seem so obvious that no one bothers to look further at the merits of a proposal clobbered by the cliché. The wheels of group thinking grind to a halt on the cliché.

How can you undo the effects of a cliché? First, keep in mind that no two situations or problems are identical. Second, be on guard for easy answers, proverbs, or clichés with their stopping effects. When you spot one, you can point it out as such and suggest an examination of the details of the new proposal, especially to discover if it is different from any other. For example, you might say, "That seems too pat. Are there any differences between this proposal and . . . ?" Sometimes you can counter a cliché with another proverb, or cliché; every cliché seems to have an antithesis. For instance, if someone says, "Don't put off 'til tomorrow," you might counter with, "True in some cases, but also remember that 'haste makes waste.' Now why don't we look further into this proposal?"

Lowering the Impact of Defense-Inducing Words

Some words in common usage have become associated with very negative feelings. Their connotative implications are highly unpleasant to many users. These are the "fighting" words that induce defensiveness in listeners—racial and ethnic slurs, stereotyped names, words commonly used to ridicule and scorn. When a discussant (or something he or she believes in) is called by one of these terms, instead of a rational response the reaction is often highly defensive—including angry accusations and open conflict. All constructive discussion ends. The group process is utterly disrupted. The discussant needs to be sensitive to current usage and to the meanings and feelings of other group members if this is to be avoided as much as possible. For example, a white speaker with no prejudicial intention may say "colored," and a Black listener may respond defensively—to the listener "colored" indicates that the speaker is a racist. One discussant might say "Nebraska has a socialistic form of electric power generation and distribution," meaning that all such facilities are owned by the public and managed by a board elected by the registered voters. Some Nebraskans would react to such a statement in a very defensive way, stopping forward progress of the group to wrangle about "socialism." Or perhaps one discussant expresses a judgment or suggests a solution, and another replies: "Why that's nothing but _____ !" "You're proposing _____ !" "That's _____ !" In the blanks may go any word or phrase used to label something strongly disliked or feared, and for which the respondent has a highly unpleasant connotation: *communism, facism, federal control, racism, childishness, chauvinism,* or others words used in derogation. The speaker has now been identified with something ugly or fearful. He or she may stop cold, deny and argue, or call the speaker some name. The group will likely get caught in a sidetrack of whether the subject of discussion should be called by the stigmatic term. The goal is forgotten, harmony is lost, feelings are hurt, and members lose face. Even if the group gets reoriented, residual antagonism is likely to hamper cooperation: "Nobody gets away with that!"

The use of sexist terms is a major problem for many groups. Terms that were once used interchangeably to refer to all people and to males specifically are now rejected as biased against women. For instance, the word "man" has been used in the past when the person referred to could be either male or female (patrolman, chairman, businessman). Some words have a special ending to indicate a woman, but no such ending to indicate a man: usherette, aviatrix, Jewess, and poetess are examples. Much preferred are the root forms that do not imply the sex of the person referred to: usher, aviator, Jew, and poet. Many persons resent any word that implies an inappropriate sex criterion for filling any role or performing any task, and this resentment will often disrupt a discussion. Most certainly if you view women as inherently inferior to men, beings who should be "kept in their place, the home," you are in for some serious relearning. Consciously eliminating all sexually stereotyping terms from your speaking vocabulary may be necessary if you are to avoid being disruptive in many discussions.

The worst form of stigmatizing is out-and-out name-calling. Adrenalin rises and physiologically we prepare to fight when called by such names as "pig," "male chauvinist," or "nigger." Such behavior is sure to turn attention from the issues before a group, reduce trust, and evoke defensive reactions.

What can you do to prevent, reduce, and alleviate stigmatizing? First, recognize that persons have feelings about everything, and these feelings are not to be rejected. Then, be aware that your feelings and evaluations are just that—YOUR feelings or the other person's—and not characteristics of some objective reality outside yourself. Some labelling and stigmatizing are likely to occur when persons express how they feel about things. We can reduce it in ourselves, using phrases to remind others and ourselves that our judgments are our judgments: "I don't like . . ." or "It seems to *me* that . . . ," for example. When someone expresses a stigma or red-flag term, another participant or designated leader can directly reduce the danger of direct and wasteful conflict or defensiveness by inviting contrasting feelings and points of view, first restating the stigmatic statement in unloaded terms. For example: "Joe has called the ACTION program phony and fascistic. That's one point of view. What are some others?" "Okay, Helen's belief is that public power is socialistic. Are there other ways of looking at it?" Rephrasing might go like this (to "Cops are brutal pigs"): "Joe feels that police officers are insensitive and brutal in their dealing with the public. Has this been the experience of others?" Thus by replacing the stigma terms with more denotative ones and having obtained other evaluations and feelings, one can then ask for a description of the idea or proposal based on more complete information. Talk can now be directed to the facts of the situation and the goals of the group.

If no one is ready or willing to express a point of view contrary to that of the stigmatizer, the designated leader can sometimes help remove the block to objectivity by playing the devil's advocate. He or she expresses a point of view contrary to that of the stigmatizer, indicating that it is one that ought to be considered in order to objectively weigh the proposal from all points of view and on its own merits. For instance, he or she might say: "Joan has called the loan fund socialistic. Let's consider another judgment of it that I've heard expressed by. . . . They say it helps students develop independence."

All of this points to the importance of trying to develop group norms against the use of stigma terms, and an objective examination of all evidence and points of view. A periodic examination of the values and norms implicit in the language we choose and the ways we express our feelings and beliefs can be quite constructive in a group plagued by language barriers to communication.

Organize Your Remarks

In addition to choosing words with care, how you put them together can make a great deal of difference in the responses others make to your messages. A useful comment does not come at random, nor is it randomly organized. Outstanding fluency—the ability to speak smoothly and with apparent ease— is not essential to being a valuable discussant, but clarity is. How you organize your remarks can make a great deal of difference in how easy it is for others to interpret your remarks as you intended.

The syntax of your remarks should be conventional and clear. For example, to say "Year last of all automobiles per cent seventeen recalled from the past five years were" would call attention to your unusual word arrangement in the sentence (syntax) and away from the content of the remark. The words are the same, but syntactic structure gives very different implications to "ate the rabbit" and "the rabbit ate." "It no way won't work somehow" would leave everyone confused. Conventional sentences that are simple, direct, and clear, will facilitate mutual understandings. Clarity thus results both from choosing words likely to have similar referents for both you and listeners, and from arranging them by the syntactical rules of English. Thus you would say "Last year seventeen per cent of all autos made in the past five years were recalled," or "There are two features of this plan that probably will not work."

Speak concisely. If listeners appear bored or restive, you may have spoken at too great length. Try to state your ideas as simply and briefly as possible. Some participants restate every point several times, or take two hundred words to say what could be stated in twenty. This reduces the opportunity for others to participate, and often results in the long speech being tuned out by others. If you notice that others restate your ideas more briefly than you, you should work for a concise style. For instance, the length of the following sentence makes it confusing: "Although I have no doubt about the possible efficacy of the operations of this proposal, there remain unresolved complications about it that might eventuate at some indeterminate point if untoward circumstances tending toward time slippages were to arise and signal-exchange operations were conducted." To be concise and clear one could say "This plan would fail if someone received a late signal or was not prepared to act when he got the signal."

State one point at a time. This is not an inviolable rule, but generally speaking, you should not contribute more than one idea in a single speech. A several-point speech is definitely out. A group can discuss only one idea at a time; confusion is likely to result if you try to make several points at once. A comment in which you attempt to give all the data on an issue or present a series of points is likely to be too involved to be grasped and responded to. How would you respond to this? "Many persons are injured when bumpers fail. Furthermore, I think brakes need to be designed to prevent fading, and then there is the problem of ignition systems that stop the car when powerful radio signals hit them." One person might begin to reply about brakes, while another was thinking about how the ignition systems could be perfected, and another was thinking about a wreck when his or her bumper failed—confusion! As a rule, one issue or idea at a time, unless you are setting up an order for discussing several items, and you say so.

Organize your statements. A useful comment does not come at random, nor is it randomly expressed. A general pattern to follow is this: relate the contribution to what has already been said by another; state the idea; develop and support it; connect the contribution to the topic or phase of the problem being discussed. You will notice that this format provides an answer to the three basic questions to be asked when evaluating any extended contribution: What is the point? How do you know? How does it matter at this time? For example:

Helen, you said many magazine articles have been cut out. I also found that every encyclopedia had articles removed from it. The librarian told me it costs about $1,000.00 per year to replace damaged encyclopedias. So we can see that a serious part of the problem is the loss of widely used reference materials.

State Your Opinions Directly

It is common to hear someone state an apparent question that is actually an indirect or evasive way of stating an opinion. The form is that of a question, but the function is that of expressing an opinion. Such verbal constructions are often ambiguous, leaving the responder in a double-bind where whatever he or she says can be attacked. The classic example is "Have you stopped beating your kid?" instead of saying directly "I think you were a child beater." "It's a nice day?" on close examination suggests "I think this is an unpleasant day." To increase your sensitivity to the evasive tactic of substituting question-form statements for direct affirmations, try exercise two at the end of this chapter.

Statements that have been called "rhetorical questions" are not questions at all; these are the so-called "leading questions" that suggest the right answer. For example: "Wouldn't it be a good idea to brainstorm this question?" "Why don't we recommend that the school buy a bus to transport debate teams?" or "Don't you think prostitution should be legalized?" When a discussant hears a rhetorical question he or she can often clarify or prevent confusion by restating it as a declarative sentence, such as: "You seem to think we should brainstorm this issue. I agree." "You are recommending that the school buy a bus for the debate team." "You seem to favor legalizing prostitution."

Ask Clear, Specific Questions

Every affirmative statement is an answer to some implied question, whether or not the question has been stated. It has often been said that "To know how to ask the right questions is the mark of an educated person." The entire process of dialectic—a search for truth through discussion—is a search for the best possible answers to questions. Effective discussions are always that, a search for answers to questions. First, we will consider the general questions that indicate the goal of a discussion, and then the specific types of questions that will be raised along the journey to the goal.

Group-goal questions. True discussions always involve a search for answers on the part of participants: answers about each other, about how to solve or ameliorate personal problems, about the meaning of some object, about the status of something, about the quality of something, or about what policy or course of action to pursue. Sometimes the goal of the group is stated as a question ("What should be done to reduce accidents at the 73rd and

Jones intersection?"); sometimes (as in a therapy group) it is not, but only implied. When an answer has already been determined by someone with power and authority, only pseudo-discussion can occur in which the participants are coerced to arrive at the "right" answer. If you suspect this is the case, ask what the *real* purpose of the meeting is. Trying to get persons to think that they have had a hand in reaching an answer when it has actually been predetermined is a crass form of manipulation. If the group does not have in its area of freedom the right to answer the questions, then it should not be called a discussion. Let the "head" or authority who has decided announce the decision, and try to sell it.

A number of criteria in the form of questions need to be applied to the formulation of the general questions to which a small group may address its discussion. If the answer to any of these questions is *no,* the discussion will in all probability be chaotic and vacuous, the interaction listless and apathetic, and the output satisfactory to no one. The general goal question should be revised.

1. Is this question of interest to the members? (Do they need an answer to it?)
2. Is the question within the area of freedom of the group? (Unless the group has the authority or ability to do something about its answer, the question has been worded inappropriately for them.)
3. Is the question within the competence of the group to answer? (If the members do not have or cannot obtain the kinds of skills and information needed to answer the question, they cannot answer it validly. For instance, a group of laymen could not answer the question "How do Russian missile guidance systems compare with those of American missiles?")
4. Is the question sufficiently clear for all members to understand the goal similarly? ("What's wrong with American education?" is an example of a very fuzzy question. The referent might be public schools, private schools, or both. Is only formal schooling to be discussed, or all activities that educate? At what levels will the discussants direct their attention: elementary, secondary, post-secondary, professional, technical?)
5. Is the question sufficiently delimited to be dealt with thoroughly in the time available to the group? (Vague terms in a goal question often need to be made more concrete if the group is to make any real progress toward producing valid answers or solutions that will work.)

Very often the content of a discussion can be greatly improved by simply asking the question, "What question are we now discussing?" An open statement of the question or issue and its implications will reveal what is wrong when a group seems to be going awry. After examining the frequency with which themes or topics are switched in many discussions, it often appears as if no one knows what the issue is much of the time. Many discussions could be characterized as answers looking for questions. Both *what* we ask and *how* we ask it are vital to the communication among members of a small group.

Two characteristics of the way in which questions are formulated are of special concern. First, all questions can be classified as either *answerable* or *unanswerable*. As Weinburg pointed out, just because we can put a question mark after a string of words does not mean we have asked a meaningful or answerable question. If "answers" are given to an unanswerable question and we are unable to choose among them on any objective basis, there is no way to tell which is the correct or best answer.[5] To illustrate, consider the following: "What is the population of China today?" "What was the population of Omaha according to the 1976 census?" "How fast can a greyhound run?" and "Why did God punish the Martins by burning their house?" Most persons would agree that a factual answer, based on specific methods of census taking, could provide an objective answer to the first question even though such an answer may not now be available. Thus it is *potentially* answerable, but not answerable at the moment without exensive nonverbal activity. The second is readily answerable; records will give a specific incontrovertible answer to what the report says. The third question is ambiguous because it contains variable terms—it can only be answered when specific conditions are stated naming the dog, and such conditions as time and place. Thus it could be made meaningful by asking, "How fast did Diamond Jack run in the third race at the Atokad Greyhound Race Track on July 3, 1973?" The fourth question is meaningless, because it refers to nonobjective concepts, unobservables. That question assumes some personal force called God, and that this God took direct causative action. To answer it, what would we observe? Under what conditions? How? Such a "question" cannot be answered by any known means, so there is nothing to be gained by discussing it except confusion and conflict. You can help a group by pointing this out, and suggesting that the question either be dropped as meaningless or else be rephrased in a meaningful way that provides for some sort of observational answer (e.g., "What beliefs do each of us have about why the Martins' house may have burned?"—our beliefs can at least be stated and observed *as our beliefs*).

Second, all questions can be classified as *limited* or *open-ended*. Limited questions ask for a specific, brief answer, such as information, or if another person agrees or disagrees with some proposition. Such questions do not encourage elaboration or different points of view. Implied in a limited question is that there are only one, two, or a very few possible responses. Once a short answer has been given, there is no room for further response. For example: "How old are you?" "Do you think age is related to wisdom?" "Did you like that movie?" "When must we submit our report?" or "Which side do you think is right, the students or the administration?" Especially be wary of questions that suggest a one- or two-valued orientation. Although there are useful two-valued ways of classifying things, in most cases such thinking leads us to overlook matters of degree. Few things are either all good or all bad, all black or all white. If something were pure black, no light would reflect from it. But even lampblack reflects some light. Digitalis is poisonous in some quantities, but a powerful medicine in other quantities. To ask, "Is this painting beautiful?" is to imply that it is either all beautiful or all ugly. As a rule, phrase questions in terms of degree, not as either-or.

Open-ended questions imply a wide variety of possible answers, encouraging elaboration and numerous points of view. They imply more than a one-word or brief answer, with room for many responses. For example: "How beautiful do you think she is?" "What did you like about the movie?" "What are the relative merits of both the students' and the administration's points of view?" "Can anyone tell me more about that?"

Questions during discussions. Questions asked during the course of a discussion can be classified according to the function of the implied response (or, the kind of content each question indicates). Questions may be concerned with orientation, procedure, socio-emotional state, information, interpretation and opinion, or solution and policy. The first three types are concerned with issues of group process; the last three types are concerned with the group task.

Questions of orientation seek answers that will orient the group and help determine its goals. Early in a discussion it is important that the interdependent purposes, the area of freedom, and the type of end results that the discussion is to achieve be established. Questions seeking such information and decisions are most helpful if asked explicitly during this time, and may be needed whenever the group seems to lack a clear goal. Some questions of orientation may need to be of the limited type, such as when asking about the group's area of freedom. Consider the following examples:

"What are the purposes of this meeting?"

"How many nominees are we to report for each position to be filled?"

"Should we be trying to reach an agreement on what is the best policy regarding capital punishment, or just understanding the arguments for various proposed policies?"

"Where are we now? We were discussing the extent of the problem, but now we seem to be talking about a possible solution to it."

Procedural questions are relatively infrequent when compared with those seeking information, opinions and policies or solutions, but they are vital if coordinated teamwork is to be achieved. The procedural questioner asks such things as how to coordinate activity of group members, what to do next, or what discussion technique to follow. Here are some examples:

"What agenda will we follow today?"

"How should we organize this discussion?"

"How shall we proceed to evaluate this list of ideas?"

"How can we get our conclusions written up and reported to the Senate?"

Hirokawa found that effective problem solving groups spent significantly more time discussing and agreeing upon procedural matters than did ineffective groups.[6] When no procedure for the group to follow has been agreed upon (or announced), or if you do not understand what to do next or who is to do what for the group, that is a good indication that a question of procedure will facilitate group productivity.

Questions about socio-emotional states ask how members are feeling toward each other and the group as a whole. If a group member's nonverbal behaviors seem to indicate annoyance, anger, boredom, frustration, or alienation from the rest of the group, a question about what the person is feeling might help to bring the tension out in the open and thus permit the group to deal with it before a serious interpersonal clash occurs or a potentially valuable member is lost to the group. When you feel some negative or positive affect toward the group, asking if others feel likewise may help the group correct a previously unrecognized problem with its goal, procedures, or ways of interacting. Contrariwise, a socio-emotional question might get members to express positive feelings toward another or the group as a whole, thus heightening the group's cohesiveness. In a continuing group it is almost always more productive to deal with budding tensions and interpersonal conflicts before they become serious, rather than to hope the tensions will go away.

Questions of information are those that ask for specific statements of fact. They may refer to observations of something that has occurred, to what somebody said earlier, or for clarification of some statement. The answers should be limited to such reports without interpretations or inferences being confused with the fact; confusion often arises when a question of fact is responded to with a guess, hunch, theory, or pet belief. A fact as such is not discussable; it can merely be reported and possibly verified by further observation. Examples of meaningful questions of information or fact (those that can be answered from observations based on specific steps or operations) illustrate this type:

"What factors did the fire chief say contributed to the burning of the Martins' house?" (To verify, ask him or ask someone who heard him.)

"How did you do on the English CLEP exam?"

"What did you say, Sally, was the number of abortions in University Hospital last year?"

"By 'police' did you mean all law enforcement officers or only uniformed patrolmen?"

"What does anybody know about the extent of crimes of violence in our city?"

The answers to such questions may be true or false, depending on whether or not the answer conforms to what happened. The accuracy is discussable, but a fact itself is not subject to discussion—only to observation. It is important to determine whether what appears to be a question of information is really such, or if it is ambiguous or meaningless (does not refer to any observable event).

Questions of interpretation, opinion, or judgment are those concerned with the meaning of a fact or group of facts. Such questions ask not what happened, but what the facts mean to discussants. Since the answers are matters of opinion, there is much room for different answers. Many groups have as their goal the answering of such questions. For example, a grand jury collects information, then decides whether or not to file charges against a suspect. A so-called "fact-finding" committee of a legislature first ascertains what has happened, then interprets the meanings of these facts and may even recommend policy actions. The facts about heroin usage in a particular city will undoubtedly be judged as indicating a serious (or not so serious) problem. Examples of this type of question, such as the following, can be found in any discussion:

"Has auto theft increased in seriousness in our city since 1975?"

"How have the attitudes of college students changed since 1970?"

"What conditions appear to have contributed to the decline in the number of family-owned farms?"

"How effective is capital punishment in reducing the murder rate?"

"What are the relative merits of these proposals for improving the delivery of mail?"

To answer any such question requires information, but the answer will be an interpretation of that information.

Questions of interpretation are vital in both learning and problem-solving discussions. To analyze a problem means to interpret the extent and seriousness of it; and to get at its roots means to judge how events are related. Thus questions of "What caused this?" are invariably questions of interpretation. It is vital to keep in mind that answers are not absolute and totally objective, as can be the answers to questions of fact. There is room for disagreement among reasonable persons. The goal of a group is to arrive at the best *group* judgment possible.

Questions of value are special types of questions of interpretation. They call for judgments about the merit or worth of something. A comparison is always involved or implied in the answer to a question of value. This may be a comparison to some specific criterion (standard of judgment) or to a similar type of object or idea. For example:

"Is it more beneficial to humanity in the long run to supply food to starving people in over-populated countries or to let them starve?"

"Which political party has done more to improve the living conditions of the poor?"

"How effective is busing in achieving equality of educational opportunity for all children?"

"What are the benefits of a liberal education in the technological world?"

When individual and personal valuations are called for, it is important to remember that there is no need for agreement. There is no sense arguing about answers to such questions as: "Is this a good painting?" "Do you like this poem?" or "Is pork or chicken better?" A learning group has no need to agree on matters of value, but merely to understand what the questions imply and the basis for different answers to them. On the other hand, a group trying to arrive at a solution to a problem, when facing a choice among possible courses of action, must agree on the values or criteria in order to arrive at a specific recommendation or plan of action. For such a problem-solving group, arriving at agreement on values may well be essential if they are ever to agree on a solution.

Questions of policy ask, "What should be done to . . . ?" The key word is *should*. Such a question asks for a solution to a problem or a general plan of action. For example: "How many credits of science should be required for liberal arts graduates?" "What should we do to reduce littering in our town?" Obviously, answers to such questions that will be acceptable to all members of a group can be found after answers to questions of interpretation and value have been agreed upon. When communication breaks down in a group trying to agree upon a solution, it is usually wise to raise questions of value, asking what criteria are actually being applied. It may also be necessary to collect more facts and interpret them. The patterns for problem-solving discussion provide for discussion of fact, interpretation, value, and policy in that order. But sometimes the discussion is too sketchy at some stage in the process of problem solving to provide a basis for agreement on a policy statement. In this event the group may need to backtrack to answer questions of fact, interpretation, or value previously overlooked. When initially asking for possible solutions to a problem, it is often better to phrase the question as "What *might* be done to . . . ?" in order to encourage a variety of ideas before any discussion of their pros and cons is undertaken.

Develop Rhetorical Sensitivity

You are likely to make your verbal message encoding as productive of mutual understanding among group members as possible only if you develop the attitude toward communicating that has been called "rhetorical sensitivity."[7] Hart, Carlson, and Eadie described rhetorical sensitivity as "an attitude toward encoding spoken messages" that involves ". . . thinking about what should be said and then a way of deciding how to say it."[8] This mind-set is said to have five constituent parts that are all relevant to encoding in small group communication:

1. *Acceptance of personal complexity,* which means that the speaker views persons as having many selves, only some of which will be involved in the role(s) taken by a discussant in a particular group.

2. *Avoidance of communicative rigidity,* which implies that the person is free from rigid ways of encoding and interacting, and so is free to speak and act in a variety of ways in different group situations.
3. *Interaction consciousness,* which is a high degree of awareness of the process of interaction leading to avoidance of either sacrificing one's own ideas and feelings in order to please or placate others, or rampant egoism leading to speaking without regard to the needs and feelings of other participants.
4. *Appreciation of the communicability of ideas,* indicative that not *all* of our ideas and feelings ought to be uttered in a given discussion even if to express some of them might make us feel better temporarily. The criterion for utterance by a rhetorically sensitive person would be "will communication of this feeling or idea facilitate achievement of my personal goal and our group goals at this moment?"
5. *Tolerance for inventional searching,* which suggests that the speaker realizes that there may be many ways to express an idea, and so he or she consciously searches in mind for the most effective way to evoke a desired response from fellow discussants before speaking.[9]

The rhetorically sensitive discussant occupies a midway position between two extreme attitudes toward verbal encoding: "noble selves" who "see any variation from their personal norms as hypocritical, as a denial of integrity," and "rhetorical reflectors" who have no Self to call their own. For each . . . situation they present a new self."[10] Thus the rhetorically sensitive discussant would be one who neither says just anything and everything that comes to mind ("let it all hang out") nor one who tries to figure out the position of the majority (or high status members) and reflects that without personal conviction (the "yes-man" type).

At this time there is no evidence that the scale developed to measure rhetorical sensitivity predicts how well discussants function in various types of discussion groups. But developing an attitude of rhetorical sensitivity, especially of interaction consciousness, likely will help you to encode in ways that are both true to your self and yet clear and palatable to fellow group members. Being rhetorically sensitive should help you contribute to mutual understanding and such output variables as group cohesiveness and consensus decisions.

Nonverbal Codes

Up to this point we have examined only verbal signals in the process of communication, but the nonverbal components of messages are equally as important as the verbal in determining listeners' interpretations and responses. Furthermore, a large proportion of the interaction among discussants is done with signals that are entirely nonverbal. Birdwhistle has estimated that sixty-five per cent of meaning when persons communicate is the result of nonverbal signals.[11] Mehrabian put the percentage of meaning derived from nonverbal cues during face-to-face interaction as high as ninety-three per cent.[12] Four implications of communicating via nonverbal signals are especially important to keep in mind when considering what happens during the process of discussion:

1. You cannot *not* communicate in a face-to-face small group. Nonverbal cues go out from you constantly; you cannot stop them. Even if you sit relatively immobile and impassive, that behavior will be seen and responded to by others, possibly with distrust, dislike, worry about what you are up to or what is wrong with you. Another way to put it is that in a group "nothing never happens" with anyone.
2. Many nonverbal cues are highly ambiguous when not clarified verbally. For instance, a smile can mean friendship, agreement, disdain, gloating, private reverie, or just about anything.
3. In any case where the words signal one attitude or idea to a perceiver and the nonverbal cues signal another, the receiver is more likely to believe the nonverbal signals. Thus if you say "I'm really interested in that idea" in a flat tone while looking at notes in front of you, the previous speaker to whom you are responding is almost certain to believe that you do not care what he or she suggested.
4. Our feelings are communicated primarily by our nonverbal signals. These signals can rarely be concealed from sensitive persons in the close proximity of a small group. Integrity or sincerity is the only means to prevent tension from the mixed messages that result when a discussant attempts to deceive, bluff, or play manipulative games with other members of a small group. As Rosenfeld wrote,

Within a few seconds after you enter a group you are ready to pass judgments on the other members. You are ready to predict which members will be friends, which will be hard workers, and which trouble-makers. But if someone dared to ask how you made these judgments, you would probably be hard-put to provide an articulate answer. Is it the clothes they wore? The shape and smell of their bodies? How they combed their hair? Maybe it's the way they sat, or where they sat, or how they moved their bodies when they turned to look at you? . . . It's possible that the shape, size, color, or decorations of the room "turned you off."[13]

Functions of Nonverbal Signals in Small Group Communication

Nonverbal signals serve six major functions during group interaction: supplementing the verbal code, substituting for words, contradicting verbal statements, expressing emotions, regulating the interaction, and indicating status relationships. Being aware of these functions can help you act in ways that will be appropriate when responding to others and make your own signals more clear and unambiguous to them.

Supplementing the verbal. A movement or gesture may effectively *repeat* what is being said, as when a person points to item three on a chart at the same time he says "now look at the third item on our list of ideas." Such repeating makes the verbal message doubly clear. Other nonverbal messages serve to complement or elaborate what is said. For instance, a discussant might shake his head from side to side while saying, "I cannot accept that suggestion. I consider it immoral," in a voice louder and more strained than usual, or hold up three fingers while saying "There are three things in support of your suggestion."

Some nonverbal signals give emphasis or accent the verbal message. A nod of the head, increased force on a particular word or phrase, and a shake of the finger can all indicate "this is an especially important thought or word I am now uttering." Thus by repeating, complementing, and emphasizing, nonverbal signals can supplement the verbal.

Figure 6.5 Nonverbal signals supplement the verbal ones.

Substituting for words. Many gestures are substitutes for words. You are probably familiar with the American Sign Language that is used for communication among persons who cannot hear speech. A back-and-forth nod of the head is often used to indicate agreement or to bid at an auction without saying anything. If the chairperson of a small group asks "Do you want to vote on this?" and then sees one person shaking her head from side to side, no vote will be taken at that time. A finger movement can indicate to another discussant that you want him to lean closer to you, or a circle made with the thumb and forefinger can say in effect "I approve" or "I'm okay." Because only one person can be speaking at a time in an orderly discussion, a great deal of the communicating among members is done with nonverbal substitutes for words. Not to be aware of these, or not to consciously look for them, will mean that you are missing many important potential messages among the group members.

Contradicting verbal messages. When something that a person says in a discussion doesn't seem to "ring true," often that is because the nonverbal cues contradict the words uttered. Members of therapy and encounter groups are especially likely to watch for contradictory nonverbal messages, but they occur in other learning and problem solving discussions when someone is lying, conning, or has mixed feelings. For instance, someone might say "Yes, I'll go along with that," but in such a way that you expect him to give no real support to the idea. When you observe nonverbal messages that seem to contradict what someone is saying, it will usually pay to point this out and ask what the person means. For example, "You said you like your boyfriend, but something about the way you said it sounded as if you really don't care very much for him. What do you feel?"

Expressing emotions. As the previous example indicated, our feelings are communicated more often by nonverbal cues than by what we say. Try saying "I like you" in a variety of ways, and notice how each seems to indicate a very different feeling. Sitting close to another person can indicate more positive feelings for him or her than any words will convey. Starkweather reported that some vocal aspects of anxiety were immediately detectable.[14] Davitz and Davitz were able to associate particular voice characteristics with both active and passive feelings.[15]

Regulating interaction. Certain nonverbal messages control or direct the flow of interaction among group members. A designated discussion leader may use nods of the head, eye contact, and hand movements to indicate who should speak next when two or more persons have indicated a desire to do so. Favorable nods encourage a speaker to continue, whereas a lack of overt response or looking away often signals "shut up." Persons will show they want to speak by leaning forward, raising a hand or finger, opening the mouth, and possibly by uttering a nonverbal sound such as "uh." Hand signals may be used to speed up a dawdling speaker, or slow someone who is rushing. So it is that nonverbal cues are the primary means of regulating the flow of verbal interaction in discussion groups.

Figure 6.6 Nonverbal signals regulate interaction.

Indicating status relationships. It has previously been pointed out that sitting at the end of a table may indicate leader status or desire for a high degree of influence in a small group. A feeling of relative superiority is often indicated by staking out a larger than average amount of territory at a table (with books, etc.), suddenly getting very close to another, a penetrating stare, a loud voice, and a patronizing pat or other touch.[16] Relatively high status persons tend to have more relaxed posture than lower status group members. On the other hand, uncrossing arms and legs, unbuttoning a coat, and general relaxation of the body often signal openness and a feeling of equality.[17] Body orientation, the angle at which a participant's shoulders and legs are turned in relation to the group as a whole or another person, indicate how much one feels a part of the group, and often that one is more committed to a subgroup than to the group as a whole.[18]

Types of Nonverbal Signals

Although we usually respond to a pattern of simultaneous nonverbal signals rather than to a single cue, nonetheless it is important to be aware of the variety of types of such cues to help you avoid overlooking some of them. There are many ways of classifying nonverbal signals. Those which are listed below seem to play an especially important role in communication among members of small groups.

Paraverbal cues. These are the characteristics of voice and utterances other than words from which listeners interpret meanings of speakers. Included are such variables as pitch, rate and fluency of utterance, dialectical variations, force, tone quality, and silences (pauses). Listeners tend to agree on the characteristics they ascribe to speakers based on vocal cues, as shown by extensive research since the 1930s.[19] Included are such characteristics as aptitudes and interests, personality traits, adjustment, ethnic group, education, anxiety, and other emotional states.[20] The tone of voice has been recognized as an excellent indicator of a person's self-concept and mood. How we react to statements such as "I agree" or "Okay" depends much more on the pitch patterns and tone of voice than on the words themselves. Anxiety about communicating has been related to nonfluencies such as interjections ("uh"), repetitions, hesitations, sentence corrections, and even stuttering. To discover how much you infer from vocal cues, tape record a discussion. Everyone in the group should listen just to the voices, trying to ignore the words, and then write a description of the mood, feelings, or attitudes of each other person in the group. A comparison of the results often shows strikingly high agreement.

Facial Expression. Facial expression is highly indicative of feelings and moods. Without a word being spoken, you can often perceive anger, support, agreement, disagreement, and other sentiments from facial expressions. Eckman, Ellsworth, and Friesen found that at least six types of emotion could be detected accurately from facial expressions.[21]

With the close physical proximity typical of small group meetings one can easily detect changing moods of fellow discussants if one is simply aware of facial expressions. It pays to look around to sense the "pulse" of the group.

Eye Contact. Americans in small groups often use eye contact to seek feedback, when they want to be spoken to, and when they want to participate more actively.[22] In a competitive relationship between two persons, direct eye contact (or staring) may indicate something like "let's fight" whereas in a cooperative group it signifies friendship and cohesiveness.[23] As previously mentioned, eye contact is used to regulate the flow of conversation among discussants. Averting the look from another is usually taken as a sign that one wishes not to speak. Persons who seek and provide eye contact are often regarded as more believable than those who offer limited eye contact.

Eye movements can also signal disgust, dislike, superiority, or inferiority. In short, the eyes provide many important clues in human interchange.

Movements. Body movements and gestures signify much to the sensitive observer. A gatekeeper's nod may indicate who should speak next. Leaning toward another person in the group usually indicates interest, whereas leaning away indicates the opposite. However, leaning away during a discussion held out-of-doors might simply indicate being relaxed. A lot of twisting and shuffling of feet may indicate frustration or impatience with the pace of group progress. Members' movements often signal that it is time for the meeting to end.

Body angle. The importance of body angle has already been described. Noting it can help you judge who is vitally involved and who feels less interested or left out.

Dress and Accessories. These are often cues to status as members get acquainted in a small group. Crosses, social organization pins, jewelry, hair styles, and type of clothing often say much about how a person sees self, reference group memberships from which one derives norms, and personal values.

Any single nonverbal cue may be meaningless or highly ambiguous. But if you are careful to observe all the types of nonverbal cues a person is sending, you will gain a great deal of information helpful in relating effectively and in interpreting his or her verbal messages.

Listening in Small Group Communication

Communicating for mutual understanding during discussions depends as much on how you listen as it does on how you encode your ideas and feelings. Listening has been defined as a "selective process of attending to, hearing understanding, and remembering aural (and, at times visual) symbols."[24] "Hearing," the reception by the ear of sound waves and transformation of them into auditory nerve signals, is only a part of listening. A person with acute hearing may be a poor listener, whereas a person with considerable hearing loss may be a very capable listener in small group discussions, where hearing is usually not a problem.

It is much easier to detect that a fellow communicator is not listening well in a dyad than in a small group. In a group of several persons one member can avoid speaking for relatively long periods of time. Only when irrelevant comments indicate the speaker is unaware of what was said earlier is poor listening likely to be revealed.

Pitfalls to Effective Listening

If you discover that you do not listen well, the first step you must take is to identify the bad habits that are interfering with your attending to and understanding others. Here are five common behavioral patterns that are frequent sources of poor listening by discussants.

1. *Preparing to reply before fully understanding a question or statement by a fellow discussant.* You cannot both listen to your own internal dialog as you think of what to say and listen to what another person is saying. Group members who know each other will often think they know what a person will say long before he or she has finished a statement, jump to a conclusion, and then get ready to reply without listening to the full statement or attending closely to the nonverbal components of the message.

2. *Focussing on irrelevancies and distractions.* Instead of keeping the attention focussed on what other members are saying or signalling nonverbally, some members let themselves be distracted and attend to background noises, furnishings, statements made by persons not in the group, or other less-than-ideal environmental conditions. Some will pay undue attention to a speaker's dialect or personal mannerisms, and thus miss his or her meaning. As one woman from Georgia said to group members, "Dammit, listen to what I have to say, not to how I speak. I can't change that now. It makes me really mad when someone says 'Oh, how you talk is so cute I just can't pay attention to what you are saying.' "

3. *Getting unduly emotionally or ego involved.* When we feel defensive, we often quit listening while we invent ways to defend and attack. But then is when we may most of all need to listen to understand the source of the irritation: it may be a very real clash in values, one person assuming a position of superiority, or simply a different way of verbalizing the same belief or value. A tip: when you get so emotionally involved that you literally cannot feel the seat of your pants, it is time to relax a bit, back off, and try to understand as exactly as possible the meaning of the speaker to whom you are responding so strongly. Take another look! Especially watch out for your "fighting" or trigger words when used by another.

4. *Sidetracking.* Another discussant mentions some experience or idea, and you begin a reverie as you recall some past experience that the statement triggered. Meanwhile, something else has been said that you missed. Watch out for the tendency to sidetrack into your personal storehouse of memories while others are still speaking.

5. *Not listening when someone presents a belief or idea contrary to one of your deep seated convictions.* This is closed-mindedness in action. Such behavior is often hard to change, for it rests on basic attitudes such as were discussed in chapter 3. But if you are aware of your biases and convictions, you can then at least try to compensate by extra diligence in attending to and interpreting what another is saying that is contrary to your belief.

Listening Actively to Understand and Evaluate

Effective listening is an active process, requiring as much effort as speaking. Unless we listen closely, we will not have all the information needed to make sound decisions. Often several discussants in turn say almost the same thing, as if they had never heard what the first person said. This wastes time. Of course during the early stages of the emergence of a new group, while roles are in flux, not much listening may be in evidence as members vie for status and roles. But if this continues at length something needs to be done.

It is especially important to listen to understand the other person's meaning before reacting. The sidetracking and irrelevancy that result from half listening are costly of time and goodwill. A good test of your listening is to restate, in your own words, the meaning of the previous speaker. My own discussion classes often do this as an exercise to develop effective listening. Each discussant is required to restate the prior speaker's ideas to the person's satisfaction. If the restatement is not accepted as accurate, then the new speaker loses the floor. In many groups, more than fifty percent of the restatements are rejected as being inaccurate or incomplete. If misunderstanding is so common even when great effort to understand is being made, how common must it be in ordinary discussions?

One effect of listening to understand is a slowing down of the discussion. One cannot listen well while thinking up what to say next. If you are not used to listening so carefully that you could restate what another has said to his or her satisfaction, at first you may find you have nothing to say for a moment after the discussant has finished. But keep at it; soon you will find yourself making spontaneous responses in place of strategically preplanned remarks. Your comments will be more relevant to what preceded, and cooperation will be enhanced in your groups.

Only when you are sure you understand another person's point of view should you evaluate his or her comment. Then critical listening is in order. Was the comment pertinent? Is there a basis in evidence and experience for what was said? Is the statement logically valid? Does he or she present a biased picture of events? Good listening is a process of understanding what the speaker meant from his or her point of view, and then evaluating the significance and dependability of his or her comments.

A part of good listening during discussions is to be an open responder. This was previously explained in "The Complete Communicative Transaction" (p. 127). Only overt feedback can provide the speaker with the responses he or she needs. Positive feedback indicating that a message has been received and understood can take the vocal form of an "um-hum," "gotcha," or "yeah," or such nonverbal gestures as head nodding, smiling, frowning, changing of body angle, or hand gesturing. More expansive forms of these cues usually indicate agreement. Some listeners get in the habit of "pseudolistening" in which they emit such moves and gestures mechanically, misleading the sender. Pseudolistening is often more damaging to mutual perception than ambiguous responses, such as just looking at the person, for the speaker at first thinks the responder understands or agrees, then in time may cease to place any confidence in responses from such a person.

When you cannot hear adequately or do not have confidence that you understood, negative feedback should be supplied. Such responses do not necessarily mean that you disagree; the extensiveness of the move or vocal range seems to be the determining factor in whether a negative nonverbal response is perceived as disagreement or simply as a sign of not hearing or understanding. If speakers frequently seem not to perceive or to misunderstand your responses, most likely your responses are ambiguous and need to be amplified or complemented with more vigorous verbal and nonverbal signals.

Written Messages Among Small Group Members

Efficient communication within a continuing group depends upon records and reports of meetings. Although learning groups rarely keep records of their meetings since the outcomes are individual learnings, problem-solving groups always should. Even a single-meeting *ad hoc* group usually benefits from a written report of the meeting, as a reminder to all members of what was discussed and decided, and to assure that all agree with the understanding of the secretary or reporter. Most committees of larger groups are required to keep records of their meetings, and they usually must submit reports not only to all members of the committee, but also to the parent organization (and sometimes to other interested groups). For example, at the university where I work, the committees of the Faculty Senate must write reports of each meeting, and the reports are distributed to all members of the Senate and sometimes to selected administrators.

The purpose of such reports is to preserve a record of the essential *content* of the discussion, not of the process. The format and type of detail included in meeting reports may take various forms, depending upon the nature of the group, its objectives, and the type of report is must submit to others.

The reports of some committees and judicial groups must, as directed by the constitution of the organization, be kept in the form of minutes with a record of all items on the agenda, including reports, actions by consent, motions, and votes. Such a report does not necessarily indicate that the committee employed all possible parliamentary rules, but only that it kept complete records of all actions and voted where necessary to confirm decisions. Here is an example of committee minutes that you could use as a guide:

Minutes of April 12, 1977 Meeting of Committee A

Committee A held a special meeting at 1:30 P.M. on Thursday, April 14, 1977 in room 14 of the Jones Library.

    Attendance: Walter Bradley, Marlynn Jones, George Smith, Barbara Trekheld, and Michael Williams.

    Absent were Jantha Calamus and Peter Shiuoka.

    1. The minutes of the April 4 meeting were approved as distributed.

    2. Two nominations for membership in the graduate faculty were considered. A subcommittee of Bradley and Trekheld repored that their investigation indicated that Dr. Robert Jordon met all criteria for Membership. Williams moved that Professor Jordon be recommended to Dean Bryant for Membership in the Graduate Faculty. The vote was unanimously in favor.

    The nomination of Professor Andrea Long was discussed; it was concluded that she met all criteria, and that the nomination had been processed properly. Jones moved that Professor Long be recommended for appointment to the Graduate Faculty. The motion was passed unanimously.

3. Encouragement of grant activity. Discussion next centered on the question of how to encourage more faculty members to submit proposals for funding grants. Several ideas were discussed. Bradley moved that we recommend to President Yardley that:

a. A policy be established to grant reduced teaching loads to all professorial faculty who submit two or more grant proposals in a semester; and

b. That ten percent of all grant overhead be returned to the department that obtained the grant for use in any appropriate way.

This motion was approved unanimously.

4. It was agreed that our next meeting will be in Carter Hall 241 on Friday, May 6, at 1:30 P.M. All members were asked to send agenda items to Professor Jones by April 24.

5. The meeting was adjourned at 3:45 P.M.

Submitted by,
Marlynn Jones, Chair

More typically the report of a problem-solving group takes the form of a brief summary of attendance, time and place of the meeting, the purpose of the meeting, the problem(s) discussed, the findings, the ideas considered, any criteria used to weigh ideas, the final solution accepted by the group, and who is responsible for what action. The following report is given as a model that you may use as a guide for format, or modify to suit the needs of particular groups and meetings.

Report of February Meeting of the Field Trial Committee
Pine Ridge Beagle Club
Time and Place of Meeting: 7:30 P.M. at home of Henry Lewis, February 4, 1974.

Attendance:	Joe Hamilton, Marshall Frazier, Henry Lewis, George Brown, and Jack Brilhart. Absent was Mark Jones.
Purpose:	The committee met to select dates for the 1974 licensed trial, and to prepare a slate of judges to recommend at the next membership meeting.
Findings:	The predicted entry, based on past records and AKC registration trends, will be 10–15 15″ males, 15–20 15″ females, 20–25 13″ males, and 25–30 13″ females.
	A letter from AKC indicated we could hold our trial on September 5–8, September 30–October 3, or November 5–6. Because of costs, it was felt we should have two judges cover all classes.
Criteria for Judges:	1. They should have attended an AKC seminar, and give performance priority over style.
	2. They should have a reputation for tact.
	3. They should live within 400 miles in order to hold down transportation costs.
Possible Judges:	Twelve names were proposed by the committee: Jack Jones, Evlyn Smith, Tim Coasley, Mike O'Neil, Harry Lampdon, Pete Bradovich, Ed Ponza, Mack Lambert, Walt Smith, Betty Candler, Jim Johnson, and Bugs Gower.

Decisons:	We decided to recommend a 3-day trial, September 30–October 2, with both 15″ classes the first day, followed by 13″ males and 13″ females. Earlier might be too hot, and later runs into the Hawkeye trial dates. For judges we nominated: Pete Bradovich, Betty Candler, Jack Jones, and Harry Lampdon.
Action:	Chairman Hamilton will write to AKC requesting approval for the dates elected. Secretary Lewis will call the four judges to determine if they are available.

Reported by,
Henry Lewis, Secretary

Such records as the above will help members recall from meeting to meeting just what facts were presented, what assignments were accepted for research, what progress was made toward finding a commonly accepted solution, and so on. Without such a written report, each meeting of a group tends to "begin from scratch." Much time is wasted, and often members forget what was decided, leading to needless argument and even open conflict. Further, such a report can give a sense of accomplishment to the group and help to foster cohesiveness among members.

It is wise for each member to keep some record of the meeting as it progresses, but the writing of the report (or "minutes") is usually the assigned duty of the chair or an appointed recorder (or "secretary"). Regardless, even as the content of the discussion is the responsibility and the property of all members, so is the report. It is usually unwise to report *who* suggested what solution or idea, or who presented what information. Sometimes this could be threatening to the members, and so may stifle creativity if they fear the responses of some superior administrator in an organization (e.g., the Chancellor in the case of a university committee, or the instructor in the case of a class committee). So record all information, all ideas, all accepted criteria, all decisions, and all responsibilities for action—but only in the latter case report the name unless legal minutes are required.

Summary

Human communicating is a highly complex transactional process that involves many transformations of signals, individual vagaries, and symbolic encoding. Hence, intense attention to both encoding and listening are required if members of small groups are to achieve perceptual congruency. Productive discussants display both rhetorical sensitivity as they select and arrange their verbal messages, and sensitivity to the nonverbal cues both they and fellow discussants emit. They ask appropriate questions to clarify both the process and content of discussion. They are active listeners who try to understand the messages of fellow group members so well that they could paraphrase acceptably to speakers. Finally, they are capable of writing reports and minutes in concise form as a record of group effort and progress.

Exercises

1. See how well you understand the kinds of statements and behaviors that foster defensiveness and openness-trust in a group, and how these relate to a cooperative vs. competitive climate by matching the following:

   _____ certainty   A. cooperative relationships
   _____ control   B. competitive relationships
   _____ description
   _____ empathy
   _____ evaluation
   _____ neutrality
   _____ problem solving
   _____ provisionalism
   _____ spontaneity
   _____ strategies

2. Carry on a conversation with two or three other persons in which you can only make statements in the form of questions. Leading or rhetorical questions are okay. Discuss what you learn from doing this.

3. From your experience in small group discussions, describe an instance of miscommunication resulting from one of the following types of verbalizations. Be specific in describing what was said and what happened in response.

   ambiguity or vagueness
   cliché
   sexist language
   racist language or ethnic slur

4. As you listen to a tape-recorded discussion, make up a sheet listing each of the *types* of questions, thus getting a frequency count of each type. Also record each actual question and the appropriateness of the response to it. Compare your results with those of other members of your group who listen to the same recorded discussion.

5. With others, listen to a tape-recorded discussion. Each time the group seems to be discussing a new question or issue, stop the recorder, write out what you judge the question under discussion to be, and the logical-psychological implications of it. Compare results with others listening to the same discussion.

6. Practice the rule that "each discussant must rephrase in his own words his or her understanding of the previous speaker's meanings (ideas *and* feelings) to that speaker's *complete* satisfaction (as indicated verbally or by a head nod) before he or she may have the floor and add anything to the discussion." If the rephrasing is not accepted, the original

speaker may then clarify, the rephraser may try again, or someone else may try. One member of the group should not participate, but keep an accurate count of the number of times rephrasings are accepted and rejected. Be sure to count each attempt to rephrase. Discuss the implications of listening, how to improve communication, and how you felt during this project.

7. During fishbowl discussions (one group in center engaged in discussion, encircled by nonparticipating observers), the observers should rate each participant on each of the polar scales of defensive vs. supportive communication, by making an X in the appropriate space:

evaluative	___ : ___ : ___ : ___ : ___ : ___ : ____	descriptive
controlling	___ : ___ : ___ : ___ : ___ : ___ : ____	problem-solving
strategic	___ : ___ : ___ : ___ : ___ : ___ : ____	spontaneous
neutral	___ : ___ : ___ : ___ : ___ : ___ : ____	empathic
superior	___ : ___ : ___ : ___ : ___ : ___ : ____	equal
certain	___ : ___ : ___ : ___ : ___ : ___ : ____	provisional
	1 2 3 4 5 6 7	

8. In a practice session, group discussants should first refrain from giving any bodily or vocal responses to comments of others (i.e., no head nods, leaning forward, hand gestures while another talks, "un-huh" comments, facial expressions, etc.) for about ten minutes. Then, during the next ten minutes, everyone should react nonverbally (both physically and vocally) as fully and completely as possible. Members should then describe how they felt in each situation, why, and what this shows about group communication.

9. During a fishbowl discussion, any observer may call "freeze" at any time, at which point each discussant should remain motionless without changing even so much as eye direction. Then the observer asks each other observer to comment on what each discussant's posture, position in the group, eye direction, and nonverbal behavior seems to indicate about his or her feelings toward the group. After this, both observers and participants may discuss the implications of these observer comments and the basis for them.

10. Each member of a small group should write up a formal report of the discussion. Distribute these to all group members. Evaluate them in a discussion, seeking to determine guidelines for an adequate report.

11. This is a test of sensitivity to nonverbal visual cues in small group discussion. Each of the three photographs that follow shows a small group engaged in discussion. Study each photo carefully, then discuss with four or five classmates your perceptions and responses to it. What do you judge each person shown to be thinking-feeling? On what specific nonverbal cues do you base your interpretation of each person? What functions do these nonverbal cues seem to be serving?

communication within the small group 159

Bibliography

Cathcart, Robert S., and Samovar, Larry A., eds., *Small Group Communication: A Reader,* 3rd ed., Dubuque: Wm. C. Brown Company Publishers, 1979; section III.

Gulley, Halbert E., and Leathers, Dale G., *Communication and Group Process: Techniques for Improving the Quality of Small-Group Communication,* 3rd ed., New York: Holt, Rinehart and Winston, Inc., 1977; especially parts 1 and 3.

Hart, Roderick R., Carlson, Robert E., and Eadie, William F., "Attitudes toward Communication and the Assessment of Rhetorical Sensitivity," *Communication Monographs* 47 (1980), pp. 1–22.

Hayakawa, S. I., *Language in Thought and Action,* New York: Harcourt, Brace and Company, 1949.

Knapp, Mark L., *Nonverbal Communication in Human Interaction,* 2nd ed., New York: Holt, Rinehart and Winston, 1978.

Rosenfeld, Lawrence B., *Human Interaction in the Small Group Setting,* Columbus, Ohio: Charles E. Merrill Publishing Company, 1973.

References

1. Reprinted with permission from Wm. C. Brown Company Publishers and the author, Stephen W. King, "The Nature of Communication," in Robert S. Cathcart and Larry A. Samovar (eds.), *Small Group Communication: A Reader,* 3rd ed. Dubuque, Ia.: Wm. C. Brown Company Publishers, 1979, pp. 271–81.

2. William V. Haney, *Communication and Organizational Behavior,* 3rd ed. (Homewood, Ill.: Richard D. Irwin, 1973), p. 246.

3. Dale G. Leathers, "Process Disruption and Measurement in Small Group Communication," *Quarterly Journal of Speech* 55 (1969), pp. 288–98.

4. H. Kahane, *Logic and Contemporary Rhetoric: The Use of Logic in Everyday Life* (Belmont, Cal.: Wadsworth Publishing Co., Inc., 1976), p. 102.

5. Harry L. Weinberg, *Levels of Knowing and Existence* (New York: Harper & Row, Publishers, 1959), pp. 213–16.

6. Randy Y. Hirokawa "A Comparative Analysis of Communication Patterns within Effective and Ineffective Decision-Making Groups," *Communication Monographs* 47 (1980), pp. 312–21.

7. Roderick P. Hart and Don M. Burks, "Rhetorical Sensitivity and Social Interaction," *Speech Monographs* 39 (1972), p. 75.

8. Roderick P. Hart, Robert E. Carlson, and William F. Eadie, "Attitudes toward Communication and the Assessment of Rhetorical Sensitivity," *Communication Monographs* 47 (1980), p. 2.

9. *Loc Cit.*

10. Donald Darnell and Wayne Brockriede, *Persons Communicating* (Englewood Cliffs, N.J.: Prentice-Hall, 1976), pp. 176–78.

11. Ray L. Birdwhistle, Lecture at Nebraska Psychiatric Institute; Omaha, Nebraska; May 11, 1972.

12. Albert Mehrabian, *Nonverbal Communication* (Chicago: Aldine-Atherton, 1972).

13. Lawrence R. Rosenfeld, *Now That We're All Here: Relations in Small Groups* (Columbus, O.: Charles E. Merrill Publishing Company, 1976), p. 31.

14. J. Starkweather, "Vocal Communication of Personality and Human Feelings," *Journal of Communication* 11 (1961), pp. 63–72.

15. Joel R. Davitz and Lois J. Davitz, "Nonverbal Vocal Communication of Feeling," *Journal of Communication* 11 (1961), pp. 81–86.

16. Erving Goffman, *Relation in Public* (New York: Harper and Row, 1971), pp. 32–48.

17. Gerald I. Nierenberg and H. H. Calero, *How to Read a Person Like a Book* (New York: Pocket Books, 1973), p. 46.

18. Stewart L. Tubbs, *A Systems Approach to Small Group Interaction* (Redding, Mass.: Addison-Wesley, 1978), p. 185.

19. N. D. Addington, "The Relationship of Selected Vocal Characteristics to Personality Perception," *Speech Monographs* 35 (1968), p. 492, and Ernest Kramer, "Judgment of Personal Characteristics and Emotions from Nonverbal Properties of Speech," *Psychological Bulletin* 60 (1963), pp. 408–20.

20. Joel R. Davitz and Lois Davitz, "Nonverbal Vocal Communication of Feelings," *Journal of Communication* 11 (1961), pp. 81–86.

21. Paul Eckman, P. Ellsworth, and W. V. Friesen, *Emotion in the Human Face: Guidelines for Research and an Integration of Findings* (New York: Pergamon Press, 1971).

22. James McCroskey, Carl Larson, and M. Knapp, *An Introduction to Interpersonal Communication* (Englewood Cliffs, N.J.: Prentice-Hall, 1971), pp. 110–14.

23. R. V. Exline, "Explorations in the Process of Person Perception: Visual Interaction in Relation to Competition, Sex, and the Need for Affiliation," *Journal of Personality* 31 (1963), pp. 1–20.

24. Larry L. Barker, *Listening Behavior* (Englewood Cliffs, N.J.: Prentice-Hall, 1971), p. 17.

7

which shall it be? decision making in small groups

Study Objectives

As a result of your study and application of chapter 7 you should be able to:

1. Distinguish between the concepts "problem solving" and "decision making," and be able to define each of these terms.

2. Describe the relative output advantages of decision making in matters of judgment by individuals and groups.

3. Understand the differences among decision making by consensus, majority vote, averaging, expert, and leader, and be able to list advantages and disadvantages of each method.

4. Relate the five procedural guidelines for making group decisions by consensus.

5. Make major decisions in groups of peers by consensus.

Key Terms

Consensus decision   a choice among alternatives, which all members of a group agree is the best they can make that will be acceptable to all members.

Criterion   a criterion is a standard for judging among alternatives, often stated as a question; plural is *criteria*.

Decision making   choosing among alternatives.

Groupthink   conformity of lower-status members to the beliefs and opinions of a high-status member or majority of a group.

Majority decision   decision made by vote, with at least 51 percent voting for the chosen alternative.

Many choices have to be made by small groups—when to meet, where to meet, whether or not to accept a statement as true, how to word a recommendation, whether or not a defendant is guilty, what punishment or reward to give, which of several applicants shall receive a scholarship, or which of the proposed solutions to adopt. Some of these will be very important, some relatively trivial in their consequences for the group's task achievement and future functioning. In this chapter we will be concerned with a number of ways in which such decisions are made by groups, and the implications of these procedures.

Decision Making Is Not Problem Solving

Some writers have confused the terms "decision making" and "problem solving," but there is a major difference between the two group process variables implied by these terms. Decision making refers to the act of *choosing* between two or more possible alternatives, whereas problem solving always includes the freedom to *create* alternatives.[1] Problem solving refers to a many-stage procedure through which an individual or group moves from a state of dissatisfaction with something to a plan for arriving at a satisfactory condition. Problem solving entails a series of steps such as determining what is wrong, establishing a goal, developing a detailed plan for correcting the problem, and implementing that plan. So the process of problem solving includes numerous decisions long before the group is ready to choose a solution and implement it. In chapter 7 we are concerned with how these decisions are made, not with the problem solving procedure *per se*.

Of course one could say that some groups have the "problem" of choosing among alternatives provided to them. But their work in choosing is only a step in the larger process of problem solving, which in such a case involves other persons or groups. Many groups have authority to engage in only a limited part of the problem solving process, such as committees assigned to investigate a situation and interpret their findings, but not to recommend a solution or take concrete action. An example of a decision-making group with no freedom to invent or propose alternatives is a screening committee of students, faculty members, and administrators asked to recommend one of several applicants for the position of college ombudsman. As I use the term, this is *not* a "problem solving" group. The entire problem solving procedure, of which their work is only one step, would include the feeling that something was wrong in the way the college was functioning, some determination of the nature and causes of that problem, the decision that the best possible course of action as a solution was to appoint an ombudsman, and recruitment of applicants for the job. Our hypothetical screening committee is only making one decision in the lengthy process of problem solving.

effective group discussion

Group vs. Individual Decision Making

Before reading further, *rank* the following ways for making decisions in a small group from 1 (most preferred) to 7 (least preferred).

_____ A. Let the leader of the group decide because he or she should have the right to make the decision. After all, the leader has the responsibilities.

_____ B. Find out who is most expert on the topic, and let him or her decide what is best for the group.

_____ C. Decide by chance, such as flipping a coin, rolling a die, or drawing straws.

_____ D. Determine the average of what group members think.

_____ E. Wait it out. A decision will finally emerge, or maybe if you wait long enough a decision will not be necessary.

_____ F. Take a vote, and the majority rules. This is the American way to decide after the issues have been discussed.

_____ G. Keep talking until you can arrive at a basic agreement from everyone as to what the decision should be. Everyone should participate in discussion until all agree you have arrived at the best possible decision the group can reach.

If possible to do so, compare your rankings with those of several other persons in a small group of classmates. *Be sure to explain your reasons for your rankings, and listen to understand the reasons of the other persons in your group.*

Deciding among alternatives by a group rather than an individual invariably takes more time. A group of persons must often discuss at great length before making a decision. Even if they do not, just the time to get together can be quite expensive. Certain types of decisions can be made better by an individual than by a group if the individual is truly expert in the matter and the group members are not, or if there is some clear and unequivocal basis for making the decision. An expert on cleaning agents might make a better decision on how to treat an unusual stain in a carpet than would many persons not so informed. A skilled woodsman could better decide how to fell a tree than could a group of novices. But when it comes to an issue such as how to proceed in coordinating group effort, all members must concur or the decision is not going to work. Most of the major issues confronted by groups have no single best answer, but call for judgments based on a range of information no one member alone possesses. When there is no information sufficient to make an absolutely certain decision, groups tend to make decisions superior to those of individuals. Often the sole criterion for validating a decision is its acceptance by the persons who must put it into effect; there is no external criterion to which it can be compared. Possibly in time the quality of the decision can be appraised, but even then there will be no way to know for certain if one of the alternatives rejected would have been better.

Maier presented a formula for the evaluation of decision making that fits this situation: $ED = Q \times A$.[2] In this formula *ED* refers to the effectiveness of a decision, *Q* refers to the potential technical quality of the decision, and *A* to the acceptance it receives from persons involved. A classic field experiment reported by Coch and French demonstrated that when workers had a voice in deciding how to put a change of work routine into effect they were more productive and less inclined to be absent, quit, and file grievances than when the decision was made entirely by experts and their superiors.[3] Other researchers have demonstrated that group decisions by non-experts were qualitatively superior to those made by the same individuals or averages of the decisions made by the individuals. In these experiments there was a criterion of excellence previously established by agreement among a panel of experts not known to the experimental subjects.[4] From an analysis of many major political decisions Janis concluded and argued forcefully that decision making by a high status member of a group or a minority of such persons often leads to disastrous outcomes.[5] Thus the evidence is clear that in such matters groups tend to make decisions superior to those made by individuals.

It was once thought that group decisions are more conservative and mediocre than those made by individuals.[6] But this belief was corrected by a series of studies that found groups more willing than individuals to make high-risk decisions when the payoff is high. Stoner first reported that decisions made by groups tended to be more risky (lower odds for success) than decisions made by individual members of the groups working alone.[7] Subsequent studies confirmed that in many cases groups will make risky decisions, but also found that in some conditions the group decisions are more conservative than those originally made by individual members. When the stakes are very high—such as when the lives of participants or loved ones are at stake—when moral values are involved, or when members share norms favoring caution, the tendency is for the group to make even more conservative decisions than do individual members acting alone.[8] Many theories were advanced in attempts to explain the tendency for groups to make risky decisions: responsibility was shared in case a decision made by a group proved to be the wrong one; high-risk takers are more persuasive than conservative discussants; our society has norms that encourage risk taking. Regardless of the reason, it has been shown beyond doubt that groups do not make more mediocre, cautious, and traditional decisions than do individuals. Groups often achieve what is called the "assembly effect," a decision qualitatively and affectively superior to what could have been decided by even the most expert of its members or a simple adding or averaging of the skills and wisdom of the members. The *procedures* that a group follows in making decisions may be more important than sharing responsibility, individual persuasiveness, or societal values, but this issue has not been explored thoroughly in research.

Methods of Decision Making in Small Groups

How decisions are made is vital to the output of task groups. As has been previously stated, output variables of solution quality, member commitment and effort to make a solution work, member satisfaction with both solutions and group process, and cohesiveness are all affected by methods used by the group to make decisions.

There are at least six different ways in which decisions are made by and for small groups: by consensus, by majority vote, by averaging individual ideas, by a minority, by an expert member, and by an authoritarian leader (head). If you are reading this book for a course in small group communication, discussion, or group dynamics, to get the full impact of differences among these methods you can do the activities explained below for each method.

Decision by Consensus

A consensus decision is one that all members agree is the best they can *all* accept or agree to; it is not necessarily the most preferred decision of all members. Deciding by consensus produces superior results in quality, in member satisfaction with the decision, and in acceptance of the result. But reaching consensus usually takes more time than any other method of deciding, especially if unanimity is achieved, and sometimes consensus is not possible. Unanimity is a state of perfect consensus in which every member of a group believes that the decision reached is the best that could be made, not just the best that the group could agree upon. Often this is not possible. All members of a group understand a consensus decision and the reasons for it, and all will usually support it even though it is not the decision one or a few persons would have preferred. The process of arriving at a consensus gives all members a chance to express how they feel about it, and an equitable chance to influence the final outcome.

Consensus depends on careful listening so that all important information and points of view are understood similarly by all discussants. A consensual decision is often a synergistic outcome in which the group produces something superior to a summation of individual ideas and thinking. In arriving at a consensus, conflicts and differences of opinion must be viewed as a means for clarification and testing of alternatives, not as interpersonal competition for power. Guidelines for making decisions by consensus were outlined by Hall:

1. Don't argue stubbornly for your own position. Present your position as clearly and logically as possible, being sure you listen to all reactions and consider them carefully.

2. When a stalemate seems to have occurred, avoid looking at it as a situation in which someone must win and someone else lose. Rather, see if you can find a next best alternative that is acceptable to everyone. This may take conscious effort.
3. When an agreement is reached too easily and quickly, be on guard. Don't change your position simply to avoid conflict and reach agreement quickly. Through discussion, be certain that everyone accepts the solution for similar or complementary reasons.
4. Don't use such techniques as majority vote, averaging, coin tossing, or swapping off.
5. Seek out differences of opinion; they are to be expected and can be most helpful in testing ideas. Get every member involved in the decision-making process. If you have a wide range of information and ideas the group has a better chance of finding a truly excellent solution.

If you are enrolled in a class, the learning activity that follows was designed to give you such an experience. Before doing anything else, read the hypothetical case "Lost on the Moon," and rank the items as instructed.

Lost on the Moon

Your spaceship has just crash-landed on the moon. You were scheduled to rendevous with a mother ship 200 miles away on the lighted surface of the moon, but the rough landing has ruined your ship and destroyed all the equipment on board except for 15 items listed below. Your crew's survival depends on reaching the mother ship, so you must choose the most critical items available for the trip. Your task is to rank the 15 items in terms of their importance for survival. Place number 1 by the most important, number 2 by the second most important, and so on through number 15.

_____ Box of matches

_____ Food concentrate

_____ Fifty feet of nylon rope

_____ Parachute silk

_____ Solar-powered portable heating unit

_____ Two .45-caliber pistols

_____ One case of dehydrated milk

_____ Two 100-pound tanks of oxygen

_____ Stellar map (of the moon's constellations)

_____ Self-inflating life raft

_____ Magnetic compass

_____ Five gallons of water

_____ Signal flares

_____ First-aid kit containing injection needles

_____ Solar-powered FM receiver-transmitter

As soon as everyone has ranked all 15 items without consulting anyone else, your class should be formed into groups of five or six members each. Following the rules for decision making by consensus as closely as possible, arrive at a ranking for your group. As soon as your group has completed a consensus ranking, each member should complete a copy of the "Postdecision Reaction Sheet."

Postdecision Reaction Sheet. On a sheet of paper record your answers to the following questions; then give the answers to your group's coordinator who will record them on one sheet of paper, compute the averages, and report them to your instructor who may record them on a chalkboard for discussion by the entire class.

1. How much chance to influence the group decision do you feel you had?

1	2	3	4	5	6	7	8	9

   (none)   (a great deal)

2. How satisfied are you with the result of your group's decision-making discussion?

1	2	3	4	5	6	7	8	9

   (very dissatisfied)   (very satisfied)

3. How well do you think other members of the group listened to and understood you?

1	2	3	4	5	6	7	8	9

   (not at all)   (completely)

4. How much commitment do you feel to your group's decisions?

1	2	3	4	5	6	7	8	9

   (none)   (very much)

5. What adjective best describes the atmosphere in your group during the discussion? _____

(Note: you will complete this same form after each of the next three exercises.)

Your instructor may now want you to score both your individual and group answers. Scoring is done by computing error points with a known "best" answer. This "best" answer was arrived at by a group of experts in the National Aeronautics and Space Administration's Crew Equipment Research Department in Houston. Your instructor has a copy of the "best" answer, and will explain how to do the scoring.[9]

Decision by Majority Vote

Majority vote is the basis for deciding in most large, democratic groups. As soon as 51 percent of the members voting support one alternative, the decision has been reached. Voting in a small group can be done by voice ("aye"), a show of hands, or even by ballot (slips of paper). This method of deciding is much easier and faster than consensus as a rule, but all too frequently the members in the minority ("losers") are not satisfied that their ideas have been fully understood and considered or that the best possible decision the group could make has been achieved. Not only does the quality of the decision frequently suffer, but also the cohesiveness and commitment to the decision. In some committees the constitution of the parent organization requires that votes be taken and recorded on major issues. If so, the group can discuss until a consensus decision has emerged, then vote to confirm it "legally."

The following learning activity will give you a guided experience in making a group decision by majority vote:

Decision making by majority vote. Divide the class into different groups from those used for the exercise in making decisions by consensus, with five, seven, or nine members in each group. Discuss your opinions about the following five propositions for not more than ten minutes. Then vote for them by a show of hands, with one member tallying the vote. If no alternative gets a majority, vote again between the two alternatives that receive the most votes.

A. Sex is an expression of love and belongs in a close, enduring relationship, with or without marriage.
B. Sex is simply a biological function; there is no reason not to experiment with it. Sex can be for showing liking, for fun, or simply for learning how to handle it.
C. Sex is a natural expression of friendship or love.
D. Sex apart from marriage violates the law of God. We believe persons should remain virgin until married.
E. Sex in and of itself is not bad, but it can lead young persons into situations they are not ready for and cannot handle.[10]

Now complete the Postdecision Reaction Sheet for this activity.

Decision by Expert

When a group contains one member with much greater knowledge than other members, the group may let this person decide an issue and then inform the group of the decision. In some cases this may indeed provide a technically excellent decision. But letting the expert decide for a group has drawbacks: only the expert may understand the reasons for the decision, beliefs and values of other members may be violated, important information held by other members may not be available to the expert, and other members may not work well to carry out the decision. In short, if the expert has a truly superior solution, taking time to make it a consensus of the group may be well worthwhile. To explore this method of decision making, you can do the next learning activity.

Decision by the group expert. Look over the following three alternatives. They concern a serious issue in a course on small group communication. You can use the same groups formed for the previous exercise. Spend not more than five minutes deciding who in your group is most expert on the subject of grading. That person will rank the three alternatives from 1 (best) to 3 (poorest), and announce his or her first choice as the decision for the group when the group is called on to announce its recommendation to the entire class. Meanwhile, you should also rank them in private. After your group expert has announced the recommendation from your group, complete the Postdecision Reaction Sheet.

_____ The instructor should grade each student on participation during classroom discussions.

_____ Students should grade each other on class participation, and each gets the average of all grades received from classmates.

_____ Participation during classroom discussions in a course such as this makes for phoniness and competition. It should not be graded.

Decision by Leader

Sometimes a designated or emergent leader makes a decision and announces it for the group. This may be done after some discussion of the facts, ideas, and issues involved; in other cases, an authoritarian leader will think the problem through alone and simply state his or her decision without discussion. The result may or may not be a good one in light of the facts of the problem situation, but other outcomes will often be resentment from other group members, lowered cohesiveness, halfhearted support for the decision, and a loss of effective influence on later decisions. Indeed, the members may not only "drag their heels," but even work to make the solution fail, as classic studies in management have shown.

Decision by the leader. The class is first divided into new small groups of five or six members each. One person in each group is appointed as leader by the instructor, or elected by the group members to occupy that role. Then each group member should choose from the list below one social activity for your class as a means to getting better acquainted, increasing class cohesiveness, and relaxing.

A. Hold a pot-luck dinner or picnic at an appropriate location on campus.

B. Attend an intercollegiate sports event together, followed by a dance in the student union building.

C. Arrange a class social hour in a private party room at a nearby bar or lounge.

D. Attend a movie together (selected by leader), followed by informal discussion of the film over soft drinks and coffee in a comfortable private room on campus.

As soon as each person has made a choice, hold a five-minute discussion of the pros and cons of these social activities. The leader will then *announce* to the rest of the group which of the social activities your group will recommend to the entire class, and explain why it is the best possible decision in his or her judgment. As soon as the leader has made this announcement, complete the Postdecision Reaction Sheet, tabulate the responses, and compare them with those from other groups in your class.

Other Methods of Making Decisions

Decisions can also be made in small groups by random choice among the available alternatives (coin toss, drawing, etc.), averaging a set of member ranks or ratings, or allowing a subcommittee to decide. All of these have little to favor them except convenience and saving of time. None makes optimum use of information or the reasoning of all members. You can compute the average ranks for members of your class groups in the "Lost on the Moon" exercise (if you did it) and compare them to the group consensus decisions. In groups where I have done this about 90 per cent of the time the group consensus decisions have been superior to the averages. Another way to compare decision making by averaging with consensus is to have one person bring a small jar filled with beans. Each person examines the jar carefully and records a best guess of the number of beans in the jar. These guesses are collected on slips of paper and tabulated by the person having the correct count. Then the group discusses the number until a consensus is achieved. The average of the individual guesses and the consensus numbers can then be compared with the actual count.

Summary

There are numerous ways by which decisions are made in and for small groups. When there is an absolute standard of "correctness" or a formula for decision making, then an individual skilled in the procedure for making the decision should usually make it and explain it to the group. For example, in many groups a skilled mathematician can work out statistics for the group. However, groups far excel individuals—even "experts"—in matters of judgment where no alternative can be confirmed as the "best" when the decision is made. Substantive or task decisions faced by groups are most often of this sort. In such cases the quality of a decision can best be estimated from these process and output criteria: (1) To what degree was the information and thinking of *all* group members used? (2) How satisfied are members with the decision, and how committed are they to working for it? and (3) To what degree has the decision-making procedure improved the cooperativeness and cohesiveness among members?

Group decisions take longer to make than do individual ones, but extensive research shows them to be superior for a number of reasons. Although arriving at a majority takes longer than averaging, and arriving at a consensus takes longer than to get a simple majority, the results are usually worth the extra time expended. First, complementary knowledge of members is pooled to provide a better understanding of the situation and the merits of alternatives. Second, persons perform better on many tasks when acting in the presence of others. Discussants often stimulate each other to recall information and invent creative alternatives that could not have been done by working alone. Third, conscientious, confident, and creative persons tend to be more active in decision-making discussions than do less well-prepared persons. Fourth, mistakes in individual thinking are often detected and corrected by other members during honest conflict about alternatives. As a general rule, discussing until consensus emerges among members is the most effective way in the long run to make decisions for small groups.

Bibliography

Coch, Lester, and French, John R. P., Jr., "Overcoming Resistance to Change," *Human Relations* 1 (1948), pp. 512–32.

Hall, Jay, "Decisions, Decisions, Decisions," *Psychology Today* 5 (November, 1971), pp. 51–54, 86–87.

Janis, Irving L., *Victims of Groupthink,* Boston: Houghton Mifflin Company, 1973.

Johnson, David W., and Johnson, Frank P., *Joining Together: Group Theory and Group Skills*, Englewood Cliffs, N.J.: Prentice-Hall, Inc., 1972, especially chapter 3.

Shaw, Marvin E., *Group Dynamics*, 2nd ed., New York: McGraw-Hill Book Company, 1976, especially chapter 3.

References

1. Norman R. F. Maier, *Problem Solving and Creativity in Individuals and Groups*, (Belmont, Cal.: Brooks/Cole Publishing Company, 1970), p. 445.
2. Norman R. F. Maier, *Problem Solving Discussions and Conferences* (New York: McGraw-Hill, 1963), p. 5.
3. Lester Coch and John R. P. French, Jr., "Overcoming Resistance to Change," *Human Relations* 1 (1948), pp. 512–32.
4. Jay Hall, "Decisions, Decisions, Decisions," *Psychology Today* 5 (November 1971), pp. 51–54, 86–87.
5. Irving L. Janis, *Victims of Groupthink* (Boston: Houghton Mifflin Company, 1973).

6. William H. Whyte, Jr., *The Organization Man* (Garden City, N.Y.: Doubleday, 1957).
7. J. A. F. Stoner, "A Comparison of Individual and Group Decisions Involving Risk," (Unpublished master's thesis, Massachusetts Institute of Technology, 1961).
8. For a concise summary of this research, see Marvin E. Shaw, *Group Dynamics*, 2nd ed. (New York: McGraw-Hill Book Company, 1976), pp. 70–77.
9. Both the exercise and the scoring were provided by Hall, p. 51.
10. Adapted from David W. Johnson and Frank P. Johnson, *Joining Together: Group Theory and Group Skills* (Englewood Cliffs, N.J.: Prentice-Hall, 1975), p. 63.

8

problem solving group discussions

Study Objectives

As a result of studying chapter 8 you should be able to:

1. Analyze any problem into the three major components of (1) undesirable present situation, (2) obstacles, and (3) goal.

2. List and explain the importance of seven dimensions of a problem when developing a sequence of steps for problem solving.

3. Present a rationale for following a step-by-step procedure of some sort during problem-solving discussions, or at least of determining that none of these steps has been overlooked by the group.

4. List and explain seven principles that serve as guidelines for developing specific problem-solving procedures.

5. Distinguish among four general patterns for organizing problem-solving discussions, and adapt each to specific problems for which it is appropriate.

Key Terms

Brainstorming   a procedure for releasing the creative potential of a group of discussants in which all criticism is ruled out for a period of time, the group works for a large number of ideas, and building on each other's suggestions is encouraged.

Cooperative requirements   the degree to which coordinated efforts of group members are essential to satisfactory completion of a group task.

Creative problem-solving sequence   a six-step procedure for problem solving in which brainstorming is used to generate possible solutions prior to any discussion of criteria.

Developmental discussion   a pattern for organizing discussion in which the specific issues that comprise the problem are discussed thoroughly prior to any consideration of solutions.

Ideal solution sequence   a procedure for problem solving that puts emphasis on the acceptability of possible solutions to the persons who will be directly involved with them; after analysis of the unsatisfactory situation and goal, the next stage is to consider what would be an ideal solution from the point of view of all parties who will be affected by any change.

PERT   acronym for Program Evaluation and Review Technique, a procedure for planning the details involved in implementing the solution to a complex problem in which many persons and resources are coordinated.

Population familiarity   degree to which members of a group (or society) are familiar with the nature of a problem and experienced in solving similar problems or performing similar tasks.

Problem   an undesired state of affairs, or the difference between what is expected and what is actually happening; included are conditions (causes) producing the undesired state, obstacles, and some goal (desired state).

Problem question a question calling the attention of a group to a problem without suggesting any particular type of solution.

Problem solving procedure through which an individual or group proceeds through time in the attempt to find a way to move from an unsatisfactory condition to a more satisfactory one (goal).

    Intuitive problem solving that is nonsystematic, impulsive, or not characterized by step-by-step procedure.

    Systematic following a definite series of steps; organized problem solving following a definite sequence.

Reflective thinking sequence a generic term for systematic thinking when trying to solve a problem; a systematic procedure for organizing group problem-solving discussion that tends to put emphasis on criteria and quality as opposed to quantity and innovativeness in thinking up possible solutions, and in which solutions may be evaluated as soon as proposed.

Solution question formulation of a problem as a question in which a solution to the problem is suggested or implied.

Solution multiplicity characteristic of a problem; when high, many alternatives are possible as solutions.

Single question sequence a systematic problem-solving procedure focusing attention on a central issue and subquestions implied in a problem situation.

Task difficulty degree to which a problem is characterized by complexity requiring extensive effort, knowledge, and skills for solution.

In chapter 7, *problem solving* was defined as a multi-step procedure beginning with some dissatisfaction with a present state of affairs and ending with a plan of action to produce a satisfactory state of affairs. Many decisions are involved in problem solving, ideally made in a sequence depending on the nature of the specific problem. The humorous definition that "a camel is a horse designed by a committee" reflects concern for the quality of solutions developed by groups despite findings by small group researchers that groups are generally superior to individuals in solving many types of problems.[1]

Have you noticed how easy it is to overlook some important fact when you tackle a problem alone? Do you find your thoughts often coming in a random, jumbled, helter-skelter fashion? Have you regretted decisions made before all the needed evidence was considered or possible alternatives explored? If individual thinking is often haphazard, consider what can happen when a group of persons try to think together toward a common aim. Each person may have a different way of approaching the subject or problem. If each follows his or her own lead, there will not be a group discussion, but individuals talking to themselves. Perhaps you have noticed how often conversation is shallow and vacuous, shifting aimlessly from topic to topic, with no one getting his or her feelings and meanings clearly expressed about anything. Berg used a technique of content analysis to locate the themes in discussions by task-oriented groups. He reported that these groups averaged changing themes or topics every 58 seconds. "Though the same themes frequently reappeared several times, groups were often unable to complete discussion of these topics." Although his procedure for theme analysis contributed somewhat to the finding that the themes were discussed very briefly, the conclusion that these problem-solving discussions were badly organized is inescapable.[2] Bormann also reported that the average amount of time groups of many types stuck to a topic was about one minute.[3] It seems apparent that engaging in sustained and organized problem-solving discussion is not easy. If you ask most educated persons how to solve a problem, they will say something like "get the facts, weigh the alternatives, and make a decision." That's not too bad a procedure, but extensive observation of both individual and group problem solving reveals all sorts of procedures, mostly haphazard and unsystematic, more intuitive than analytical. Problem solving by groups, if it is to be maximally effective, requires systematic procedures to coordinate the thinking of several persons, just as playing winning football requires systematic coordination of the actions of all players during each play and an overall game plan.

In the all too typical problem-solving discussion, someone outlines a problem, then immediately someone else suggests what to do to solve it, followed by a brief period of discussion evaluating this idea. Then another idea is suggested, discussed, and dropped. Maybe at this point the group goes back to talking about the problem. A third idea for solving the problem is proposed, and possibly forgotten along with the first two. Finally, time begins to run out and a decision is made quickly, usually the last idea discussed, even though the proposals made earlier might have solved the problem more effectively. All too often the group adjourns without making plans for actually getting anything done.

In order to provide a basis for improving problem solving, chapter 8 defines the concept "problem," analyzes the major dimensions and types of problems, provides evidence that problem-solving procedures can be improved by both individuals and groups, reviews research that indicates what can be done to improve it, and provides specific guidelines and sequences for improving the efficiency and effectiveness of problem-solving discussions.

Problem

How a group can best proceed depends on the nature of the problem with which it is concerned. We need to understand the concept "problem," then the variables of any problem and the major types of problems groups address.

All problems consist of three major components: an undesirable present situation, a goal, and obstacles to achievement of that goal. Figure 8.1 illustrates this three-part conception of a problem, both in general and with an example of a specific problem a family group might face. *Problem solving* is thus defined as the procedure undertaken to overcome the obstacles in order to move from the undesirable present situation to the goal. A problem does not exist unless someone perceives or "encounters" it. For example, one person might find nothing wrong with home heating bills of $1,000.00 per year, whereas another person with a limited income would feel that when heating costs reach $500.00 a serious problem exists. Many Americans would feel they had encountered a problem if their residence lacked indoor plumbing, whereas many people in the world would not consider this a problem.

A goal to which there are no obstacles does not present a problem. Persons cannot engage in *group* problem solving until they collectively define the problem, agreeing on what needs to be changed, the desired goal, and the obstacles that must be overcome to reach it. Sometimes the process of describing the problem leads to changes in the goal, for effective solutions are those that succeed in overcoming obstacles. *Unless a group has the power to overcome the obstacles, it cannot solve the problem.* Unsurmountable obstacles thus necessitate changes in our goals; we can only learn to live with situations we have no power to change. Recognizing what *cannot* be changed (at least for now) and accepting it, as well as recognizing what can be changed and finding ways to change it, are both included in problem-solving behavior. Understanding the details and causes of obstacles lying between the present situation and the goal is essential to the achievement of acceptable solutions.

A similar definition of the concept "problem" as it might be used in the business world is advanced by Kepner and Tregoe:

A problem is a deviation between what *should* be happening and what *actually* is happening that is important enough to make someone think the deviation ought to be corrected.[4]

Figure 8.1 Components of a problem.

Problem Components

In general:	**Undesirable present situation:** we are here	**Obstacles**	**Goal:** we want to be here
A specific problem:	House heating bills are averaging over $600 per year	Price of fuel; 40-year-old house with many air leaks; little insulation; limited building skills; doors must be opened frequently; cannot afford new house, etc.	House heating costs of less than $300 per year

Figure 8.2 Kepner-Tregoe model of a problem.

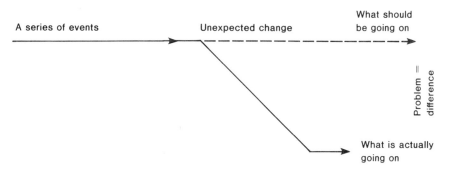

This concept of a problem was diagrammed by Kepner and Tregoe as shown in Figure 8.2. The "problem" is the difference between what *should* be going on (desired state of affairs) and what is *actually* going on (present undesired state of affairs). The goal is to get the course of events to lead back to the desired state, "what should be going on." A group using this model of a problem must determine the details of the difference: what is wrong. Then they must decide what produced or caused the unexpected change in order to create an appropriate solution. The Kepner and Tregoe model of a problem may help you to map out such problems as a change in the frequency of accidents, a machine that is not running properly, or even a change in the relationships among members of a family. Regardless of the model, a group does not understand a problem adequately to come up with an effective solution until all members agree on what is the desired situation, what is the actual situation, and the causes or obstacles producing the difference.

Problems (and problem solving) go on and on. Often, solving one problem leads to others. For example, if a woodburning furnace, chain saw, and log splitter were purchased as a solution to the high cost of heating, keeping the chimney free of creosote would likely be one of several new problems the homeowner would encounter growing out of the solution to high heating bills. A high-speed railway to reduce travel time between cities could lead to such problems as dangerous crossings, destruction of communities, and loss of crop producing land.

Problem Characteristics

Shaw used a complex statistical procedure to determine the major dimensions of a set of 104 tasks used in studies of small group process. This resulted in six task variables or dimensions. Five of these dimensions are characteristics of all problems discussed by problem-solving groups: *difficulty, solution multiplicity, intrinsic interest, cooperative requirements,* and *population familiarity*.[5] To help you analyze the problems facing groups in which you participate we will examine each of these task characteristics, plus two other important characteristics—the *acceptance-technical dimension*, and the *area of freedom of the group*.

Task difficulty refers to the amount of complexity, effort, knowledge, and skill needed to achieve the goal. The amount and kind of leadership services needed will vary with the difficulty. Group performance on difficult problems was found to be better when members could express their feelings and opinions about possible solutions openly than when such expressions were artificially restricted.[6] Interestingly, one researcher found that groups discussing difficult tasks were more confident of their solutions than were groups discussing relatively simple problems.[7] Of course what appears to be an insurmountable obstacle to one person may appear routine to another. Simple problems may be solved quickly with very little concern about procedure, whereas complex problems may require many meetings, a highly detailed problem-solving procedure to guide this extended activity, and considerable attention to how well members are cooperating. Only the very general components of the problem-solving procedure will be the same in discussions of simple and complex problems (how to lay out our garden vs. developing a differentiated salary schedule for teachers).

Solution multiplicity refers to the number of conceivable or feasible alternatives for solving the problem. To illustrate, there are usually only a few ways to obtain potable water for a farmhouse, but innumerable ways to decorate and arrange the living room. Few research studies of this problem dimension have been reported. Shaw and Blum found that "directive" leadership was more effective when a very low number of alternatives was possible, whereas "nondirective" leadership was more effective with problems for which more alternative solutions were possible.[8] In an unpublished study, I found that the majority of group members preferred a several-step procedure to a simple two-step outline for guiding their discussion when both a limited number (nine) and an unlimited number of alternative solutions were possible. However, nine is still a relatively high number of alternatives compared to the problems used by Shaw and Blum. Several studies of "creative" problem solving have shown that highly structured "brainstorming" procedures evoke more possible solutions and more ideas rated "good" than do simple outlines or no outline to guide the discussions. In all of these investigations, the outline of the problem-solving procedure was provided and more-or-less imposed on the group by a designated leader or the experimenter.[9] Any outline, sequence, or procedure for guiding a problem-solving discussion should be selected in part on the basis of the extent to which the problem is characterized by "solution multiplicity."

Intrinsic interest was defined by Shaw as ". . . the degree to which the task in and of itself is interesting, motivating, and attractive to the group members."[10] A task that discussants feel is highly important is likely to be more interesting to them than one they consider of little importance. Interest is also related to the degree to which the solution will directly affect them in some way. However, the challenge and enjoyment of participation is what "intrinsic interest" primarily refers to—members find it exciting to discuss the problem. Berkowitz found that when members were extremely involved with the task, they preferred sharing in procedural control, whereas strong procedural control of the discussion by a designated leader was preferred when the task was of less direct interest to them.[11] My personal experience and observation of numerous groups supports this finding. If interest is very high, members will not at first want to stick closely to any procedural outline, but will more readily do so when initial feelings and ideas have been expressed ("ventilated").

Ideally, persons in groups would discuss only problems of intrinsic interest to them, but this ideal situation is often not present. In the world of organizations and committees, persons are assigned to task groups or serve on continuing committees that must deal with a variety of problems, some of little interest to them. When intrinsic interest appears to be low, this needs to be discussed by the group, possibly leading to a change of attitude toward the problem, a modification of it, or a request that it be assigned to some other group.

Cooperative requirements refers to the degree to which coordinated efforts are essential to satisfactory completion of a group task. It is obvious that a consensus decision about the solution to a complex problem will require a high level of cooperation when members initially have different perceptions of the problem and different values and ideas about what ought to be done to solve it. The complexity of a problem and cooperative requirements are thus intertwined variables. Discussions of problems requiring high levels of cooperation will usually be inefficient and unproductive unless some procedure for problem solving is understood and accepted by all members. Essential leadership services will be those that assure that members' behaviors are provided at the time when needed, and that a win-win relationship is maintained among members. Coordination of thought can be just as vital in problem solving as is coordination of movement in offensive plays of a football team. Special procedures such as the "nominal group technique" have been developed to insure such coordination of effort and talk in problem solving groups.

Population familiarity refers to the degree to which members have previous experience with the task and possess information essential to the successful completion of it. If other factors are the same, groups with experienced members tend to perform better than groups of inexperienced members.[12] Several writers have stressed the danger that participants experienced in solving problems similar to the one being discussed may be less imaginative or openminded in thinking of solutions than will less experienced members, even to the extent of squelching creative ideas. A procedure such as brainstorming can be used to offset any such tendency.[13] Shared knowledge about the problem prior to discussing it will facilitate rapid progress toward goal agreement and consensus on a solution. A more extended period of investigation, sharing of information, and developing the details of the problem will be required if members are not well informed about it.

The importance of the **acceptance-technical dimension** of problems was stressed by Maier.[14] This dimension concerns the degree to which the solution must be acceptable to persons who will be affected by it, rather than simply being feasible technically. For instance, outlawing the consumption of alcohol and preaching the evils of drunkenness have been tried as solutions to the social problems created by alcoholism. Both failed as solutions. They were not accepted—persons broke the law or refused to believe the preaching—because they did not take into account the importance of the acceptance-technical dimension. So it may be with problems of smaller compass, such as lawns being damaged by foot traffic or making money more durable (consider the Susan B. Anthony dollar). Only persons discussing problems that are primarily technical or mechanical in nature can ignore the acceptance factor, such as how to stop the killing of persons by toxic fumes from burning plastic or the crushing of bodies when inadequate bumpers and structural members collapse in an auto crash. The degree of human acceptance necessary for a solution to achieve the goal is always a dimension of the problem that needs to be considered if a truly effective remedy is to be found.

The **area of freedom of the group** was defined in chapter 3 as the amount of authority given a group, which is related to the type of general question that the group discusses. As mentioned in chapter 5, problem solving groups may seek answers to questions of interpretation ("fact"), value, or policy. Problems of interpretation require the group to assemble a body of information and interpret it with some generalization. Such is the work of the so-called "fact finding" or investigative committee—for example, a team of detectives working on a bank robbery, a grand jury trying to determine if there is sufficient evidence to prosecute, or a legislative study committee trying to decide if there is a need for a statute to control use of ground water. The solution for such a group is a decision about the meaning to be given to the body of relevant data. Their problem-solving procedure would entail less steps than that of a group dealing with a question of value, which requires not only interpreting data, but also deciding on the relative worth of something: "How worthwhile is a liberal education in a technical world?" "Which make and model of small truck will be most economical for delivering auto parts to garages in our city?" "How effective has the present welfare program been in reducing poverty?" A question of policy implies one further step in the problem-solving process, a decision as to what *should* be done: "What should be done to reduce destructive behavior at rock concerts?" "What should be done to reduce the murder rate in Dallas?" When facing such problems, a group must locate, select, and interpret a body of information, make value judgments about such matters as rights of suspects versus protection of the innocent, and decide on a general policy to be implemented when dealing with all specific problems of the sort discussed by the group.

In one sense, all of these types of questions as problems for discussion are more alike than different. Interpreting information often requires making value judgments among conflicting testimony, statistics, and other information. A judgment that a serious problem exists implies that a policy for dealing with it is needed. An answer to a question of value not only depends on interpretation of information, but also implies some alternative that can be considered a general policy. For example, if several makes of truck are evaluated, obviously the policy implied is to buy the best one, and if a liberal education is truly worthwhile, the policy of encouraging a person to obtain one is indicated. Determining what *ought* to be done is clearly making the value judgment that the policy decided upon is superior to others. In all three types of questions the problem faced by the group entails a "felt difficulty": a body of information is not adequately understood for us to feel comfortable with it, a need to rank or establish priorities among alternatives, or a feeling of need for a general guideline to action in a recurrent type of problem.

Yet none of these questions implies a *complete* problem-solving procedure. Problem solving has not been finished until some definite *action has been taken* to remove obstacles to a desired goal. With that in mind, participants in discussions can formulate their goals clearly not in terms of what "should" be done, but in terms of "what will we do to . . ." or "what action will be taken to. . . ." Only *advisory* (or study) groups discuss problems and then terminate their work with a body of interpreted knowledge, value judgments, or statements of policy. Their final action as a group solution is to report, advise, or recommend. Thus a complete formulation of their problem would include a question such as this: "What course of action will we recommend to the city council as a means of reducing traffic deaths?" or "What will we report as the relative merits of six makes of cars under consideration as police cruisers?" In the later example, the final action of the group within its area of freedom will be to recommend a specific make of car, not to purchase the cars or even decide that they will be purchased. Groups having the area of freedom to act on a problem are responsible for taking definite action to solve the problem, or see that others do so—they can complete the total process of solving a problem. For instance, a safety committee with authority may shut down a dangerous mine until their solution to the danger has been put into effect. In short, the complete process of problem solving ends with taking action, not merely with a recommendation.

In summary, it is vital to consider all the major dimensions of any problem when seeking to solve it: the degree to which there are few or many possible alternatives, the complexity of the problem, the amount of cooperation required among group members, the human acceptance-technical factor, and the area of freedom of the group.

Organizing Problem-Solving Discussions

All thinking involved in problem solving goes on within the nervous systems of individual persons; a group does not "think" in some mystical way. How persons solve problems as individuals has been explored by many scholars.

How Systematic and Orderly?

Persons have been classified as primarily "intuitive" or "systematic" problem solvers. According to this theory, *intuitive problem solvers* size up a problem, then somehow come up with a solution without conscious effort or following any organized procedure. Whatever happens between defining the problem and finding a solution occurs on a pre-conscious level that cannot be observed. Perhaps you have mulled over a problem for sometime, been unable to think of a solution, and then suddenly been aware of a solution at some later time when not consciously working on the problem. This is the so-called "Eureka!" or "Ah-ha!" experience. Quite possibly your mind continued working on the problem fairly systematically even though you had stopped thinking about it on a conscious level.

Systematic thinkers, on the other extreme, are said to go through a series of mental steps such as those described by John Dewey in his famous book, *How We Think*.[15] Dewey, a philosopher in the early part of the twentieth century, asked his students to recall how they solved various problems. From their descriptions he formulated a five-step model of a systematic problem-solving procedure that he called "reflective thinking." This model did not fit exactly with how his individual students described their mental operations, but was a general pattern that he felt they more or less followed. The result was

. . . a consecutive ordering in such a way that each [step] determines the next as its proper outcome. . . . The successive portions of the reflective thought grow out of one another and support one another; they do not come and go in a medley.[16]

1. "*Awareness of a felt difficulty*" is variously described as "whatever perplexes or challenges the mind" and "an ambiguity to be resolved" such as which fork in the road to take when one has no road map.
2. "*Definition of the difficulty*" is stage 2, involving a detailed exploration of the problem. "The essence of critical thinking is suspended judgment, and the essence of this suspense is inquiry to determine the nature of the problem before proceeding to attempt its solution." Necessary for this step is the ". . . ability to 'turn things over,' to look at matters deliberately, to judge whether the amount and kind of evidence requisite for decision is at hand, and if not, to tell where and how to seek such evidence."
3. "*Occurrence of a suggested explanation or possible solution*" is the third stage of Dewey's idealized procedure. He urges the problem solver to suspend decision making until many solutions are available for comparison: ". . . *cultivation of a variety of alternative suggestions* is an important factor in good thinking."
4. "*The rational elaboration of an idea*" is stage 4 of Dewey's model. At this point implications of the alternatives discovered during stage 3 are explored. Some ideas might be rejected, some modified, some accepted: "Suggestions at first seemingly remote and wild are frequently so transformed by being elaborated into what follows from them as to become apt and fruitful."
5. "*Corroboration of an idea and formation of a concluding belief*" is the final step in Dewey's model of problem-solving thought. At this point the remaining ideas are evaluated, including an experimental test if that is possible, before making a final decision on a course of action to achieve the goal.[17]

Dewey never observed how his students actually went through the mental procedures in problem solving, only their reports from memory. Obviously, they may have made their procedures appear more orderly and rational than they actually were. You might try recalling how you actually went about solving a few problems, and see how well your procedure compares with that which Dewey describes. If you are like me, you may find that you have solved different problems with a variety of different procedures, both in intuitive and systematic ways depending on how complex, interesting, vital, and open to a variety of alternatives the problem was, and the amount of time and resources available. The majority of writers of textbooks in discussion and small group communication present Dewey's sequence of systematic individual problem solving as a model for organizing group problem-solving discussions, often with the addition of one, two, or three additional steps. However, Dewey is *not* concerned with how to organize discussions of problem-solving groups, or even if they should be organized around some sequence or outline. He does not include the necessary final step of how to get the solution put into effect.

He does state forcefully that this model of reflective thinking should be varied to fit different types of problems:

The disciplined . . . mind . . . is the mind able to judge how far each of these steps needs to be carried in any particular situation. No cast-iron rules can be laid down. Each case has to be dealt with as it arises, on the basis of its importance and the context in which it occurs. To take too much pain in one case is as foolish—as illogical—as to take too little in another.[18]

Despite Dewey's urging that training in reflective thinking should be the core of education, the question remains of whether or not individuals and groups can learn to follow a complex problem-solving sequence, especially in light of Berg's finding that attention span is very short with frequent shifts in the theme being discussed. "Content analysis" is the general technique used by Berg and others who do thematic analyses of discussions. The definitions and procedures one uses for a content analysis determine to a large degree what one finds. Using a different basis for theme analysis, I found that some groups average fifteen or more minutes per theme in two-hour discussions.[19] In my technique, brief sidetracks onto a different topic were not counted as a change of theme unless the group did not come back to the issue under discussion previous to the tangential remarks. These groups were led by persons specially trained for the role who attempted to keep discussion centered on one major issue at a time. This indicates that a group can stick to a major issue or a stage in problem solving.

One of the most common complaints about discussions is that they are *not* organized, but jump back and forth among issues. Two recent studies have shown that perceived quality of discussions is related to how systematically they appear to have been organized. Gouran, Brown, and Henry had students in a group communication course evaluate the quality of audio recorded discussions and the behaviors of the discussants, then later rate these same characteristics of discussions in which they themselves had participated. A major conclusion of the study confirms the importance of procedures that maintain goal orientation and systematic examination of issues:

The results in general indicate that behaviors contributing to the substance of a decision-making discussion, such as introducing relevant issues, amplifying ideas, and documenting assertions, as well as procedural behaviors, such as maintaining goal orientation and pursuing issues systematically, had greater weight on perceptions of quality than the extent of individual member involvement and behaviors focused on maintaining or improving the social-emotional climate. . . .[20]

In the other study, Jurma trained leaders to act both in structuring and nonstructuring roles. The results indicate beneficial outcomes from structuring problem-solving discussions. In the nonstructuring style, the leaders were vague and offered no information, procedural suggestions, or guidance to the group. In the structuring style they offered considerable procedural guidance to see that the issues in the problem were discussed, that goals were set by the group, and that the group was reminded of the passage of time. Independent evaluators rated the discussions led by structuring leaders as significantly better than those led by nonstructuring leaders. Low-task oriented participants were significantly more satisfied with both the leaders and outcomes of the structured discussions. This is an important finding, for low-task persons are those most likely to be intuitive problem solvers, not high in need for procedural organization, and more inclined to non-task comments during discussions than are high-task oriented participants.[21]

Putnam set out to establish a scale for measuring a participant's general preference for a high or low degree of procedural order during discussions. She concluded that an individual's preference for a certain degree of structure could be superseded at times by more potent needs, such as time pressure or a struggle for leader status would produce. She suggested that group norms may have more to do with how much a continuing group organizes its discussions than preferences of individual members.[22] Although the question has not yet been investigated by any researcher, I suspect that the more experience one has in problem-solving discussions that are organized and orderly the more one prefers to follow a general outline of some problem-solving procedure.

Previously alluded to was the study by Brilhart and Jochem in which we found that significantly more students participating in experimental problem-solving discussions preferred a complex five-stage problem-solving sequence— the "Creative Problem-Solving Sequence" of problem description and analysis, generation of possible solutions, determination of criteria, evaluation of possible solutions, and decision on final solution—to a simple three-stage process of problem analysis, discussion of solutions, and decision.[23] In a later study I found that when leaders followed a structured problem-solving sequence, the large majority of statements made by participants were relevant to the phase of problem solving announced by the leader and only a small proportion were irrelevant to that phase.[24] Sharp found that problem-solving discussants whose contributions were ranked high by both fellow discussants and observers scored significantly higher on a test of reflective thinking skill than did discussants ranked low on performance in the problem-solving discussions.[25] Ability to engage in systematic, step-by-step problem-solving procedures seems to be important to being judged an effective contributor to problem-solving discussions. We know that some persons tend to prefer low levels of structure (unsystematic) during problem-solving discussions. But this preference *may* well be subject to change as one gains experience and skill in small groups.

Both instructor and student may well ask if one can learn to follow a procedural outline of several steps in problem solving. The answer appears to be yes, at least to some degree. It is extremely doubtful that there are pure "intuitive" or "systematic" types of thinkers. Most of us at times do each. More important than some inherited tendency is what we have *learned* previously from family members, peers, schooling, and the small groups in which we have been members. Two psychologists, Nisbett and Ross, have shown forcefully that relying on intuitive problem solving and inference making leads to many errors. Their evidence includes the finding that we arrive at better solutions to problems if we learn to replace simplistic intuitive strategies with the systematics and statistical principles of the formal scientist.[26] Further support for this conclusion comes from the work of Sternberg, who has studied the ways in which persons who do well on problems in IQ tests proceed to solve them. The difference between those who do well on a wide variety of such mental tests and those who do poorly lies primarily in how they process the information presented. Those who are most successful follow a definite sequence in which they first set up a procedure for tackling the problem, then routinely follow it step by step. If it does not work, they then try a different approach, but their overall strategy tends to be exhaustive of the possible answers, requiring more steps than are taken by persons who do less well. Small children cannot do some of the steps involved. Expert and beginning chess players likewise are differentiated by the procedures they follow in dealing with a problem. Sternberg believes that impulsive problem solvers can be taught to do better by showing them how their erroneous procedures lead to erroneous solutions, and then how to proceed more systematically and effectively.[27] Certainly one must *learn* how to follow the strict problem solving procedures of the scientist in attacking research problems. Few individuals naturally or "intuitively" follow a "scientific method" as any of us who has taught a research methods course can testify. Mechanics must learn how to diagnose and correct problems in cars, following a definite sequence akin to that followed by winners of the game "twenty questions." They do not learn this just by developing skills with wrenches and gear pullers. Likewise, the medical student is taught to follow a step-by-step procedure in diagnosing and treating medical problems. I believe strongly that very few persons are so inflexible that they cannot learn to follow systematic procedures or that they are so recalcitrant that they will not do so in a group discussion *if they have seen the benefits from doing so are guided by norms favoring organized, relevant comments* and *are following an outline or procedure agreed upon by the group.* Often, of course, groups contain members who do not think systematically in solving problems. Then it may be necessary to accept considerable skipping about among the stages of problem solving, but if the group makes a point of consciously adopting a procedure and develops norms for such, this difficulty can be reduced through time in a continuing group.

Sequences for Problem-Solving Discussions—Some General Principles

Focus on the problem before thinking and talking about how to solve it.

What would you think if you drove into a garage with a car that was running poorly and the mechanic almost immediately said, "What you need to fix this buggy is a new carburetor and a set of spark plugs." If your reaction is like mine, you would get out of there as fast as your ailing auto would let you. A competent mechanic, after asking questions about how the car was acting and observing how it ran, might put it on an electronic engine analyzer. After gathering information by these means he or she would make a tentative diagnosis, which would be checked by direct examination of the suspected parts. Only then would the mechanic say something like, "The problem is that two of your valves are burned, and the carburetor is so badly worn that it won't stay adjusted properly."

Our two hypothetical mechanics illustrate one of the most common failings in group (and individual) problem solving: solution centeredness. Irving Lee, after observing many problem-solving conferences and discussions, found that in most of the groups he studied there was "a deeply held assumption that because the problem was announced it was understood. People seemed too often to consider a complaint equivalent to a description, a charge the same as a specification."[28]Maier, after many years of studying problem-solving discussions in business and industry, stated that "participants as well as disssion leaders focus on the objective of arriving at a solution and fail to give due consideration to an exploration of the problem."[29] Groups tend to act like a surgeon who scheduled an operation when a patient complained of a pain in his abdomen, like a judge who handed down a decision as soon as he had read the indictment, or like the hunter who shot at a noise in the bushes and killed his son. This tendency to short-circuit on the analysis and encoding of the problem was the major error found by Sternberg in his studies of how persons worked IQ test problems.

Time spent on problem analysis often makes solution finding and consensus much easier than if the group gets too quickly into "how to solve it." A very thorough description of the problem, discussion of goals, and analysis of the obstacles will in many cases lead to a solution that is almost obvious—after such detailed encoding of the problem. The "single question" sequence for problem solving especially applies to this principle.

Failure to initially discuss the problem adequately leads to both process and output variables that are undesirable:

1. *Partisanship is encouraged.* Participants spend a lot of time arguing the merits of their pet proposals. Often this is due to their having different ideas about the group objective, factual information not having been shared, and a failure to discuss what may have caused the unsatisfactory situation. Only when members first agree on the nature of the problem are they likely to be able to agree on what to do about it; otherwise the group may become hopelessly split or generate interpersonal tensions that hurt future group work.
2. *Time is wasted.* Solution-at-once methods often result in a sort of pinwheel pattern. Ths problem is mentioned; someone proposes a solution that is argued at length; someone points out that an important aspect of the problem has been neglected; someone then goes back to the problem to see if this is so. This problem-solution cycle may be repeated indefinitely, wasting time on solutions that do not fit the facts of the case. At first, focus on what has gone wrong rather than what shall be done about it.

3. *Ineffectual solutions tend to be adopted.* There is a tendency to spend much time debating the first and most obvious solutions, which are usually taken bodily from other situations and are not based on the facts of the present case. New, innovative ideas are not considered. When a careful analysis of the combination of forces and conditions producing the problem ("causes") has not been made, often only symptoms are treated with the basic problem getting worse instead of being solved. To illustrate, think of what will happen if you try to solve the problem of a headache by taking pain killers when the cause is inadequate handling of stress or a brain tumor. Maier and Maier found that a "developmental pattern," while taking more patience and skill on the part of the designated leader, produced a better quality of decision than did a simpler problem-solution ("free") pattern.[30] The "developmental pattern" breaks the problem into a series of distinct issues and steps. It forces the group to map out the problem thoroughly and systematically. In a "free" discussion the group tries to find a solution without following any systematic outline to guide the analysis of the problem. In a similar study, Maier and Solem found that a leader technique for delaying the group decision produced solutions to a "change of work procedure" problem superior to those solutions produced when "free" discussion was permitted.[31]

Begin with a Problem Question

How a problem is formulated into a question by (or to) a group can make a great difference in what happens in the problem-solving process. It is often important to begin with a "problem question" rather than a "solution question." A *problem question* asks what might or should be done to achieve a goal, whereas a *solution question* contains a suggestion of a solution, and merely asks how to put it into effect. Of course a group with the limited freedom only to act upon a policy decided by someone else or to carry out a previously decided solution does begin with a solution question, but this is only a small part of the total problem-solving procedure. If your group has authority to search for, invent, and decide on a solution, *always* begin with a *problem question.*[32] The differences in the two types of general questions are illustrated in Figure 8.3.

How can I transfer a man who is popular in the work group but slows down the work of others?

What can be done to alleviate complaints about inadequate parking space at our college?

How will we reduce shoplifting in our store?

How will we get more students to shape up by taking physical education?

What action shall we take in the case of Joe Blevins who is accused of cheating on Professor Lamdeau's exam?

Figure 8.3 Differences between *Problem Questions* and *Solution Questions*.

Solution Questions	Problem Questions
One type of action is suggested.	*Many alternative solutions* implied, none suggested.
Focus is on *what to do*.	Focus is on *what's wrong*.

How can we reduce the amount of oil being imported into the United States?

How can we get more persons to build solar-heated and solar-cooled houses?

Map the Problem Thoroughly

To help develop an attitude and norms fostering thorough problem analysis, think of the problem at the start as an uncharted map with only vague boundaries. The first step is for the group to make this into as complete a map of the problem as possible, using all the relevant data available to the group. The participants should share all they know about the situation: facts, complaints, conditions, circumstances, factors, details, happenings, relationships, disturbances, effects, etc. In short, what have you heard, read, and observed that bears in any way on the problem? What have other members heard, read, and observed? What does this all add up to?

Such mapping should be as precise and detailed as possible. You might be guided by such examples as the investigation of a murder by a team of trained detectives, the investigation of a plane crash by the Federal Aviation Administration, or the investigation by medical researchers of a series of deaths from some unknown disease. As Kepner and Tregoe pointed out, one of the greatest dangers is that a group will too quickly accept an apparent cause without adequate gathering of facts, analysis, and interpretation of them— "jumping to a conclusion about cause." Instead of being very critical in comparison of possible causative forces, discussants may collect arguments in support of a pet theory, resist other possible explanations of the problem, and pridefully fight to protect their theories of why things are not satisfactory. It is very important to "closely examine each hypothesis, looking for loopholes, for inconsistencies, for exceptions, for partial explanations," even with regard to one's own brainchildren.[33]

Perhaps the greatest obstacle to problem-centered thinking is the leader or member who comes to the group with the problem all solved in his or her mind. The presenter of a problem to a group must therefore set aside the solution and focus on the goal he or she wants to achieve if true discussion is to occur. Even in a consultative discussion where one member brings a problem to the group for advice, the discussion will frequently bring that person to see the problem very differently. Being willing to explore any and all solutions without having a favorite is an essential attitude for problem-solving discussion. Clarifying relationships between goals, obstacles, and the present state of affairs must be done if the solution is to be maximally effective. Remember, also, to focus on what *can* be done, what obstacles *can* be overcome.

Figure 8.4 illustrates this process of gathering and sharing information to map out a problem so that all members have virtually the same understanding of it. The large outer circle represents the entire problem in a context. Each of the four members of the group (A, B, C, D) has some information about the problem, a unique personal map represented by one of the four inner circles. Some of the information is shared by two members (light shading), some by three members (dark shading), and some by all four members (dark center area), when the discussion gets underway. As the discussants share their information in a systematic analysis of the problem, they come to have at least very similar images or maps of the problem; no longer do they have four problems, but a shared problem. This map of the situation facing them is far better than any one or two members could have constructed (indicated by the circle in the right half of figure 8.4).

Figure 8.4   "Maps" of a problem before and after discussion.

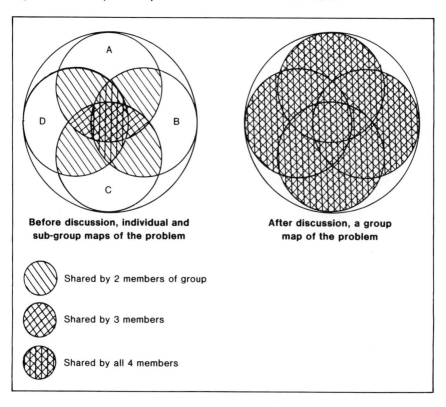

Before discussion, individual and
sub-group maps of the problem

After discussion, a group
map of the problem

Shared by 2 members of group

Shared by 3 members

Shared by all 4 members

Be Sure the Group Agrees on Criteria

Many times there is a lack of "reality testing" before a decision is made final. Other times, a group cannot agree on which of two or more possible solutions to adopt. If the problem has been fully explored, the most likely source of difficulty is a lack of clear-cut standards, criteria, or objectives. In many discussions there is a need for two considerations of criteria: first, when formulating the specific objectives of the group; second, when stating specific standards to be used in judging among solutions. Until agreement (explicit or intuitive) is reached on criteria, agreement on a solution is unlikely.

Many criteria are expressions of values shared by members of a group. Rubenstein gave an example of a problem that brought out very different values from different persons, and thus disagreement over the appropriate course of action (solution). Imagine that a man is in a small boat with his mother, wife, and child. The boat capsizes. The man is the only person in the boat who can swim. He can save only one of the other three persons. Which one should he save? Rubenstein found that all the Arabs he asked would save the mother, explaining that a man can always get another wife and children but not another mother. Of 100 American college freshmen asked this same question, 60 said they would save the wife and 40 the child. These Americans laughed at the idea of saving the mother. Why these great differences in choices? The criteria, based on different values, are different for most Arabs and most Americans. Hence, said Rubenstein: This is the problem of problems, the subjective element of problem solving and decision making. Man's value system, his priorities, guide his behavior as manifested in problem solving and decision making. Two people using the same rational tools of problem solving may arrive at different solutions because they operate from different frames of values, and therefore, their behavior is different.[34] So a consensus of values relevant to the problem must be arrived at before a group can arrive at a consensus decision. It may take much time for a group to search out common values and beliefs. This is an important function of fantasy chains, the establishment of common frames of values. When a group cannot seem to agree on a solution, look for differences in values, bring these up for discussion, and see if it is possible to agree. It may *not* be.

From the beginning of the discussion, the group needs to be clearly aware of the limitations placed upon its area of freedom. The group that tries to make decisions affecting matters over which it has no authority will be both confused and frustrated. For example, the area of freedom for a group of university students includes recommending changes in teaching methods, but students have no authority to make or enforce policy governing such changes. A committee may be given power to recommend plans for the building, but not to make the final decision and contract for the building. Any policy decision or plan of action must be judged by whether or not it fits into the group's area of freedom. Thus, if a committee is authorized to spend up to $500.00, it must evaluate all possible ideas by that absolute criterion.

It is important to rank criteria, giving priority to those that must be met. Ideas proposed can be rated *yes* or *no* on whether they meet all the absolute criteria, and from *excellent* to *poor* on how well they measure up to the less important criteria.

Single words, such as *efficient*, are not criteria, but categories of criteria. Such words are so vague that they are meaningless when applied to possible solutions. They can be used to find specific criteria. Criteria should be worded as questions or absolute statements. For example, the following criteria might be applied to plans for a club's annual banquet:

Absolute— Must not cost over $400.00 for entertainment.
　　　　　Must be enjoyable to both members and their families.
Questions— How convenient is the location for members?
　　　　　How comfortable is the room?

The importance of valid facts as criteria is suggested by Maier. Any solution not based on unchallenged facts or interpretations of facts available to the group should be rejected, and any solution based only on challenged information or interpretations should not be given further consideration.[35]

Defer Judgment When Seeking Solutions

Instead of evaluating each possible solution when it is first proposed, it is more efficient to defer judgment until a complete list of possible solutions has been produced. Much of the research already cited indicates that the process of *idea gathering* should be separated from *idea evaluation*. Judgment stifles unusual and novel ideas. It is a good idea to list the proposed solutions on a chart or chalkboard. Encouragement should be given to combine, modify, or build upon previous suggestions.

For some types of problems, there are few options open to a group. If so, some discussion of each idea when it is proposed may be appropriate, but no final decision should be made until all alternatives that group members can think of have been recorded. At other times a very thorough exploration of the problem and causes will lead to a sudden insight into a solution. In such a case, the group should still try to think of other ideas with which the first one can be compared— "What *else* might we do?" If nothing is discovered, that solution should still be evaluated very thoroughly, and in the process it may undergo considerable revision and improvement.

Brainstorm

Occasionally a problem-solving group may want to engage in a full-fledged brainstorming discussion. Brainstorming depends on the deferment of judgment; many auxiliary skills and techniques can be used to advantage. Brainstorming can be applied to any problem if there is a wide range of possible solutions, none of which can in advance be said to be just right. The process of brainstorming can be applied to any phase of the discussion: finding information (What information do we need? How might we get this information?),

Figure 8.5 Brainstorming produces lots of ideas.

finding criteria (What criteria might we use to test ideas?), finding ideas (What might we do?), or implementation (How might we put our decision into effect?). In addition to what has been said about creative problem solving, the following rules of brainstorming should be presented to the group:

1. *All criticism is ruled out while brainstorming.*
2. *The wilder the ideas, the better.* Even offbeat, impractical suggestions may suggest practical ideas to other members.
3. *Quantity is wanted.* The more ideas, the more likelihood of good ones.
4. *Combination and improvement are wanted.* If you see a way to improve on a previous idea, snap your fingers to get attention so it can be recorded at once.

It is often advantageous to have in the discussion group both persons with experience and persons quite new to the specific problem (for a fresh point of view). A full-time recorder is needed to write down ideas as fast as they are suggested. Sometimes this can be done with a tape recorder, but a visual record that all can see is best. Be sure the recorder gets all ideas in accurate form.

The flow of possible solutions can sometimes be increased by asking idea-spurring questions. One can ask: "How can we adapt (modify, rearrange, reverse, combine, minimize, maximize) *any general solution*?" A concrete suggestion can be used to open up creative thinking in a whole area. For example, someone might suggest: "Place a guard at each door." The leader could then ask, "What else might be done to increase security?" When the group seems to have run out of ideas, try reviewing the list rapidly; then ask for a definite number of additional suggestions to see if you can get more ideas. Usually you will get many more, including some very good ones.

A few warnings about applying brainstorming should be mentioned. A thorough job of creating new ideas, based on a full understanding of the problem, takes time. If time is short, use a more conventional and simple pattern. Be sure to stop all criticism, whether stated or implied by voice or manner. Everyone must feel completely free to express any idea that occurs to him or her as a possible solution. There are a few persons who seem to be unable to separate ideation from evaluation. If a few attempts fail to stop a person from criticizing ideas, ask him to follow the rules, stay quiet, or leave the group. The problem must be clear, carefully analyzed, and closely limited and defined. Broad, sweeping problems must be broken down into subproblems. Vague generalities cannot be put into action, so be sure to clarify and elaborate all courses of action before adopting them.

Use Constructive Argument to Avoid Groupthink

As mentioned earlier, Irving Janis has used the term *groupthink* to refer to conformity to the belief of a head person or a majority in a group. Groupthink sometimes occurs when members begin to think they are infallible, or that the ideas of high status members should not be challenged. Leaders who promote their own solutions invite groupthink, but this phenomenon can occur in any group. Examples of the results of groupthink outcomes are the invasion of the Bay of Pigs, the decision to escalate the United States involvement in South Vietnam, and the Watergate espionage. Contributing to groupthink are pressures for consensus at the price of repressing doubts and contradictory evidence, cohesiveness based on less than open communication, a lack of critical scrutiny of all pros and cons, a failure to look for more alternatives, a failure to examine moral or ethical considerations, stereotyping of opposing groups, pressure from high status members, ignoring of facts and interpretations that do not support a majority view, failure to consult with available experts, and an illusion of unanimity based on suppression of doubts.[36]

Appropriate norms or rules for arguing can do much to produce constructive argument. Any problem-solving group needs norms such as those that follow. If your group is suffering from groupthink it might be a good idea to make a copy of these for everybody to discuss at one meeting.

1. Arguments should not lead to some persons being perceived as winners and other members as losers; everyone wins when a more creative, adequate solution is achieved.
2. Each member of the group should participate openly, expressing feelings, ideas, and positions. Even intuitions and hunches should be expressed and evaluated.

effective group discussion

3. Members should insist on exploring the assumptions and implications of every idea; it is especially important that the person who first suggests a solution ask for such critical evaluation of the idea.
4. Every response to one's ideas should be valued and taken seriously. Every idea deserves an interested hearing.
5. Members should be critical of *all* ideas, but not of the members who express the ideas. Disagreement should not be person-centered but idea-centered. No one should try to put another on the defensive if the best possible thinking is to be done. Uptight discussants do not think clearly.
6. Members should frequently state what they think are the positions, feelings, and values of others with whose ideas they disagree. This will avoid much bypassing, and needless secondary tension.
7. All ideas should be evaluated on their own merits, not on the basis of who suggests them. In so far as possible, status power should be equalized so all members have the same chance to participate and be listened to, regardless of position or power in the external structure of the group or even role in the group.
8. The importance of teamwork in striving for consensus decisions that all can support should be stressed, perhaps often.
9. Controversy should be introduced when there is enough time to discuss the point at issue thoroughly, not just before the meeting must adjourn.
10. Trickery, bargaining, manipulation, and deception should be assiduously avoided, and pointed out and rebuked if detected.[37]

Plan How to Implement and Follow Up

Many times a group will arrive to no avail at a policy decision, a solution to a problem, a resolution, or some advice. No plans are made for putting a policy into effect or to see how recommendations are received. Every problem-solving discussion should terminate in some plan for action; no such group should consider its work finished until agreement is reached on who is to do exactly what, by what time, and how. If a committee is to make recommendations to a parent body, the committee should decide who will make the report, when he or she will make it, and in what form. If this report is to be made at a membership meeting, the committee members may then decide to prepare seconding or supporting speeches, may decide how to prepare the general membership to accept their recommendations, and so forth. A neighborhood group that has decided to turn a vacant lot into a playground would have to plan how to get legal clearances, who to get to do the work, where to get the materials (or at least from whom), and how to check on the use children get from the playground. No good chairperson or leader of a problem-solving group would fail to see that the group worked out details of how to put their decisions into effect.

Phillips has suggested the use of PERT (Program Evaluation and Review Technique) as an adjunct to the discussion process for working out the details of a complex solution.[38] It can be very useful for implementing a complex plan of action such as is involved in constructing a building, conducting a promotional campaign, scheduling the making of a movie, producing a play, etc. PERT involves identifying all events that must take place in sequences, estimating the time and resources needed for each, determining the allocation of personnel and material, and deciding whether a target date can likely be achieved. Although not needed for most plans of action, it is an excellent means for working out a plan based on statistical estimates rather than personal whim or guesswork. You may want to study it in one of the many excellent manuals on the process, but it must be practiced, not merely read about. Regardless of whether or not you study and apply PERT be sure that your decisions will be converted into observable events, that definite actions are taken by designated members of the group, and that some procedure for monitoring is arranged to be sure that the solution is carried out as intended and that the desired state of affairs is achieved.

Specific Sequences for Organizing Problem-Solving Discussions

With the general principles explained in the preceding section as a background, we can now examine specific patterns or sequences of steps for guiding a group's problem-solving activity. A number of scientific investigations of specific sequences have been made, from which one clear and consistent finding has emerged, as stated by Mabry and Barnes:

. . . research does not produce unequivocal evidence supporting or disconforming the utility of reflective thinking models in groups. But it does unequivocally support the advantage of some sort of rational decision making agenda.[39]

Early on in this line of research Maier and Maier compared a problem-solving sequence they called "developmental" with "free" discussions in which no particular sequence was followed. In a developmental discussion the designated leader posed a series of questions about the details and causes of the problem before permitting discussion of what to do about it. After these questions had been discussed by the group, they could then follow any procedure to arrive at a solution. Blind judgments by experts in the subject matter of the problem showed that the groups following the developmental pattern produced significantly more high quality solutions than did groups involved in free discussions (the leader asked no particular questions to get the group to map out the problem). An important process effect was also found: the developmental outline required more skill and tact on the part of the leader, or an outcome could be resentment by members at having their remarks restricted to one issue at a time. Members of these experimental groups were all managerial personnel in an organizational development program coordinated by Maier, but they were not necessarily trained in the logic and self-restraint required for reflective-type thinking.[40]

The effects of three different patterns for problem-solving discussion were compared experimentally by Brilhart and Jochem. A creative problem-solving pattern produced more possible solutions, and more solutions judged to be good ideas by independent judges. Participants preferred the complex creative problem-solving outline to a simpler pattern of "problem-possible solutions-final solution." Significantly more subjects also preferred a creative problem-solving pattern in which possible solutions preceded criteria to one in which discussion of criteria preceded possible solutions. Several subjects indicated that they felt discussing criteria first reduced their freedom to express novel ideas.[41] In a subsequent unpublished study, I compared the creative problem-solving sequence and a simpler reflective thinking sequence in which each idea was evaluated when first mentioned. Discussants in this later study made decisions on problems that affected them personally: how to distribute grade points among themselves, and the date of the final examination in their speech course. Again, significantly more subjects preferred the detailed creative problem-solving pattern after using both.

Bayless also reported that subjects in his study of sequences for organizing group problem solving felt that following a several-step procedure had helped them to reach a solution.[42]

Following up in this line of research, Larson used student groups to discuss industrial relations problems for which a "best" solution was known. This "best" solution was one of five alternatives supplied to the groups from which they had to choose. Four different problem-solving sequences were compared: the "no pattern," in which the group was given the problem to solve but no outline of steps to follow; the "single question" sequence, which is much like Maier's developmental pattern; the "ideal solution" format, which focuses attention on the wants and values of persons affected by the decision; and the "reflective thinking" form, based on the model presented by Dewey. Any of the three prescriptive patterns for guiding group discussion produced significantly more correct solutions than did the "no pattern" discussions. The merit of some outline of problem solving for organizing discussions was thus clearly demonstrated.[43]

The Reflective Thinking Sequence

This name has been given to a variety of patterns based on the model Dewey originated, with several changes to fit group interaction. This pattern could be employed if there is only a very limited range of possible solutions.

I. What is the nature of the problems facing us (present state of affairs, goal, and obstacles and causes of the problem)?
   A. What exactly are we concerned about?
      1. Is the question or assignment clear to us?
      2. Do we need to define any terms?
      3. What is our area of freedom?

B. What do we find unsatisfactory about the present situation?
   1. What exactly is wrong?
      a. Who is affected and in what ways?
      b. Under what conditions (when, where)?
   2. How serious do we judge the problem to be?
   3. What additional information do we need to adequately describe the extent and nature of the problem?
C. What goal(s) do we hope to achieve?
D. What obstacles to achieving this goal exist?
   1. What obstacles must be removed in order to achieve the goal?
   2. Are there any causative conditions that we can ascertain?
E. How can we summarize the problem, including the present situation, the goal, and the obstacles to it?
   1. Do we all agree on this formulation of the problem?
   2. Should we subdivide it into subproblems?
      a. If so, what are they?
      b. In what order shall we take them up?
II. By what criteria shall we judge our ideas? (This step may not always be necessary.)
III. What solutions are feasible?
IV. What seems to be the best possible solution?
V. How will we put our solution into effect?

The Creative Problem-Solving Sequence

The creative problem-solving sequence was developed as a discussion procedure for applying research findings about human creativity. It is based on the work of Alex Osborn, Sidney J. Parnes, and others associated with the Creative Problem Solving Institute. The pattern is most fittingly applied to problems for which there are many possible solutions, such as how to improve some product, alternative uses for idle buildings or tools, or any situation where imagination is called for.

I. What is the nature of the problem facing us (present state, obstacles, causes, goals)?
   A. What are we talking about?
      1. Is the question or assignment clear to us?
      2. Do we need to define any terms or concepts?
   B. What is our area of freedom?
      1. Are we to plan and take action, advise, or what?
      2. What sort of end product should we produce through our discussion?
   C. What has been happening that is unsatisfactory?
      1. What is wrong? How do we know?
      2. Who or what is affected, and under what conditions?
      3. How serious do we judge the problem to be?

effective group discussion

4. Have any corrective actions previously been tried that did not work?
5. What additional information do we need to adequately assess the extent and the nature of the problem?

D. What is the desired situation or goal we hope to achieve?

E. What factors seem to have caused this problem?
1. Are there any causative conditions of which we can be certain?
2. What obstacles must we remove to achieve the desired situation?

F. How can we summarize the problem to include the present situation, the desired situation, the difference, the causes, and the obstacles?
1. Do we all agree on this statement of the problem?
2. Should we divide it into any subproblems?
a. If so, what are they?
b. In what order should we take them up?

II. What might be done to solve the problem (or first subproblem)? (Here the group brainstorms for possible solutions.)

III. By what criteria shall we judge our possible solutions?
A. What absolute criteria must a solution meet?
B. What relative standards shall we apply? (List and rank these values and standards by group agreement.)

IV. What are the relative merits of our possible solutions?
A. What ideas can we screen out as unsupported by uncontested facts?
B. Can we combine and simplify our list of possible solutions in any way?
C. How well do the remaining ideas measure up to the criteria?

V. How will we put our solution into effect?
A. Who will do what, when, and how?
B. Do we need any follow-up or check procedures?

The creative problem-solving sequence could, of course, be repeated from II to V for each set of subproblems.

Ideal Solution Pattern

This pattern is especially suited to discussion of problems that will affect different groups of persons with different interests, or which must have the support of various types of persons with different concerns and values. For example, a change in traffic law would be of real concern to motorists, police officers, insurance companies, and businesses, at least. If the success of a policy or solution will be determined in large part by how well persons with different frames of reference will accept it, the ideal solution model of problem-solving is the procedure that should be followed. The second major step (II) in the procedure is to explore the desires of persons who would be directly affected by any change from the present situation. Thus, the discussants are urged to consider what *other* persons want, would accept, and make effective in achieving the goals of the group. The prohibitionists who succeeded in getting the United States Constitution amended to outlaw beverage alcohol may well have had a medically sound idea, but they failed to consider what the outcome would be when a large segment of the public rejected the solution. As a result, prohibition was not enforceable, and may have contributed directly to the growth of organized crime of other types. To understand the types of problems that the ideal solution pattern may be helpful with, consider the following problem questions:

Where should we five members of the Lamas family go for vacation next summer?

What courses should be offered by our department next semester?

What should be the law governing gambling in Idaho?

I. What is the nature of the problem? (The rest of this section of the analytic outline would be very much like that for creative problem solving.)

II. What would be an ideal solution from the point of view of each interested person or group? (A separate question, then, for each group, as:)
   A. Merchants?
   B. Customers?
   C. Manufacturers?
   D. Others?

III. What *can* be changed in the present situation? (That is, what solutions are possible? What *could* be done?)

IV. What solution best approximates the ideal? (Here the group synthesizes and decides on the final solution to apply or recommend.)

V. How will we put this solution into effect?

Sometimes you may not want to use this entire procedure for problem solving but simply ask questions during the analysis of the problem to get the group to consider various points of view. You would then use the group's findings about these as criteria when evaluating possible solutions to determine if they are realistic. That, of course, is the purpose of the ideal solution model.

Single Question Pattern

This format was created out of an analysis of differences in the behaviors of successful and unsuccessful problem solvers studied by Bloom and Broder, and was adapted to group problem solving by Larson for the study cited above.[44] Like the ideal solution pattern, Larson found it produced more choices of the best alternative than did the reflective thinking sequence.

I. What is the single question that, when answered, means the group knows how to accomplish its purpose?

II. What sub-questions must we answer before we can answer the single question we have formulated?

III. Do we have sufficient information to answer the sub-questions with confidence?

    A. If yes, what are our answers? (Then go on to step V.)

    B. If no, the group continues to IV or adjourns to look up answers, then meets again to proceed with Step IV.

IV. What are the most reasonable answers to the sub-questions?

V. Assuming our answers to the sub-questions are correct, what is the best solution to the problem. (Of course, a final step may be needed.)

VI. How will we put this solution into effect?[45]

Problem Solving Sequences in Relation to Problem Characteristics

Groups often find it somewhat frustrating and inhibiting to follow an outline of a problem-solving procedure. Indeed, they will usually deviate at times from any outline, but the value of a definite sequence will usually be so apparent that deviations from it can be kept rather brief. This will be much less of a chore for the group if the procedure chosen is suited to the specific problem, and if the group decides on the actual sequence to follow. Less changes in the procedure will be needed if the sequence of problem-solving steps is adapted to the problem. Often it is best to combine stages from two or more of the model outlines presented in the preceding section of this chapter. Below is a table of problem characteristics matched with the step(s) needed in the problem-solving sequence to deal adequately with each characteristic. This table may be helpful to you when planning an outline for a group to follow during a problem-solving discussion.

Problem Characteristic	Needed Problem-Solving Step
1. Difficulty is high.	1. Problem mapping, as presented in Single Question format, or Stage I of Reflective Thinking and Creative Problem Solving formats.
2. Multiple solutions are possible.	2. Ideation, Step II of Creative Problem Solving sequence, possibly including "brainstorming."
3. Intrinsic interest is high.	3. A period of "ventilation" before a systematic problem solving sequence.
4. Cooperative requirements are high.	4. If not already clear to all, a "criteria" step may be helpful, as in Stage III of Creative Problem Solving sequence.
5. Population familiarity is low.	5. Many subquestions will be needed in Step I to thoroughly map out the problem. The Single Question format may be especially appropriate.

Problem Characteristic	Needed Problem-Solving Step
6. A high level of acceptance for the solution is required.	6. Be sure to include Step II of the Ideal Solution format.
7. A high level of technical quality is required.	7. The Reflective Thinking sequence may be most suitable.
8. Area of freedom is for the complete process of problem solving.	8. Any complete problem-solving sequence, depending on other characteristics.
9. Area of freedom is limited to advising, or one or a few stages of problem solving.	9. The sequence should be shortened to emphasize only those steps in which the group has authority.

The Discussion Leader's Outline

Some discussion leaders get so involved in trying to follow a long, complex outline that they seem to be unable to listen well and adapt to what is happening in the discussion. Such a leader needs a relatively short, simple outline of the pattern for problem solving that the group has decided to follow for organizing its thinking and talking. A very abbreviated outline of the problem-solving sequence can be put on a chart or blackboard for all to see. A longer outline of questions can be duplicated and a copy given to each member of the group. Study carefully the following example of a leader's outline for guiding a group through the process of creative problem solving on a specific problem. Notice how the general questions from the model outlines above have been worded in terms of the specific problem. The leader, in actually using this outline, further revised his questions to fit the group's findings. He kept notes on his copy of the outline, modifying it as the group proceeded.

Problem Question. How might theft and mutilation of materials in the university library be reduced to a minimum?

I. What is the nature of the theft and mutilation now occurring in the library?
   A. Is the question clear to all of us?
   B. What limitations must we consider in our discussion?
      1. We can only recommend and advise; we are to draw up a proposal to be offered to the library committee.
      2. Do we want to place any other limits on our discussion of the problem at this time?
   C. What has been happening?
      1. What has been stolen or mutilated?
      2. How extensive and serious is this loss?
      3. What factors seem to contribute to the problem?
         a. In the library;
         b. In the classroom;
         c. Students and society at large;
         d. Other.

4. Have any steps been taken to reduce the loss? If so, how did they work?
   D. Can we summarize our findings and formulate the goal we want to achieve?
II. In view of the findings, what *might* we do to reduce theft and mutilation of library materials?
   A. Types of materials (books, periodicals, etc.)?
   B. Any rearrangements?
   C. Additional facilities or staff?
   D. Publicity or campaigns?
   E. Other ideas?
      [Notice that the leader does not have any proposed solutions on this outline, but only general headings to encourage the group to think up solutions.]
III. By what criteria shall we judge our ideas for reducing theft and mutilation?
   A. Are there any absolute standards by which to judge them?
   B. What features should a solution have?
IV. How well does each idea measure up to our criteria?
   A. Can we now combine or synthesize any ideas?
   B. Are there any ideas that we can reject at face value as being unrelated to the facts or causes we have identified?
   C. How does each remaining idea measure up to our criteria?
V. What will we recommend to the senate library committee?
VI. How will we prepare and present the report?
   A. Who will write our actual report?
   B. How will we present it?
   C. Do we want to check up on what the librarian does with our recommendations?

Next is a much simpler leader's outline following the reflective thinking sequence:

I. What sort of written final exam should we have for our class?
   A. How much authority (area of freedom) do we have?
   B. What facts and feelings should we take into account as we seek to answer this question?
II. What are our objectives (criteria) in deciding on the type of exam?
   A. Learning objectives?
   B. Grades?
   C. Type of preparation and study?
   D. Fairness to all?
III. What types of written final exam might we have?
IV. What are the advantages and disadvantages of each?
V. What will be the form of our written exam?

Summary

In this chapter we have considered many process variables of discussions for which the purpose is to solve some problem shared by group members. The concept "problem" was defined as consisting of an unsatisfactory condition, a goal, and obstacles to achievement of that goal. Before embarking on the actual problem-solving process, a group may first need to ventilate feelings and ideas about the problem, then they should consider the characteristics of the specific problem on seven major variables in order to adopt a procedure suitable to both the problem and the members.

It is not always possible to organize problem-solving discussions closely to the steps of a specific procedure, but doing so as much as possible will help keep the discussion coherent, goal-oriented, and efficient. Whatever specific procedure is used by a group, it should always begin with a thorough mapping of the details of the problem. It is usually productive to generate a list of possible alternatives before discussing their relative merits unless an obvious solution appears to all members. The group may need to spend time discussing criteria if these are not already clear and accepted by all members from the problem analysis stage. If acceptance is a major factor, a definite stage of discussion should be devoted to it. Every idea should be evaluated until a consensus (or at least a majority) decision emerges. Then the group is ready to work out a specific procedure for putting the solution into effect.

Depending on the nature of the problem, the most appropriate sequence could be a version of reflective thinking, creative problem solving (including brainstorming), the ideal solution procedure, or the single question format. These formats should be applied with considerable flexibility, adapting them to the specific problem. If the group has a designated leader, his or her duties will often include drafting a tentative sequence outline for the group to consider before getting deeply into the discussion. Such an outline should be relatively brief, easy for all members to understand, accept, and follow its logic. Any definite sequence for organizing the discussion is likely to produce a final solution and satisfaction superior to what would be achieved if no special attention and effort were devoted to the procedure by which the group thinking and talking will be organized.

Exercises

1. Select two problems you currently are faced with. Write each as a problem question. Then decide what is *unsatisfactory* about the present state of affairs, the *goal* you hope to achieve, and the *obstacles* that lie in the road to achieving the goal. Write these in the following format:

   Problem question—

   What is unsatisfactory—

   Goal—

   Obstacles—

2. As a *class*, select a problem affecting all members of the class—such as the type of final exam for the course, or some campus issue. Now *describe* the problem on each of the seven characteristics (variables) of a problem presented in this chapter.

3. As a *class,* select a problem in which all are interested which is appropriate for each of the four major sequences of problem solving presented in the chapter (reflective thinking, creative problem solving, ideal solution, and single question). You will then have four problem questions. Write a brief leader's outline for guiding discussion of each problem, adapting the model sequence to the actual problem.

   Now compare your outlines with those prepared by three or four fellow students. As a group write one outline for each problem so that the sequence of questions is acceptable to all members of your subgroup.

4. Your instructor may assign you to actually discuss the four problems. If so, after each evaluate how satisfied you are with the solution decided upon by your group, the discussion itself, the procedure you followed, and your participation.

Bibliography

Dewey, John, *How We Think*, Boston: D. C. Heath & Company, 1910.

Kepner, Charles H., and Tregoe, Benjamin B., *The Rational Manager*, New York: McGraw-Hill Book Company, 1965.

Maier, Norman R. F., *Problem Solving and Creativity in Individuals and Groups*, Belmont, Calif.: Brooks/Cole Publishing Company, 1970.

———, *Problem-Solving Discussions and Conferences*, New York: McGraw-Hill Book Company, 1963.

Osborn, Alex F., *Applied Imagination* (rev. ed.), New York: Charles Scribner's Sons, 1957.

Rubenstein, Moshe F., *Patterns of Problem Solving*, Englewood Cliffs, N.J.: Prentice-Hall, Inc., 1975, especially chapter 1.

Shaw, Marvin E., *Group Dynamics*, (2nd ed.), New York: McGraw-Hill Book Company, 1976, pp. 58–69 and 312–38.

References

1. Marvin E. Shaw, *Group Dynamics*, 2nd ed. (McGraw-Hill, 1976), pp. 58–65.
2. David M. Berg, "A Descriptive Analysis of the Distribution and Duration of Themes Discussed by Task-oriented Small Groups," *Speech Monographs* 34 (1967), pp. 172–75.
3. Earnest G. Bormann and Nancy C. Bormann, *Effective Small Group Communication*, 2nd ed. (Minneapolis: Burgess Publishing Company, 1976), p. 132.

4. Charles H. Kepner and Benjamin B. Tregoe, *The Rational Manager* (New York: McGraw-Hill Book Company, 1965), p. 20.

5. *Group Dynamics*, pp. 310–12.

6. Marvin E. Shaw and J. M. Blum, "Effects of Leadership Style upon Group Performance As a Function of Task Structure," *Journal of Personality and Social Psychology* 3 (1966), pp. 238–42.

7. J. R. Hackman, "Effects of Task Characteristics on Group Products," *Journal of Experimental Social Psychology* 4 (1968), pp. 162–87.

8. "Effects of Leadership Style. . . ."

9. See, for example, John K. Brilhart and Lurene M. Jochem, "Effects of Different Patterns on Outcomes of Problem-Solving Discussion," *Journal of Applied Psychology* 48 (1964), pp. 175–79; Ovid L. Bayless, "An Alternative Model for Problem Solving Discussion, *Journal of Communication* 17 (1967), pp. 188–97; Sidney J. Parnes and Arnold Meadow, "Effects of 'Brainstorming' Instruction on Creative Problem-Solving by Trained and Untrained Subjects," *Journal of Educational Psychology* 50 (1959), pp. 171–76.

10. Marvin E. Shaw, *Group Dynamics*, p. 311.

11. Leonard Berkowitz, "Sharing Leadership in Small Decision-Making Groups," *Journal of Abnormal and Social Psychology* 48 (1953), pp. 231–38.

12. James H. Davis, *Group Performance* (Reading, Mass.: Addison-Wesley Publishing Company, 1969).

13. Alex F. Osborn, *Applied Imagination*, rev. ed. (New York: Charles Scribner's Sons, 1957).

14. Norman R. F. Maier, *Problem-Solving Discussions and Conferences* (New York: McGraw-Hill, 1963), pp. 5–15.

15. (Boston: D. C. Heath, 1910).

16. *Ibid.,* pp. 2–3.

17. *Ibid.,* pp. 9–75.

18. *Ibid.,* p. 78.

19. John K. Brilhart, "An Exploratory Study of Relations between the Evaluating Process and Associated Behavior of Participants in Six Study-Discussion Groups" (Ph.D. dissertation, Pennsylvania State University, 1962), pp. 258–77.

20. Dennis S. Gouran, Candace Brown, and David R. Henry, "Behavioral Correlates of Perceptions of Quality in Decision-Making Discussions," *Communication Monographs* 45 (1978), p. 62.

21. William E. Jurma, "Effects of Leader Structuring Style and Task-Orientation Characteristics of Group Members," *Communication Monographs* 46 (1979), pp. 282–95.

22. Linda L. Putnam, "Preference for Procedural Order in Task-Oriented Small Groups," *Communication Monographs* 46 (1979), pp. 193–218.

23. Brilhart and Jochem, "Effects of Different Patterns. . ."

24. John K. Brilhart, "An Experimental Comparison of Three Techniques for Communicating a Problem-Solving Pattern to Members of a Discussion Group," *Speech Monographs* 33 (1966), pp. 168–77.
25. H. C. Pyron and H. Sharp, "A Quantitative Study of Reflective Thinking and Performance in Problem-Solving Discussion," *Journal of Communication* 13 (1963), pp. 46–53.
26. Richard Nisbett and Lee Ross, *Human Inference: Strategies and Shortcomings of Social Judgment* (Englewood Cliffs, N.J.: Prentice-Hall, 1980).
27. Robert J. Sternberg, "Stalking the IQ Quark," *Psychology Today* 13 (September 1979), pp. 42–54.
28. Irving J. Lee, *How to Talk with People* (New York: Harper & Row, Publishers, 1952), p. 62.
29. Norman R. F. Maier, *Problem-Solving Discussions and Conferences* (New York: McGraw-Hill Book Company, 1963), p. 123.
30. N. R. F. Maier and R. A. Maier, "An Experimental Test of the Effects of 'Developmental' vs. 'Free' Discussions on the Quality of Group Decisions," *Journal of Applied Psychology* 41 (1957), pp. 320–23.
31. N. R. F. Maier and A. R. Solem, "The Contribution of a Discussion Leader to the Quality of Group Thinking: The Effective Use of Minority Opinions," *Human Relations* 5 (1952), pp. 277–88.
32. Maier, *Problem Solving Discussions and Conferences*, pp. 62–97, stresses this difference, and gives excellent advice on how to formulate and present problems to a group.
33. Charles H. Kepner and Benjamin B. Tregoe, *The Rational Manager* (New York: McGraw-Hill Book Company, 1965), pp. 117–18.
34. Moshe F. Rubenstein, *Patterns of Problem Solving* (Englewood Cliffs, N.J.: Prentice-Hall, Inc., 1975), pp. 1–2.
35. Norman R. F. Maier, *Problem Solving and Creativity* (Belmont, Cal.: Brooks Publishing Company, 1970), pp. 453–55.
36. Irving L. Janis, "Groupthink," *Psychology Today* 5 (Nov., 1971), pp. 43–46, 74–76.
37. Adapted from David W. Johnson and Frank P. Johnson, *Joining Together: Group Theory and Group Skills* (Englewood Cliffs, N.J.: Prentice-Hall, Inc., 1975), pp. 154–55.
38. Gerald M. Phillips, "PERT As a Logical Adjunct to the Discussion Process," *Journal of Communication* 15 (1965), pp. 89–99. Reprinted in Cathcart and Samovar, *Small Group Conmunication*, pp. 166–76.
39. Edward R. Mabry and Richard E. Barnes, *The Dynamics of Small Group Communication* (Englewood Cliffs, N.J.: Prentice-Hall, 1980), p. 78.
40. Norman R. F. Maier and Robert A. Maier, "An Experimental Test of the Effects of 'Developmental' vs. 'Free' Discussions on the Quality of Group Decisions," *Journal of Applied Psychology* 41 (1957), pp. 320–23.

41. John K. Brilhart and Lurene M. Jochem, "Effects of Different Patterns on Outcomes of Problem-Solving Discussion," *Journal of Applied Psychology* 48 (1964), pp. 175–79.
42. Ovid L. Bayless, "An Alternative Model for Problem Solving Discussion," *Journal of Communication* 17 (1967), pp. 188–97.
43. Carl E. Larson, "Forms of Analysis and Small Group Problem-Solving," *Speech Monographs* 36 (1969), pp. 452–55.
44. Benjamin S. Bloom and Lois J. Broder, "Problem-solving Processes of College Students," in Theodore L. Harris and Wilson E. Schwahn (eds.), *Selected Readings in the Learning Process* (New York: Oxford University Press, 1961), pp. 31–79.
45. Carl E. Larson, "Forms of Analysis . . .", p. 453.

9

leadership of small group discussions

Study Objectives

As a result of your study of chapter 9 you should be able to:

1. Define and distinguish among the concepts of leadership, leader, and designated leader.

2. Explain the major theories and findings of trait, functional, style, and contingency approaches to the study of leadership.

3. Define the concept of power, and explain how power can be applied democratically in group-centered leadership.

4. Describe characteristics typical of effective discussion leaders.

5. Develop a personal philosophy of group-centered democratic leadership, and cite research supporting this style.

6. List responsibilities and functions often expected of designated discussion leaders, and both general approaches and specific techniques for providing these functions.

Key Terms

Autocratic leader a person who dominates and manipulates a group, usually for personal goals, using coercion, rewards, and positional power to influence.

Completer, leader as leader who determines what functions or behaviors are most needed for a group to perform optimally, then attempts to supply those behaviors.

Contingency approach study of how outcomes of leadership vary with differences in input or context variables; adapting leadership services to such variables.

Democratic leader person who coordinates and facilitates discussion in a small group by consent of the group, thus helping to achieve group-determined goals.

Designated leader a person appointed or elected to an acknowledged position as leader of a small group.

Discussion leader leader of a group's verbal interaction; coordinator of discussion process and procedures.

Emergent or "natural" leader member of an initially leaderless group who in time is named as "leader" by all or nearly all members.

Functions approach study of the input, process, and output functions performed by actual small group leaders.

Leader a *person* who exercises goal-oriented influence in a group, any person identified by members of a group as leader, or a designated leader.

Leadership influence exerted through communication that helps a group clarify and achieve goals; performance of a leadership function.

Power potential to influence behavior of others, derived from such bases as ability to reward, coerce, or supply needed expertise, or from personal attraction and the consent of those who follow.

Structuring leadership behaviors that function to organize and coordinate group interaction and work.

Trait approach study of personal and behavioral characteristics of both designated and emergent leaders.

It is universally believed that leaders are important in the outcomes of group discussions. But what behaviors constitute effective leadership service to a small group is not always possible to decide during the process of discussion, and agreement is lacking on what discussion leaders should do. "Leader" and "leadership" are highly abstract terms that have been used for a multitude of referents concerning personality traits, interpersonal activity, and a great variety of situations. In this book we are not concerned with a general theory of leadership for all types of leader-follower situations, but only with leadership of discussion groups in which all members have a voice in the decisions and actions of the group. Thus we can narrow our study of leadership by excluding, for the most part, such groups as work crews, combat teams, athletic teams, large organizations, and mass meetings, except when these groups are engaged in discussion.

To serve others as a leader can be a source of self-esteem, recognition, and appreciation from others. It can meet personal needs for control of both situations and other persons. It can provide the satisfaction of accomplishment, the taking on and meeting of a challenge, similar to the satisfaction experienced by a successful craftsperson or athlete. But for every potential reward of a leadership role there is the concomitant potential for failure and disappointment. Although most members of small groups of peers would like to be recognized as leader, many hesitate to take on any formal role of leader, for to do so entails high levels of responsibility and visibility. Perhaps they lack knowledge and confidence about what to do, or fear the possibility of failing and losing face. The sheer amount of work required in some discussion leader roles may stop many. Others would avoid a position of leadership because they think it requires manipulating others, and a few even go so far as to say leaders are no longer needed. But as Cathcart and Samovar say,

As yet, however, there has been no noticeable change in leaders or leadership and apparently no successful groups without leadership. Even when some members of a group consciously avoid leader roles, others arise to fill the void. The question then becomes not one of whether there should or should not be leaders, but what constitutes the most effective and desirable leadership for a given group.[1]

effective group discussion

A Learning Activity

Figure 9.1 The Sargent and Miller Leadership Scale. (F. Sargent and G. Miller, "Some Differences in Certain Communication Behaviors of Autocratic and Democratic Group Leaders," *Journal of Communication* 21 [1971], pp. 233-52.)

We are interested in the things that are important to you when you are leading a group discussion. Listed below are several pairs of statements. Read each pair of statements and place a mark in the one you believe to be of greater importance. On reacting to the statements, observe the following ground rules:

1. Place your check marks clearly and carefully.
2. Do not omit any of the items.
3. Never check both of the items.
4. Do not look back and forth through the items; make each item a separate and independent judgment.
5. Your first impression, the immediate feelings about the statements, is what we want.

1. a. _____ To give everyone a chance to express his opinion.
   b. _____ To know what the group and its members are doing.
2. a. _____ To assign members to tasks so more can be accomplished.
   b. _____ To let the members reach a decision all by themselves.
3. a. _____ To know what the group and its members are doing.
   b. _____ To help the members see how the discussion is related to the purposes of the group.
4. a. _____ To assist the group in getting along well together.
   b. _____ To help the group to what you think is their best answer.
5. a. _____ To get the job done.
   b. _____ To let the members reach a decision all by themselves.
6. a. _____ To know what the group and its members are doing.
   b. _____ To let the members reach a decision all by themselves.
7. a. _____ To get the job done.
   b. _____ To assist the group in getting along well together.
8. a. _____ To help the members see how the discussion is related to the purposes of the group.
   b. _____ To assign members to tasks so more can be accomplished.
9. a. _____ To ask questions that will cause members to do more thinking.
   b. _____ To get the job done.
10. a. _____ To let the members reach a decision all by themselves.
    b. _____ To give new information when you feel the members are ready for it.

Now turn to p. 247 to score your answers and locate your position on the autocratic-democratic style dimension of discussion leadership attitudes. You may want to discuss the items of this scale with a group of classmates. You should now be able to understand the rest of this chapter in a more uniquely personal way.

The style, functions, and communicative behaviors of leaders have been studied extensively by small group theorists and researchers since the early 1940s. Prior to that time it was widely believed that leaders were specially gifted persons who were "born to lead" and that there was little anyone could do to develop leadership skills. Even today, despite research findings to the contrary, persons often speak as if there were some mystical "quality of leadership" that if possessed makes one a leader in virtually any situation. Generals are assumed to be capable of supplying effective leadership in education or government; football captains are elected to class offices; great teachers are made chairpersons of committees—and sometimes the results are dismal. I still receive forms on which to rate former students as job applicants that contain a scale like this: "Leadership—superior ___; above average ___; average ___; below average ___."

Persons who keep abreast of research in leadership know better. Leadership is not *a* quality or personality trait; leadership involves a wide variety of communicative behaviors, personal attitudes and characteristics, most of which may differ considerably from situation to situation and group to group.

Training persons to diagnose and supply the changing leadership services needed by specific types of group situations has made many organizations more productive. Businesses and agencies constantly search for persons with attitudes and skills needed for specific positions of leadership, and then give them further specialized training in such matters as management theory and practice, human relations, listening, speaking, group dynamics, and conference leadership. Armed forces provide a variety of types of training in leadership skills for officers of all ranks. Unions conduct leadership training programs to develop special skills in their membership. In short, there is a continuing demand for persons with special leadership skills.

Money and time spent on developing discussion leadership skills are invested wisely. As we have seen, discussion is fundamental to democratic organization and cooperation. No discussion group can be effective without appropriate leadership—and that means skilled leaders. Whenever a group has a designated leader (either elected or appointed), that person can almost literally make or break the group. In my own research studies I found that the degree of success in goal achievement and member satisfaction by adult study groups was so closely related to the leader's behavior that I often said: "Let me watch the leader for fifteen minutes and I will predict whether or not the group will be successful." Countless committees and task groups have faltered and accomplished little when the chairperson did not know how to perform as leader. I once watched a dramatic change occur among faculty members of a high school when the principal was replaced. Academic departments of a university are greatly affected by the way the chairperson functions as coordinator and administrator of the faculty. A group of faculty members included in the bill of particulars calling for removal of their dean the following charge: "He is singularly inept in conducting our meetings." Yes, leaders make a great difference in how well small groups function.

But what does it take to lead *discussions* well? In a very real sense, this entire book is an attempt to answer that question: an understanding of the process dynamics of small groups, positive attitudes toward self and others, dependable and relevant knowledge, interest and commitment, sensitive listening as well as encoding skills, a belief in democratic decision making, and skills in systematic problem solving. There are specific things we can do to supply leadership services in the small groups to which we belong. In this chapter we will first consider the concepts of *leader* and *leadership,* then a variety of approaches to the study of leadership, next a philosophy of discussion leadership, and finally the special responsibilities of an appointed or elected discussion leader and some ways to meet those responsibilities so that both process and output variables of discussion are enhanced.

Leadership and Leaders

It is possible for a discussion group to have no designated leader and yet to have excellent leadership. It is also possible for a discussion group to have a leader and yet be woefully lacking in leadership. If these statements seem paradoxical, it is only because the terms *leader* and *leadership* are confusing due to overlapping meanings.

Leadership

Social scientists are virtually unanimous in defining leadership as *interpersonal influence.* Probably the most widely used definition in the area of small group communication is that by Tannenbaum, Weschler, and Massarik:

> We define leadership as *interpersonal influence, exercised in situation and directed, through the communication process, toward the attainment of a specified goal or goals.* Leadership always involves attempts on the part of a *leader* (influencer) to affect (influence) the behavior of a follower (influencee) or followers in *situation.*[2]

However, this is a general definition, not limited to small groups. Only attempts to influence behavior in an effort to achieve a *group* goal will be considered leadership in the context of small group discussion, thereby excluding behavior through which one member influences another to do something apart from or contrary to the goal of the group. Excluded would be influence irrelevant to the group's goals, such as one member influencing another to emulate his mannerisms, join him in an attempt to sabotage the group, or join him for a drink after the meeting (unless that is done to achieve greater harmony within the group).

Influence refers to the exercise of *power,* which in groups of relative equals depends on the consent of other group members to be influenced. French and Raven identified five sources of power that a designated leader may have in some degree: reward, coercive, legitimate, referent, and expert.[3] The exercise of power to influence depends upon a follower (or followers) perceiving that a leader has a power base that can be exercised, whether or not the power is actually available to the person exercising the influence. If no one follows, there is no leader. Members may be *rewarded* by giving them special attention, favors, or acknowledgement. Members who resist an attempt to influence are sometimes *coerced* by threats, lack of opportunity to speak, or ignoring them until they comply. A boss or other authority figure may use such power to virtually force acquiescence, but such behavior is not leadership.

Legitimate power stems from an acknowledged position and title. Many small group members will follow directives from a person holding such a position: a private will accept the legitimate power of his sergeant to chew him out, but would not let another private do so. A work supervisor may assign duties, but not a colleague. In the typical committee, most members will attend meetings at the call of an appointed chairperson, and will accept the agenda prepared for a meeting by that person. Most discussants let designated leaders exercise some control over the flow of verbal participation and problem-solving procedures.

Referent power is based on attraction of one person to another, or identification. Such power comes from the desire of group members to associate with an attractive leader. This is sometimes called *charisma.*

Expert power is attributed by members to another for what he or she knows and can do. A person holding a monopoly within a small group on knowledge and skills essential to overcome obstacles to a goal will have a high degree of expert power. It may matter little that he or she is not personally attractive, the holder of a position granting legitimate power, or able to either reward or punish. The expert is followed because he or she is perceived as having vital knowledge and skills.

Group-centered leadership entails the judicious use of power to serve the group's interests. Any source of power can be weakened by indiscriminate use or overuse. Members will often goldbrick or rebel if coercive power is employed, come to dislike rather than identify if referent power is used for the personal gain of the leader, or refuse to be influenced and thus remove the base of legitimate power.

The more these five power bases are concentrated in one person, the more that person can dominate and control the group, possibly leading to autocracy or decisions being made by one person. The greater the degree to which the bases of power and influence are equally distributed among the members of a small group, the more likely is verbal participation to be shared, decision making to be collaborative and by consensus, and the designated leader to serve as a coordinator rather than dominate. Sometimes when there is no legitimate leader (by appointment or election), a long struggle for the status of primary leader ensues in a group, with competitors struggling to win followers. Several studies have confirmed that such groups are ineffective unless or until a stable leadership structure (including a primary leader) emerges. A group suffering a struggle for the leader position produces poor products, dissatisfaction, and low levels of cohesiveness.[4] The conclusion is clear: someone in a group in which the bases of power are widely shared must emerge as the recognized leader or the group will be a failure in solving its problems. But what does it take to emerge as leader or to be accepted as a legitimate designated leader in a discussion group? Certainly the responsibility for leadership functions and influence are shared in successful discussion groups.

When formal organizations appoint persons to positions of control in small groups or someone is elected chairperson or leader, that person must still earn leadership from within the group. The designated leader will be challenged and tested as he or she attempts to coordinate activities of members. If that person is not able to emerge as the natural or choice leader of the group, another person will do so or the group will flounder.

Discussion leadership is the responsibility of all members of a small group; it will usually be shared by several of them. It is now believed that the tasks that were considered to be the sole responsibility of the leader (introducing the problem, guiding the discussion, probing, spreading participation, clarifying, resolving disagreements, asking questions, etc.) can better be handled by many members of a group. Some persons may have more skills at certain leadership tasks, have special knowledge, or sensitivity to what the designated leader has missed. If so, a *leadership team* emerges. If we conceive of leadership as services that help a group clarify and achieve its goals *as a group,* then it must be obvious that everyone in the group has some contribution to make to its leadership; and if not that person should not be a member.

Leaders

Even though leadership functioning may be diffused within a group, the management of a business or governmental organization will hold a designated leader responsible for the productivity of the group. Designated leaders of small groups in other settings are not free form such responsibility either: ". . . group members and outsiders tend to hold the leader accountable for group beliefs, proposals, actions, and products."[5] Thus the role or position "leader" must be clarified.

The term *leader* is used in this book to refer to any person who is viewed by group members as a leader, any person who is designated (by appointment or election) as such and who as a consequence becomes a coordinator of the efforts of group members, or to any person who at a given moment is exerting influence to help achieve group goals.

A designated leader has a special responsibility to maintain perspective and to see that all needed leadership services are performed. In this regard, Schutz described the function of a leader in a group as a *completer:* ". . . the best a leader can do is to observe what functions are not being performed by a segment of the group and enable this part to accomplish them."[6] As Schutz says, the prime requisites to being a leader are: knowing necessary group functions; sensing unfulfilled group functions; performing and getting others to perform needed functions; and being willing to take necessary action, even if personally displeasing. This concept of "leader as completer" is a powerful guide to anyone who wants to be an effective discussion leader, and emphasizes again the importance of having some image of optimal group discussion such as was presented in chapter 2.

Leader, then, is also a special role in the group. The nature of that role will depend on the person occupying it, the membership of the group (skills, expectations, and beliefs about leaders), the source of the group, the degree of development of the group as a functioning system, and the goals of the group. The ideal is for leadership functions to be shared so that each member supplies those services that he or she can do best, with the designated leader doing whatever no one else can do as well, and having a special responsibility to monitor the functioning of the group as a system in order to provide leadership services when needed (or encourage others to do so). For example, a designated committee chairperson might take notes and summarize, unless someone else is doing so for the group. The leader's role is determined by an interaction of such variables as the external situation facing the group, the expectations and beliefs of members about the leader role, and the respective skills of all members.

One-meeting groups should almost always have designated leaders. In a one-meeting group the designated leader will likely do most of the organizing, clarifying, summarizing, and other procedural tasks; concomitantly, he or she will probably do little suggesting or evaluating of ideas. In a continuing group, routines will develop with members taking on specialized roles; after a time, the designated leader may be able to participate very much like any other member. As members take on tasks of leadership and develop skill in them, the designated leader's proportion of leadership will decline. However, the designated leader will always be expected to serve as coordinator and spokesperson for the group.

Approaches to the Study of Leadership and Leaders

Four major approaches to the scientific study of leaders and leadership have developed: trait, function, style, and contingency or situational.

The Trait Approach to Leadership

Trait studies began with the assumption that leaders are a special class of people, distinguishable from "followers" in personal traits. In 1940 Bird was able to find little consistency in the research reports of leader characteristics, possibly due to inadequacies of measurement, the wide variety of types of groups and tasks studied, varying definitions, and other unspecified variables.[7] From later studies it has been shown that some general traits tend to be related to leadership. Leaders tend to exceed other group members in such characteristics as IQ, knowledge, verbal facility, and flexibility. They tend to be larger physically, and more attractive. They are also more sociable than average, as shown on measures of dependability, frequency of participation, cooperation, and popularity. They show above average initiative and persistence.[8]

A productive approach to the study of leader characteristics, especially in discussion groups, was undertaken by John Geier at the University of Minnesota. Initially leaderless groups were questioned regularly to determine which members were perceived as exerting leadership and if a consensus leader had emerged. Both directly observable behaviors of persons who emerged as leaders and traits perceived by fellow group members were examined. In the successful groups, definite consensus leaders emerged; in all groups much energy was spent on a struggle for leader status. A clear pattern of leader emergence was found with two phases to it. During the relatively short and conflict-free first phase of leader emergence, participants with three types of characteristics were eliminated from a bid for the leader spot: the uninformed members (on the problem facing the group); the infrequent participants; and the rigid or dogmatic members who expressed their opinions categorically and were not subject to the influence of other members. The second phase in the struggle for the leader position could be either relatively short or prolonged with approximately forty per cent of the group members still competing for preeminence. First, those who were authoritarian and manipulative in their methods were eliminated in favor of the more democratic. The final characteristic of behavior eliminating remaining contenders was called "offensive verbalization" by Geier, and included such behaviors as "incessant talking and stilted speech." It is also important to note that in the majority of groups where a leader emerged, another person who had contended for the leader post emerged as a "lieutenant."[9]

The Functions Approach

The functions approach to the study of small group leadership examines what leaders *do* to influence group goal clarification and achievement. Leadership behaviors may serve such functions as task achievement, structuring interaction, group development and maintenance, and helping members meet personal needs that could otherwise reduce their contributions to the group's goal achievement. Bales divided leadership functions into two broad categories, task and socio-emotional. He found that relatively few persons could perform both types of functions equally well, thus indicating the need in many groups for a leadership team of at least a task specialist and a socio-emotional specialist.[10]

Stogdill, in a major review of the literature, identified six functions of leadership from the writing of theorists:

1. Defining objectives and maintaining goal direction.

2. Providing means for goal achievement.

3. Providing and maintaining group structure.

4. Facilitating group action and interaction.

5. Maintaining group cohesiveness and member satisfaction.

6. Facilitating group task performance.[11]

It is probably obvious to you that these process functions are important to the outcomes of a group discussion, with the possible exclusion of 6. Performing these functions during discussion requires many specific types of actions. These are described and advice on how they can be provided is given in the last major section of this chapter.

The central function most often expected of a discussion leader is a co-ordinating one. Maier illustrated this function with an analogy comparing the designated discussion leader's role to that of the nerve ring in a starfish, and the other group members to its rays. When the nerve ring is intact, it connects and coordinates the rays, and the starfish is very efficient in its movements. If the ring is severed, the rays can influence each other's behaviors to a degree, but internal coordination is missing. If one ray is stimulated to step forward (perhaps to seize a clam), the adjoining rays sense the pull on them and also begin to step forward, showing coordinated behavior based on external control. But if opposite rays are stimulated simultaneously, the animal becomes locked in position as each ray tries to move in opposite directions; this can even tear the starfish in two and destroy it. The central nerve ring does none of the moving, but it coordinates the behavior of all the rays. Thus we get the coordinated behavior of a higher type organism rather than the summed efforts of five rays physically together but not coordinated unless one domi-nates the others. The ring does not do the work, but collects the information from all rays and produces an organismically unified response rather than a collection of individual responses that may or may not be interrelated. Maier likens the function of a group-centered discussion leader to that of the central nerve ring: "Thus the leader does not serve as a dominant ray and produce the solution. Rather, his function is to receive information, facilitate com-munication between the individuals, relay messages, and integrate the incom-ing responses so that a single unified response occurs."[12] Coordinating is acknowledged by virtually all writers to be the primary function of designated discussion leaders, but **how** it should be performed is a central question in small group leadership philosophy.

Recently, communication researchers have begun to study the commu-nicative functions of discussion leaders. Knutson and Holdridge found that persons who emerged as leaders in small policy discussion groups were sig-

effective group discussion

nificantly higher than others in the percentage of their remarks that were orientation behaviors.[13] The importance of verbalizing a sense of unity of purpose and identification of members with each other was presented in chapter 6. This was supported somewhat by a case study indicating that an important leadership function may be formulating and communicating a "rhetorical vision" of the bases for identification rather than conflict among group members.[14]

The Style Approach

How one acts as a leader in a discussion group depends in large part on his or her attitudes (degree of authoritarianism, of openmindedness, etc.), which collectively can be called a philosophy of leadership. "Philosophy" as used here refers to a set of beliefs, values, and ethics concerning the relationship between leaders and followers, or how a leader *ought* to act. In this sense a philosophy embraces the entire scope of functions performed by a would-be leader, the purpose of them as primarily serving self or group, and whether decisions are best made by leader or group collectively. One's style in attempting to exert leadership can be called a philosophy in action.

The style approach to the study of small group leadership gained its impetus from a study reported by White and Lippett.[15] It showed output advantages of democratic over autocratic and laissez faire styles of leading. However, the results must be generalized to adult discussion groups with caution for the groups studied were boys clubs organized to construct craft objects with the assistance of assigned adult leaders. Democratic leaders allowed the boys to decide policy issues, with encouragement and assistance from the leader. Laissez faire leaders took almost no initiative, but did respond to inquiries from the boys. Autocratic style leaders made assignments, gave orders, and rigidly controlled all verbal interaction, shutting off boys who did not agree with them.

More germane to the purpose of this book was a finding by Sargent and Miller (who developed the scale at the beginning of this chapter) that democratic leaders encouraged much more member participation in the problem-solving discussion process than did autocratic leaders. Rosenfeld and Plax found that autocratic discussion leaders asked less questions but answered more than did democratic leaders, expressed more negative reactions (coercion attempts?), and made less attempts to get others to participate actively.[16]

One line of research into the style of leaders of problem-solving discussion groups has focused on what is called "leadership structuring style," which refers primarily to what I have called "procedural leadership." As Jurma described them, "structuring leaders actively work to organize and coordinate group interaction" by helping to formulate goals and ways to achieve them, clarifying, providing task-related information, and stressing egalitarian behavior.[17] Nonstructuring designated leaders participate very little and suggest no structure or procedure, acting in a laissez faire style. A general conclusion from this line of research is that groups with structuring designated leaders are more effective in problem solving and more satisfying to the participants than are groups with assigned nonstructuring leaders.[18] Jurma found that leader structuring style made no difference to task-oriented participants, but contrary to his expectations, discussants low in task-orientation were more productive and more satisfied with both the leader and the task when the leader acted in a structuring style rather than nonstructuring. Independent judges rated discussions led by structuring leaders to be of higher quality than discussions with assigned nonstructuring leaders.[19] In summary, this line of research has produced consistent findings that a democratic structuring style produces both better task outcomes and higher member satisfaction than does either a nonstructuring or an autocratic style.

The Contingency Approach

The contingency (or situational) approach to the study of leadership in small interacting groups has investigated the general hypothesis that the style of leadership needs to be varied according to contingencies of group purpose, task complexity, organizational context, member characteristics and expectations, and other variables. When we consider all types of small groups, this hypothesis is clearly supported. Fielder developed a model of three major factors upon which appropriate leadership behaviors are contingent: leader-member relations, task structure, and position power.[20] The central thesis of Fiedler's work is that individuals' personal needs and characteristics would make them suited for leadership only in certain contingencies, and so it is more productive to match prospective leaders to situations than to try to change a person's leadership style. This theory also implies that, as a group's situation changes through time, different types of persons would be needed in the position of designated leader. Problem-solving discussion groups, according to Fiedler's theory and findings, would generally be served best by a democratic structuring leader with concern for persons rather than autocratic or nonstructuring leadership. However, in other types of situations, such as supervising police or production workers or leading primary groups, a much more autocratic or socio-emotional style of leadership would be more productive.

It has been demonstrated that what members think of as appropriate leadership functions and style is contingent upon situational variables.[21] Wood used a questionnaire to determine what members of continuing small groups with task, social, and dual task-social objectives expected of designated leaders. She named the three major factors that emerged as task guidance, interpersonal attractiveness, and team spirit. Members of both task and dual-purpose groups rated task-oriented leadership (analogous to structuring) highly important, whereas members of social groups rated interpersonal attractiveness high and task orientation low. A moderate degree of team spirit was expected of leaders in all types of groups.[22] Downs and Pickett examined contingencies of leader style and member needs. Groups of participants with high social needs were most productive with task-oriented procedural leaders, and least productive with no designated leader. Groups of persons low on interpersonal needs did equally well with designated leaders who provided task-structuring only, leaders who provided both task structuring and socio-emotional leadership, and no designated leader. Groups with members both high and low in interpersonal needs performed somewhat better without a designated leader. A complex relationship among members needs, leadership style, and member satisfaction was found, giving support to the general contingency hypothesis of leadership in small discussion groups.[23] From the research and theory we can safely conclude that a discussion leader needs to be flexible, adapting to situational contingencies, but that in almost all situations a democratic structuring approach will be productive.

Getting practical. Up to this point we have examined theory and research concerning small group leaders and leadership without prescribing any specific role functions or techniques. The rest of chapter 9 will be more prescriptive; I present a point of view about the personal philosophy that I believe you may want to adopt in order to lead discussions effectively, the functions I think you should be prepared to perform as discussion leader, and specific techniques that can be used to provide those functions. Put another way, up to now this chapter has been primarily descriptive; the rest of it will be more prescriptive. Persons from college freshmen to senior managers in large corporate structures often ask, "How should I act as discussion leader? What will I be expected to do? How can I do it?" Based on the research and theory described above and studies of specific techniques I have provided some answers to these questions, answers that I think you will find helpful. These are suggestions. Try them out. Adapt them to your specific personality and the situations you face. Use what you can. In time you should develop your own philosophy, a variety of styles to fit various group contingencies, and a wide range of techniques and skills for providing needed leadership services whether or not you hold a position of designated leader.

A Group-Centered Democratic Style of Discussion Leadership

I believe that in most situations a designated discussion leader will be most helpful to a group seeking to learn or solve problems by adopting a democratic group-centered style, with primary attention to procedural matters and secondary attention to interpersonal relations. The designated discussion leader will serve best who gladly shares the multitude of leadership functions and responsibilities while acting as a monitor of the group's processes, acting as a completer to supply needed functions, and accepting a large share of personal responsibility for the success of that group. An autocrat who seeks to push personal goals, procedures, beliefs, and solutions on a group will in most peer groups produce apathy, poor quality solutions, low levels of commitment, interpersonal conflict, and general dissatisfaction.

An autocratic discussion leader seeks to impose his or her will, belief, or solution on the group. The result is a pseudodiscussion during which the group goes through the motions of discussion but the end result is predetermined by the leader. Under an autocrat, no one speaks unless permitted by the leader. Everyone's ideas are judged by the leader. The autocrat decides on the exact order of events on the agenda and the sequence in which a problem will be discussed. He or she may listen to advice, but when the autocrat's mind is made up, the "group decision" has been made. Power resides in this one person rather than in the group. He or she acts like the dominant ray of a nerve-severed starfish rather than as a coordinating leader. Such a leader rarely announces the agenda of a meeting in advance, nor does this leader often help inform members. Armed with a private agenda and as the only fully prepared person, he or she can readily dominate the other discussants. For example, an autocrat in the classroom decides just what questions will be discussed, and the "right" answer to each. When such hard-sell tactics fail to gain support, the autocrat may attempt to coerce compliance by actions such as calling the members lazy, stupid, uncommitted, or irresponsible.

If an autocratically inclined leader lacks the power of an absolute head, he or she may use all sorts of "soft-sell" manipulative techniques to seduce agreement. An autocrat is interested in whatever will advance personal ideas and purposes, interrupting and ignoring or arguing with anything contrary, often without trying to understand the other speaker's point of view. A "divide and conquer" approach may be tried, by setting up a one-to-one communication network with a lot of "sweet talk" and politicking with promises of personal rewards to members who give support. Such an autocrat distorts summaries toward a personal purpose and states ideas with highly emotive language, sometimes coercing an agreement by preventing the group from making a decision until time for the meeting has almost run out, then pressuring others to accept his or her solution. The autocrat may coerce participation from a member who prefers not to speak by saying something like "Tim, what do you think of that?" or "Mary, don't you agree?"

On what assumptions would you base your personal style of leadership? An autocratic style rests on the beliefs that a few select persons (of which the autocrat is one) are specially endowed, that the majority are incapable or irresponsible, that the way to get persons to act is to give them personal rewards and punishments. Such premises underlie the governing techniques of dictators, paternalists, and discussion leaders who predetermine the result that their groups should reach.

A democratic style of leadership is based on the belief that the collective wisdom is greater than that of any single member, and the correlative belief that all persons affected by a decision should have a voice in making the decision. In a democratic climate, any attempt to coerce or manipulate is both immoral and impractical. Immoral because manipulation destroys the human capacity to reason and decide for one's self. Impractical because manipulation when sensed leads to apathy, resistance, or even counterforce. A democratic leader participates with the group in making decisions concerning both the procedure and substance of discussions. He or she serves the group rather than making it a servant to self-serving ends.

The democratic discussion leader, in contrast to the autocratic leader, seeks to discover the group's will and facilitate its achievement. A discussion of this sort can never be predetermined by anyone, but will be the result of interaction. With democratic leadership, discussants speak when they want to, at least within the procedural norms adopted *by the group*. All ideas are treated as group property, and judgment of them is the responsibility of the entire group. All authority for decision making resides in the group. Influence comes primarily from information, ideas, and skills in doing what is needed to achieve mutually acceptable goals. When discussion leadership is democratic, everyone has equal opportunity to prepare for discussion. Even establishing the agenda and the pattern for discussing a topic or problem is the prerogative of the group, not a single member (or leader). All power exercised by the designated leader is granted by the group for the group's good. Such a leader may suggest and encourage, but will not compel, coerce, or manipulate. Ideally, a designated leader's approval is no more important than that of any other member. Such leadership is facilitative rather than restrictive in regard to the group's area of freedom.

In practice, a democratic leader will suggest procedures, but will not impose them. He or she may suggest a plan or solution, but will be quite ready to follow any procedure or accept any solution that the group, by consensus, prefers. For example: "What do you think about . . . ," rather than, "We will. . . ."

Both autocratic and democratic styles of discussion leadership are in stark contrast to what is often called a laissez-faire style. It is not leadership, but an abdication of responsibility for leading. The laissez-faire "leader" does virtually nothing. In practice, he or she may open a discussion by saying: "It's about time we started our discussion," then sit back, exert no influence, and do virtually nothing to organize, clarify, or promote a solution. Into the void someone must step, or the group will flounder aimlessly. The usual result is either anarchy or a struggle for status. A group of skilled discussants, given this kind of appointed leader, may proceed fairly well, but all too often they waste time or an autocrat takes over. Apathy and frustration are common.

Many times a designated discussion leader is in a formal position as part of a larger organization, and so may need to exert bureaucratic leadership. As examples: a foreman is charged by his superiors with seeing that certain tasks are accomplished by the work group; a study-discussion leader is partly responsible to the organization sponsoring the study-discussion program (often a university, public library, or great books foundation); the chairperson of a committee appointed to carry out a task or to make recommendations is responsible to the parent body; a department head is bound by regulations and responsibilities that cannot be ignored. Such bureaucratic leaders must make clear the area of freedom of the group, and the limits placed on him or her and the group. It is essential that a "head" make clear when the decision will be made by the group and when he or she is only seeking information and advice on which to base a decision. Some of the topics to be discussed, the procedures to be followed during discussion, and specific recommendations or solutions to be applied can be determined by the group as a whole.

Designated task leaders (heads of departments, foremen, officers, even committee chairpersons) seeking a group decision often find the group waiting for the leader's analysis of the problem and solution to it, which the group members then tend to accept or reject apart from its merits in fact and logic. For this reason designated leaders are generally well advised to refrain from suggesting solutions, at least until after group members have suggested a number of them.

A remedy may be for a supervisor to adopt a nondirective style of leading that puts responsibility on the group for directing their activities. The leader would then exercise great self-control, withholding leadership at critical junctures, even letting the group flounder at times, so that participants will develop their own skills and motives. The nondirective leader will call attention to problems facing the group, whether of task or group maintenance, but will not solve them. On some occasions he or she may suggest and invite other alternatives, but will still leave the decision to the group. This is not an abdication of leadership. Whereas the laissez-faire "leader" does nothing, a nondirective leader works very hard, listens intently, and reflects observations back to the group: clarifying a problem, supplying information, or summarizing what he or she has noticed, but always asking the group if they agree. A nondirective leader will ask many questions and will rebound to the group questions calling for a personal opinion. In time he or she can lead democratically and still discharge all responsibilities to a superior or parent body by making clear to all group members what must be done. Once members are accustomed to accepting responsibility for making decisions that affect them, they will not often want it any other way.

Personal Characteristics of Effective Discussion Leaders

Knowing the characteristics that tend to distinguish effective discussion leaders from less influential group members should be helpful in your efforts toward becoming the best leader you can, or to select wisely whom to support as group leaders. Of course the positive attitudes toward self, others, information, and ideas described earlier as input variables are important. But from the trait studies we can now enumerate more specific behavioral and attitudinal characteristics of effective democratic leaders.

1. *Effective discussion leaders have a good grasp of the task facing the group* (whether the task be learning or problem-solving). They are informed, good at analysis, and have promising ideas for solving problems. Studies by Maier, Geier, Larson, Knutson, and Holdridge, among others, all indicate this principle.
2. *Effective discussion leaders are skilled in coordinating group members' thinking and encoding toward a goal.* They are above average in ability to engage in systematic thinking and problem solving. To be an effective designated leader, you need to be able to suggest appropriate sequences for any problem, to be skilled in detecting tangents, and in bringing a group back on track. The leader of a learning group needs to be able to provide some logical sequence of issues and themes, yet be flexible enough to encourage relevant issues and themes from all group members.
3. *Effective discussion leaders are active in participation.* They are above average for group members in frequency of verbal participation, yet not excessive talkers. They are never reticent in a small group, implying that such emergent leaders have a favorable self-concept, nor overly defensive or sensitive about being criticized or disagreed with. Morris and Hackman, like Geier, found emergent leaders to be among the most frequent participants in discussion groups (not necessarily the *most* frequent).[24] To be relatively quiet in a group is to have no chance to emerge as a leader, and to maintain the position of leader a member must be verbally active.
4. *Effective discussion leaders encode clearly and concisely.* Ability to speak well has been shown to be important to success in all social contexts. The effective discussion leader can speak to the group as a whole in clear, impartial terms, yet be able to espouse a personal point of view when that is needed. His or her remarks are concise, organized, and pertinent. Such leaders, whether designated or emergent, are rhetorically sensitive rather than tactless, and especially skilled in encoding consensus decisions. Russell found that leaders of problem-solving groups were distinguishable from other members by higher degrees of communicative skills.[25] Lashbrook also found that leaders were perceived as speaking more clearly and fluently than were other group members.[26] Discussion leaders are most certainly characterized by special facility in verbalizing the goals, values, ideas, and ideals of their groups.
5. *Effective discussion leaders are open-minded.* I found that study-discussion leaders chosen by participants as future leaders were much more conditional in the way they expressed judgments than were leaders not chosen as future leaders. Maier and Solem demonstrated that a leader who suspends judgment and encourages full consideration of minority viewpoints is more effective than one who does not.[27] I have

repeatedly given *dogmatism* and *authoritarianism tests* to students in discussion classes, and found that students most often chosen as leaders by classmates tended to score much better on these measures of open-mindedness. Haiman reported similar findings for his classes when using these scales and an *open-mindedness scale* that he devised.[28] The picture is clear: effective discussion leaders are more open-minded than average participants and can encourage open-minded consideration by participants.

6. *Effective discussion leaders are democratic and group-centered.* This characteristic was developed thoroughly in the preceding section. As Rosenfeld and Plax put it, ". . . people are equals with whom they work, the rewards and punishments are to be shared."[29]

7. *Effective discussion leaders have respect for and sensitivity to others.* Fielder, of contingency theory fame, reported that discussion leaders of productive groups displayed above average skills in human relations. Rosenfeld and Plax found that democratic discussion leaders made relatively more positive socio-emotional remarks and were more sympathetic than were autocratic leaders.[30] To adjust to the changing needs and moods of members of a group, one needs to be tuned in to the nonverbal cues that indicate these. Democratic actions rest on trust in the collective wisdom of the group and respect for the rights of all members. Several case studies have shown that building a team spirit and sense of cooperation often depends on finding and emphasizing common interests and values, which takes a high degree of sensitivity and awareness of others. The best discussion leaders are excellent listeners, patient, and able to summarize accurately.

8. *Effective discussion leaders are flexible in taking their distinctive roles.* Many studies have shown that effective discussion leaders take on roles distinctively different from those of other group members.[31] For example, I found that the most effective study-discussion leaders were those who asked more questions, gave more procedural guidance, and expressed fewer personal opinions than other members. The concept of the "leader as completer" indicates the need for role flexibility, as does Fiedler's contingency theory" of leadership. Wood observed that actual committee leaders did show such flexibility from meeting to meeting as conditions changed.[32] You are well advised to practice and develop skills in as many of the task, procedural, and maintenance functions of group interaction as possible.

9. *Effective discussion leaders share rewards and give credit to the group.* They readily praise the group for successes, not taking credit or glory to themselves. They stress teamwork and look for ways to make members feel important to the group.

Still more terms could be used to characterize the behavioral style of effective democratic discussion leaders in groups of peers, but the major findings that have shown up with some consistency in recent research have been described sufficiently for you to form an image of the ideal small group discussion leader: informed, egalitarian, organized, knowledgeable, a skilled problem solver, active and outgoing, democratic, respectful and accepting of other persons, nonmanipulative, articulate without being verbose, flexible, and group-centered.

Responsibilities, Functions, and Techniques of the Assigned Discussion Leader

A designated discussion leader cannot evade the responsibility for certain tasks and functions. Most adults are members of many small groups, and have neither the time nor the resources available to keep abreast of all details, regulations, and changes in the groups. Often we come rushing into a meeting, literally out of breath, with our minds still occupied by other matters. In this condition we try to orient ourselves to another discussion. If our leaders (or teachers) greet us with, "Well, what shall we do today?" we are likely to be irritated and to get nothing done. Students with five classes a day and businessmen with several conferences a day must place special responsibilities on designated discussion leaders. The leader in such cases has a special job to do, and doing it well will foster group cohesiveness, acceptance of solutions, and responsibility for the group's success by members. The group still retains the power to decide within its area of freedom, and can act more wisely because the leader has served it well.

Some persons avoid or even refuse assigned leader roles, such as chairing a problem-solving committee or leading a Bible discussion group, because they believe it will demand more time and effort than they can or are willing to give. Sometimes this may be valid, of course, but usually it need not be if the functions of leadership are discussed within the group and divided up on a reasonable basis. This can produce a leader team of two or more persons who share the major duties often expected of a designated leader, yet one person is still in a position to serve as liaison to other groups and organizations, and as a sort of clearinghouse within the group. This chairperson would typically plan the agenda and outline for a meeting, exert most of the structural and procedural leadership needed to keep the discussion organized, see that summaries and decisions get made, and perhaps watch out for misunderstandings to clarify as needed. A co-procedural leader might agree to take on the primary responsibility of spreading opportunity to participate verbally and watch for signs of tension that need to be dealt with. Someone else might be assigned to act as recorder for the group, writing down important information, interpretations agreed upon, ideas proposed as possible solutions, decisions reached, issues to be discussed at a later date, assignments, etc., and to write up reports and minutes (if needed) for the group. Certainly every member can assume responsibility for leadership services, for such is the very essence of being a productive discussant—to contribute to goal achievement in whatever way one can—and thus all serve as leaders from time to time. In short, *the designated leader's duties in a continuing group need not require significantly more effort and time than are expected of all group members; indeed, as a rule they should not in groups of equal members.* Still, the designated leader usually will find the duties of office burdensome unless the group deals with this issue openly and cooperatively. Many wise, experienced small group leaders refuse to proceed into the substance of extended group work until this matter has been attended to.

Some study or learning groups handle this problem of overwork by rotating the duties of primary discussion leader from meeting to meeting, but this only works well if all members are relatively equal in ability to perform that role. Coleadership assignments are often very effective in such groups. There is very little research on how coleaders function as a team, but there have been limited case studies. Some coleaders alternate major responsibility for various functions, whereas others maintain about the same relationship to each other throughout the life of a group. The Minnesota studies reported by Bormann discovered that many emergent leaders in initially leaderless task groups had a "lieutenant" who supported and generally assisted the leader in a wide variety of ways. About all we can say is that coleaders, especially if designated as such, should plan together how they will work to serve the group in the best way possible, and periodically review their relationship.

Surveys of what members of problem-solving and learning groups expect and want from designated leaders clearly indicate that structural leadership is very important. Thus an appointed or elected discussion leader must decide on the amount and kind of structural leadership to exercise. When working with peers, many leaders err on the side of too little control, a few in the direction of too much or imposing procedures without the consent of the group. Each designated leader must decide his or her own course, but should constantly review it for needed changes. This can be done by asking the group to discuss how much procedural control they desire, and with various response forms described in chapter 10. While developing a unique role the leader can experiment to find out what seems to be of most help and what is most acceptable to the group members. Generally it is wiser to supply too much rather than too little procedural control. Considering situational variables can help you optimize your leadership style and functioning:

1. *Group purpose and goals*—learning, personal-growth, and value-sharing groups usually need far less structure and control than do groups facing complex problems.
2. *Member expectations*—at least initially a designated group leader will need to conform to what members expect of the role, although this can often be changed through group discussion itself.

3. *Specific procedures and group methods often require rather strict procedural control*—brainstorming, buzz-group procedures, problem census, or the Nominal Group Technique require close procedural control, whereas a less complex pattern for organizing discussion will take far less control from a designated leader.
4. *Membership skills and maturity must be taken into account*—members with training and experience in discussion are much more able to share in leadership than are members with little or no training in discussion techniques.
5. *The leader's skill and confidence should determine how he or she acts*—it is decidedly more difficult to share tasks of procedural leadership than to monopolize them. Democratic leadership calls for skills in listening, organizing, summarizing, and timing that may take a long time to develop.
6. *Time urgency may be a factor*—occasionally a decision must be made in a hurry, in which case a group will welcome strict control on its procedures. When time is not limited and members are vitally affected by what they decide, they will need less control.
7. *Highly involved groups require less control*—when members perceive the task is important to them personally, they will often resist close procedural control by a leader. The implication is clear: the designated discussion leader should do all possible to help members realize the importance of their task, and become involved and concerned.

This brings us to specific functions that the designated discussion leader may be expected to perform, and some ways of performing them. Of course any discussion group member may provide these leadership functions, but the designated leader usually has a special responsibility to see that they are provided.

Preparing for Meetings

Planning and preparation for discussions have already been described in considerable detail in chapters concerned with input and process variables. But designated leaders often have special responsibility for agenda preparation, formulating outlines, arranging facilities, notifying members of meetings, and seeing that materials are distributed.

An *agenda* is a sequential list of topics, issues, or other items to be dealt with during a group meeting, the business to be taken up. For instance, a committee agenda may include minutes of a previous meeting, some announcements, and one or more problems to be dealt with by the group. Another meeting may have only one item on the agenda, such as a discussion of criteria to be applied to possible alternative solutions—that meeting agenda would be one step in the total group process of problem solving. A poetry study group might have four poems for discussion on its agenda. Planning the agenda is

Figure 9.2 The agenda for an actual committee meeting.

Agenda for Committee III

May 15, 1976; 12:30 p.m.; Thompson Library South, Room 17

Harry McLeroy, chairman

1. Approval of the minutes of April 22, 1976 meeting.
2. Review of nominations and appeals for Graduate Faculty Member and Fellow.
3. Preparation of a slate of nominees to positions on the Executive Graduate Council beginning January, 1977.
4. Further discussion of proposed criteria for Graduate Faculty.
5. Review of Appendix IV, p. 23 of Governance Document.

---

usually a designated leader responsibility, but in peer groups the agenda is presented to the group for approval or modification. The decision of what to actually discuss is the prerogative of the group in many instances.

Any substantive discussion of a problem or other subject matter may require the leader to prepare an outline of questions for providing systematic coverage during the discussion. Thus an agenda containing two or more problems might require two or more outlines as part of the preparation of the designated leader, however brief these might be.

Following is a checklist that you can use to make sure you have considered all you may need to do in order to be sure preparation is adequate to facilitate a productive meeting:

_____ 1. *Is there a clearly defined purpose for the meeting?* If not, no meeting should be held.

_____ 2. *Are there specific outcomes that should or must come from this meeting?* These might include interpretation of information; plans to accomplish some task, decisions, or recommendations to a parent organization or individual; a policy statement; or any other product to be achieved.

_____ 3. *Have all group members been identified and notified of the purpose, agenda, time, and place of the meeting?*

_____ 4. *How long is the meeting to run?* Most group meetings should be kept to strict time limits unless members have agreed otherwise in advance.

_____ 5. *Are all needed physical arrangements arranged?* A meeting place must be reserved and things such as informative handouts, note pads, chalk, charts, crayons, ashtrays, and possibly refreshments provided.

_____ 6. *Should group process be evaluated by the group?* If so, some plan or procedure for doing this may be needed.

Initiating Discussion

Opening remarks by a designated leader should be *as brief as possible* to accomplish the job of creating a positive atmosphere, initiating structure for the meeting, and getting discussion underway. Here are some items you should always consider in planning your opening remarks and the introductory stages of a discussion:

1. *It may be necessary, especially with a new group, to reduce primary tensions.* Members may need to be introduced to each other. An ice-breaker activity might be planned, or some brief social activity. Name tents or tags should be provided if members are not acquainted.
2. *The purpose and importance of the meeting must be described and possibly discussed, and the area of freedom (and limitations) made clear.*
3. *Some effort to create a climate of trust and informality may be needed.* This might include suggesting norms such as confidentiality of what members say, respectful active listening, and the need for cooperation. Sometimes a ventilation period of a few minutes may help get the discussants acquainted with each other's values, beliefs, backgrounds, and attitudes on the problem. This is a period of totally free, unstructured, unorganized talk usually related to the problem or task facing the group, which serves primarily a socio-emotional function. The designated leader who senses a need for ventilation and encourages it may later find the job of keeping talk organized, relevant, and objective much easier than if no ventilation of feelings and positions had occurred. It is important that ventilation not go on so long that members begin to feel that time is wasted, but long enough for them to want order and organization. Any open conflict is a good sign that it is time to get the discussion organized.
4. *Informational and structural handouts may be presented,* such as informational sheets, an agenda, outlines to guide discussion, case problems, copies of things to be discussed such as poems, etc.
5. *Supply suggested structure and procedures.* You may want the group to set these up, but be prepared to suggest. You may find it advisable to provide members with an outline for organizing the discussion, then have members modify or accept it.
6. *See that any special roles needed are established, such as recorder.*
7. *Ask a clear question to focus initial discussion of the first substantive issue on the agenda.*

Structuring Discussion

1. *Keep the group goal oriented.* Be sure the goal is clearly understood and accepted by all members. At times you will find it helpful to ask a question such as "How will this help us to achieve our goal?" or to comment "We seem to be losing sight of our objective."

Figure 9.3 Recording can help to structure discussion.

2. *A sequence for problem solving or an outline for a learning discussion can be put on a handout, a chalkboard, or a chart.* You may find it helpful to distribute a sheet explaining any procedure with which group members are not well acquainted, such as brainstorming or the Nominal Group Technique. A group that resists following an outline early in the discussion may do so gladly after some confusion and frustration set in.

3. *Summarize,* or see that a summary is made of each major step in a problem-solving discussion or of each decision reached. Ask if the summary is accepted by all members as accurate and complete. In many discussions a secretary can help summarize. It is important that the group have a complete record of findings, ideas, criteria adopted, and decisions.

4. *Make a clear transition to each new step or agenda item.* A transition can be combined with a summary. For example, "We have heard that time pressure, grade pressure, and inadequate preparation lead to plagarism on term papers. Are we ready to consider possible solutions for this problem? . . . Well, what might we recommend to reduce such cheating?" When members keep restating the same idea, you might suggest that agreement seems to have been reached, and if so the discussion can move on to the next issue.

5. *Be sure that all needed steps in the problem-solving process, items on the agenda, or issues for a learning discussion are adequately dealt with,* if at all possible. Keep track of the time so you can point out to the group what needs to be done and how much time is available. Point out anything of importance that is being overlooked.
6. *Watch for extended digressions,* and for frequent changes of theme. When you notice a digression from the outline or agenda, you can point it out, and perhaps ask the group what to do about it. If a member suggests a solution prematurely, you might ask if he or she would bring it up when the group has finished mapping out the problem. When a change of issue or irrelevant topic creeps in, or a fantasy chain has been spun out, you may suggest returning to the previous issue or step.
7. *Bring the discussion to a definite close.* This should be done not later than the time a meeting has been scheduled to end, or extended only if all members consent. Continuing groups that continually run overtime tend to lose members! The conclusion might include any or all of the following: a summary of all progress made by the group; a statement of how reports of the meeting will be distributed to members and other interested persons; comments about preparations for the next meeting; assignments for follow-up and implementation; commendations to the group for a job well done; an evaluation of the meeting to improve the group's future discussions.

Equalizing Opportunity to Participate and Influence

1. *Address your comments and questions to the group rather than individuals,* unless you want to elicit a specific item of information or respond directly to what a member has said.
2. *See that all members have an equal chance to participate verbally.* While no one should be forced to speak, neither should any member be prevented from speaking by the aggressiveness of others.
    a. You might point out in opening remarks that part of your role will be to see that everyone has an equal opportunity to get the floor, that you will be primarily a coordinator.
    b. Make a visual survey of all members every minute or two, looking for nonverbal cues that a member wants to speak. If you see such a reaction from a discussant who has had little to say, "gatekeep" the person into the discussion as soon as you can. You might cut in with a comment like, "Joe, did you want to comment on Mary's idea?" Encourage, but do not embarrass the participant if you misinterpreted the nonverbal signals by asking a question such as "Joe, what do you think about that idea?" He might not even have been listening!

    c. Sometimes a quiet member can be assigned to investigate and report on needed information.

    d. You might invite a quiet person to speak if you are sure that he or she has special knowledge or interest on an issue: "Belinda, I think you made a special study of that, didn't you?"

3. *Listen with real interest* to what an infrequent participant says, and encourage others to do so if they seem not to be listening.

4. *Try to control compulsive, dominating, or long-winded speakers.* Occasionally a member so monopolizes the conversation that either others must fight for a chance to speak, or just give up. A few will repeatedly interrupt and drown out the voices of others who are speaking. Such monopolizers must be controlled for the benefit of the group. The techniques for controlling such problem members are listed in the approximate order in which they would be used—less blunt and direct methods first, those that involve confrontation only if more tactful and subtle techniques do not work. Often highly verbal persons are valuable members of a group, and although you may need to control their aggressive or dominating tendencies, it would possibly weaken the group as much to drive them out as to let them continue putting down others.

    a. When feasible, seat talkative members where you can seem to overlook them naturally when asking questions of the group. Avoid the tendency to look at such a person when you ask a question.

    b. Establish eye contact with those who have spoken infrequently when you ask a question; avoid contact with the talkers.

    c. When a long-winded person has made a point, cut in as gatekeeper with "How do the rest of you feel about that point?" or a similar request for *others* to participate. This can be done with varying degrees of tact.

    d. Try to establish a norm by asking that each person make one point, then allow others the floor, and that persons not interrupt or drown out others.

    e. Have one person keep a count or stop-watch on each participant's remarks, then report the findings to the group and discuss them in an evaluation period.

    f. In private, ask the frequent talker to help get the quiet members to speak up more.

    g. Describe the problem openly, and ask the group to deal with it as a group.

    h. Even more drastic measures may be needed on occasion, to the point of asking the person to leave the group, but only after discussion of the troublesome behavior has failed.

5. *Avoid commenting after each member remark.* Some designated discussion leaders do this, perhaps unaware, producing a wheel network of verbal interaction. Often such leader behavior seems to come from a desire to dominate and control the ideas and decisions of the group. Most procedural leaders cannot get very deeply involved in the substance of the discussion without losing perspective. Listen, speak when you are really needed, but avoid a question-answer role or becoming the interpreter or repeater of what others say.

6. *Bounce questions of opinion back to the group,* as a rule. There is a tendency in some groups to either accept or reject designated leader opinions, so unless the group is quite well developed, you will be wise to hold your opinions until after others have expressed theirs and then express them just as another point to be considered before making a decision. So if a member asks "What do you think should be done?" you can reply with something like, "Let's see what other members think first. What do . . .?"

7. *Generally remain neutral during the argument over the merits of alternatives.* If you get heavily involved, you will then be in a poor position to see that all have equal opportunity, the discussion remains orderly and relevant, that other structuring services are provided, and—perhaps most important—to seek constructive compromises as a basis for consensus. You can and usually should react with acceptance, showing that you heard and were interested. If evaluation seems needed, encourage others to provide it.

Stimulating Creative Thinking

All too often problem-solving groups create less than imaginative products, settling for "tried and true" solutions. A thorough analysis of the problem is often a rich source of inventive alternatives. A few special techniques may help in some discussions:

1. *Apply the principle of deferred judgment* even when not brainstorming. Ask "How *might* we . . .?" rather than "How should we . . .?"

2. *When the flow of thinking seems to have dried up, encourage the group to search for a few more alternatives.* You might use this idea-spurring question: "What else can we think of to . . .?"

3. *It sometimes pays to take up various characteristics of components of the problem, one at a time:* "Is there any way to improve the appearance of . . .?" or "the durability of . . .?"

4. *Watch for suggestions that could be used to open up whole new areas of thinking, then pose a general question about the area.* For example, if someone suggests putting up signs in the library that show the cost of losses to the users, you might ask, "How else could we publicize the cost of losses to the library?"

Stimulating Critical Thinking

Although judgment may be deferred, it is essential that opinions and possible solutions be subjected to rigorous evaluation. Sometimes an atmosphere develops in which group members do not feel free to criticize or assess the potential faults of each other's ideas. Some members may be unduly defensive, there may be a tendency to conform to the thinking of high-status members, or to decide quickly without the benefit of thorough scrutiny of the evidence, reasoning, and implications of a proposal. All information and opinions should be subject to critical judgment. Here are a few things you might use to encourage evaluation without evoking undue levels of secondary tension:

1. *If the group gets solution-minded quickly, suggest more analysis of the problem.*
2. *Encourage group members to evaluate information.* For example:

    To check the relevance of evidence, you might ask, "How does this apply to our problem?" or "How is that like the situation we are discussing?"

    To evaluate the source of evidence, you might ask such questions as, "What is the source of that information?" "How well is _____ recognized in his field?" "Is this consistent with his other pronouncements on the subject?"

    To check on the credibility of information, you might ask: "Do we have any information that is contradictory?"

    To test a statistic, you might ask how it was derived or how an average was computed.

    Bring in outside experts to challenge the views of the group and its central members.

3. *See that all group members understand and accept all standards, criteria, or assumptions used in making value judgments.* For example, you might ask, "Is that criterion clear to us all?" "Is this something we want to insist upon?" or "Do we all accept that as an assumption?"

    There are a number of procedures you can follow to insure that a proposed major policy is thoroughly and critically tested before it is adopted:

    a. Ask all members to discuss tentative solutions or policies with persons outside the group;
    b. One or more members can be asked to take the role of critical evaluator and challenger of all ideas, with high priority in speaking to see that all doubts are aired openly;
    c. Subdivide the larger group into two subgroups under different leaders to evaluate all alternatives, then rejoin to iron out differences;
    d. Before reaching a binding decision on a policy of far-reaching consequence, hold a "second-chance" meeting at which all doubts, moral concerns, or untested assumptions can be explored before a final conclusion is reached by the group.

4. See that all proposed solutions are given a thorough testing before they are accepted as group decisions. Encourage the group to apply the available facts and all the criteria. Some questions you might ask:

"Do we have any evidence to indicate that this solution would be satisfactory?" "Unsatisfactory?"

"Are there any facts to support this proposal?"

"How well would this idea meet our criteria?"

"Would that proposal get at the basic problem?"

"Is there any way we can test this idea before we decide whether or not to adopt it?"

Promoting Teamwork and Cooperation

Maintenance functions require time that might otherwise be spent on productive problem solving or learning discussion. Too much time on interpersonal relations will lead to frustration with the lack of goal progress. But neglecting them can often lead to low morale or even group disintegration. The challenge for leaders is to maintain the appropriate balance of task and maintenance work. Every group will vary in the amount of maintenance leadership needed, and the same group will vary in its needs through time. It is vital that someone sense the climate of interpersonal relationships, and work to develop a team spirit in any group that must work together through time. There are many ways to do this, some of which almost any of us can do, and others that require specific personal proclivities.

Here are a few things that may help:

1. *A name for the group, and possibly other symbols can be developed.*
2. *Speak of "us" and "we," not so much of "I" and "you!"*
3. *Watch for evidence of hidden agendas at variance with group goals,* and bring these to the attention of the group as maintenance problems to be solved by it. Avoiding such matters usually encourages them to grow.
4. *If there are competing groups, a sense of common fate in a larger conflict will often help members pull together.*
5. *Keep argument focused on facts and issues.* Step in at once if any member starts an attack on another's personality or character.
6. *Don't let the discussion get so serious that persons cannot enjoy themselves.* Humor may help reduce the tensions that are generated when persons work hard together at the job of hammering out ideas. Good task leaders may have trouble with humor. Lee observed that many of the most efficient leaders were lacking in human warmth.

When men are driven, they lose spontaneity and the zestful interest in what goes on. . . . There is a very real danger that our concern with improving human communication may lead members to forget the human part of the matter. . . . We need efficiency *and* satisfyingness. One may try to rig a discussion in the image of a belt line; if he succeeds he may find that those who attend become as inert as machines without the capacity (or will) to create. [To maintain a balance in discussion, Lee suggested that designated leaders] listen with lessened tension when the bent to comedy or diversion or personal release is being manifested . . . [and] pick up the problem *after* the camaraderie or tension has been spent.[33]

Secondary tensions build, and they must be released or interpersonal friction will grow. Effective discussion is characterized by a constant shifting between the serious and the playful, the relevant and remote, kidding and criticism. Certainly you will want to let the group chain out fantasies that lead to the establishment of shared beliefs and values. The result of such tension-relieving activity is much more concerted action by group members. If you are not skilled at relieving tensions, welcome the leadership of members who are. Then bring the group back to the task outline when the fantasy chain is completed or secondary tensions have been reduced to a level where productive problem-solving discussion can again resume.

7. *If a role struggle is going on, it may help to bring it out in the open and ask the group how to resolve it.*

8. *When a group seems to be deadlocked, look for a basis on which to compromise.* Perhaps you can synthesize parts of several ideas into a consensus solution. Conferees may represent points of view that they cannot abandon or sell out, but eventually a decision must be made. For example, labor and management negotiators must eventually agree on a contract if the company is to work. To handle the problems presented by conferees representing diverse interests, we can use techniques employed by mediators of bargaining conferences. The mediator seeks to find a common ground, a *compromise* solution that all parties can accept as the *best achievable solution.* Each partisan yields something in order to obtain something. In common parlance, "half a loaf is better than none." A complete surrender by one of two or more partisans will only postpone the settlement of a basic issue.

   To encourage compromise, you may first need to point out that compromise need not be a sellout or dirty word. As Edmund Burke put it, "All government,—indeed every human benefit and enjoyment, every virtue and every prudent act,—is founded on compromise and barter."[34] Second, insist that the interests and needs of each participant are clearly understood by all other participants. Find the minimum conditions that are acceptable to every conferee, and then suggest a solution that will meet these minimums. Of course, this may take a great deal of discussion.

9. *Share rewards with the group.* Wise leaders give credit to the group, especially when they, as visible spokespersons, receive praise from parent organizations or power figures. Comments about what a fine job

the group has done, pride you have in it as one member, and acknowledgement of outstanding service provided by members can do much to build cohesiveness and team spirit.

Developing the Group and Its Members

The need for personal and group development will vary widely from person to person and group to group. A continuing group, such as a college class, a standing committee, an engineering staff, or a study-discussion group should definitely allow time for feedback and evaluation of meetings. A one-meeting discussion group, on the other hand, may have no reason to spend time evaluating the group process.

Sometimes the impetus for growth can be given by asking the group, after a discussion has ended, to examine its discussion. For example, a designated leader might ask, "How well did we do in our discussion?" or "What might we do to make our next meeting more profitable than this one?" If a group is having trouble, the leader might interrupt the discussion with some comment such as this: "We seem to be making little headway. What's wrong? How might we get more accomplished (or, relieve this tension, or make the discussion more interesting)?" The specific question should be in reaction to what the leader senses is wrong.

A class studying discussion techniques should have at least one observer for almost every discussion. The observer may break into the conversation to point out what he or she sees is hampering the group, make a brief report after the discussion, fill out rating forms that the group can discuss, or raise questions pertinent to the group's procedures. Any continuing group will benefit by doing this occasionally. A member can serve the group as an observer by focusing his or her attention for a period of time on the process instead of on the content of the interaction. Periodic evaluations of the group's performance and procedures should be made. Interpersonal feedback sessions in which members air any negative or positive feelings not previously cleared up may help a group. Advice on how to do this is provided in the final chapter. However it is done, a definite leadership service is made to a continuing group when members are made more aware of how they are participating and interacting together. In chapter 10 the role of the observer and procedures for group evaluation are explained in detail.

The preceding list of leadership functions and techniques is at best a partial one. Whatever his or her techniques, the leader must be flexible, adapting to the specific group. The main tools of the discussion leader are carefully laid plans, questions, skillful listening, clarifying comments, effective summaries, tension-relieving humor, and appropriate observations that are fed back to the entire group. Democratic, shared leadership, even when one person has been designated the leader, contributes most to group success and member development. Even heads can function as group-centered leaders much of the time during discussions by groups for which they are assigned responsibility.

Summary

Chapter 9 has explored small group leadership, especially of discussions. The first half of the chapter summarized pertinent research and theory; the second half provided prescriptive advice for those in designated leader positions. Productive discussion leadership depends on a thorough understanding of input and process variables of small groups, understanding of leadership, and personal attitudes of commitment to both self and group. Insight into self, mastery of a variety of techniques, and development of specific communicative skills all play a part in learning to be a more effective discussion leader.

Leadership, leader, and *designated leader* are similar but different concepts. Leadership was defined as group goal oriented influence, leader as anyone exerting such influence, and designated leader as anyone who is appointed, elected, or who emerges as occupant of a special position or role in a group. Influence rests on power of position, expertise, identification, and the ability to reward or coerce. Leadership implies that such power is granted to a person by the freely-given consent of those who follow, and can be shared among all group members. Small groups are most productive when a stable leadership structure has been accepted by all members.

Each of the major approaches to the study of leadership offers some insight into the phenomenon. Trait studies have indicated that certain attitudes, abilities, and skills are characteristic of accepted discussion leaders. The functions approach has indicated what leaders do and how they do it in providing for both task and socio-emotional needs of groups. In discussion, the most consistent functions seem to be those of coordinating and verbalizing group positions, but the contingency approach has stressed that style and functions must be adapted to such contextual variables as member expectations and traits, task, and other input variables. Certainly the designated leader needs a high degree of flexibility, and usually will serve as a central member of a leadership team. Sharing in the functions of leadership is vital in all small groups. Designated coleaders can share the duties, making the time and effort required of designated leaders relatively equitable and bearable. Designated discussion leaders are usually expected to make special preparations for meetings, initiate discussions, provide structure in the discussion, equalize opportunity to participate and influence, stimulate thinking, promote teamwork and cooperation, and facilitate development of a continuing group.

What follows is a personal view of the discussion leader's role written by student Tom Rogers as a summary of what he had learned from assigned leadership experiences in a course using an earlier edition of this book. You may find it helpful as you develop your own personal rules, style, and skills as leader.

I learned nine major rules to help me when leading a group. The first is to lay all the cards on the table and make sure everything is understood. Be sure everyone comprehends and agrees with the established goal or goals. Plan *as a group* how the members are to attain the goals. The second rule is to put all members at ease.

Make sure everyone feels relaxed enough to speak up when they don't understand or disagree with something. Third, be sure the group establishes some basic norms and standards to guide the group. The fourth lesson is, if you are the designated leader, work hard to stimulate the group into being inventive. The fifth and probably the most important rule is to *LISTEN* at all times. If you as leader get lost or confused because you weren't listening, the group effort is as likely to fail as you are as leader. If one does get into this predicament, be honest and clear it up right away. Another lesson equally as valuable is to be prepared. As a designated leader, one should have a grasp of the situation or problem. Prior to the meeting the leader should construct some thorough and well thought out questions. This should not wait until the last minute. The lead question should also be flexible. A leader should try to reward members for their contributions and efforts. An eighth lesson is at all times to be aware of possible miscommunication among members. If you see this happening clear it up right away. My advice to future leaders is my ninth rule— take a formal discussion course!

Exercises

1. Scoring and interpreting the Sargent and Miller Leadership Scale. The scale you filled out on p. 217 had ten items. A maximum score of 10 means you are very democratic in your responses to this test; a minimum score of 0 means you are very autocratic. Put a (1) after each item you checked as indicated in the key:

   KEY:

1. a	2. b	3. b	4. a	5. b
6. b	7. b	8. a	9. a	10. a

   Now read on in the chapter, and you will find some of the research that has been done on this scale. You may want to discuss your choices with several of your classmates.

2. Based on your most recent experiences in group discussions, complete each of the following statements about yourself:

   A. My most important strengths as a discussion leader are

   _____

   _____

   B. My most important weaknesses as a discussion leader are

   _____

   _____

   C. I plan to remove or reduce my weaknesses by _____

   _____

   _____

3. Select a case problem, preferably from your own experience, for which you do not have a solution. Prepare and distribute copies of this case to all members of your discussion group. Be sure you present all information the discussants will need to understand what is wrong in the present situation, and to decide what would be the desired situation.

During the discussion a classmate should serve as observer, rating you as a leader. Following the discussion (20–30 minutes as assigned by your instructor), the observer will guide your group in a brief evaluation of the discussion. At the class meeting after the discussion you should hand the following to your instructor: (1) a copy of the case; (2) a copy of your leader's outline; (3) a report of the discussion following the format on page 155; (4) the observer's rating sheet evaluating your leadership; (5) a brief essay in which you evaluate your functioning as leader of the discussion. You may want to make a recording of the discussion for later analysis. As you listen, make a list of:

   a. The functions you performed, how effectively you performed them, and how appropriate each was to the need of the group at the moment;
   b. Points during the discussion where you failed to supply some needed leader intervention, and what happened as a result. Did someone else eventually provide the needed function? If not, how was the group process and productivity hurt?

4. Think of leaders of small groups in which you have been a member:
   A. Who was the *worst* leader? List the characteristics and behaviors of this person (including both what he or she did and failed to do) that led to your selection. Especially list what this leader did in leading discussions;
   B. Who was the *best* leader? List the things that led to your judgment of this person as best small group leader;
   C. Now indicate those characteristics and behaviors that were most important in distinguishing between the two persons as leaders;
   D. Compare your items in step C with those of several classmates.

5. How can you determine if needed leadership services are being provided during a discussion?

6. Buzz groups should draw up lists of topics, problems, or value questions about which all members would like to learn more. Select the subject of most interest to the group, and compile a bibliography of pertinent materials. Each discussant should then do the required reading, making study notes and a tentative leader's outline. Then the group can discuss the topic, with the designated leadership rotating every fifteen to twenty minutes. One or more observers should report their findings before each new designated leader takes on his responsibilities. Some possible questions:

   "What can religion contribute to the life of a person today?"
   "What control should there be of books provided in public school libraries?"
   "How can we cope with the cost of personal transportation?"

7. Select a problem. Then have each class member prepare and deliver a leader's opening remarks for initiating a discussion of the problem. Have the class evaluate each introduction.

8. After a brief discussion, have each participant write a summary of what was said. Compare the summaries. What can you conclude?

9. Role play some problem-solving discussions (preferably using case problems presented by your instructor). Two or three problem members should be planted in each group, doing such things as pleading personal interests, sidetracking and introducing irrelevant issues, making cutting personal criticisms, talking incessantly, remaining silent, and so forth. Experiment with various leader techniques for handling these problem members and evaluate the results.

10. In a project group, plan and conduct an experiment to test the effectiveness of various leader techniques for equalizing opportunity for participation, promoting creative or critical thinking, keeping a discussion organized, and so forth.

11. Engage in four discussions of case problems supplied by your instructor. Alternate between having a designated leader and no designated leader. What differences do you observe? What are some implications of these differences?

12. Each class member should obtain one or more charts of the organization of clubs, businesses, agencies, or schools of which he or she is a member. Compare several of these organizational charts. Invite persons holding positions of headship at several levels in two or more different types of organizations to attend your class. Ask them to describe their concepts and techniques of leadership, and what is expected of them in their positions.

Bibliography

Bormann, Ernest G., *Discussion and Group Methods: Theory and Practice,* 2nd ed., New York: Harper & Row, Publishers, 1975, chapter 11.

Cathcart, Robert S., and Samovar, Larry A., eds., *Small Group Communication: A Reader,* 3rd ed., Dubuque, Iowa: Wm. C. Brown Company Publishers, 1979, section IV.

Fiedler, Fred E., *A Theory of Leadership Effectiveness,* New York: McGraw-Hill Book Company, 1967.

Maier, Norman R. F., *Problem-Solving Discussions and Conferences,* New York: McGraw-Hill Book Company, 1963.

Stogdill, Ralph M., *Handbook of Leadership: A Survey of Theory and Research,* New York: The Free Press, 1974.

Tannenbaum, Robert, Weschler, Irving R., and Massarik, Fred, *Leadership and Organization: A Behavioral Science Approach,* New York: McGraw-Hill Book Company, 1961.

References

1. Robert S. Cathcart and Larry A. Samovar, eds., *Small Group Communication, A Reader,* 3rd ed. (Dubuque, IA: Wm. C. Brown Company Publishers, 1979), p. 392.
2. Robert Tannenbaum, Irving R. Weschler, and Fred Massarik, *Leadership and Organizations: A Behavioral Science Approach* (New York: McGraw-Hill Book Company, 1961), p. 24.
3. John R. P. French and Bertram Raven, "The Bases of Social Power," in Dorwin Cartwright and Alvin Zander, eds., *Group Dynamics: Research and Theory,* 3rd ed. (New York: Harper and Row, 1968), pp. 259–69.
4. Ernest G. Bormann, *Discussion and Group Methods,* 2nd ed. (New York: Harper and Row, 1975), pp. 253–69; Nancy L. Harper and Lawrence R. Askling, "Group Communication and Quality of Task Solution in a Media Production Organization," *Communication Monographs* 47 (1980), pp. 77–100.
5. Ernest Stech and Sharon A. Ratliffe, *Working in Groups* (Skokie, IL: National Textbook Company, 1976), p. 201.
6. William C. Schutz, "The Leader As Completer," in Cathcart and Samovar, eds., *Small Group Communication,* p. 400.
7. Charles Bird, *Social Psychology* (New York: Appleton-Century-Crofts, 1940).
8. Ralph M. Stogdill, *Handbook of Leadership: A Survey of Theory and Research* (New York: The Free Press, 1974), pp. 63–82; Marvin E. Shaw, *Group Dynamics,* 2nd ed. (New York: McGraw-Hill Book Company, 1976), pp. 274–75 and chapter 6.
9. John C. Geier, "A Trait Approach to the Study of Leadership in Small Groups," *Journal of Communication* 17 (1967), pp. 316–23.
10. Robert F. Bales, "Task Roles and Social Roles in Problem Solving Groups," in E. E. Maccoby, T. M. Newcomb, and E. L. Hartley, eds., *Reading in Social Psychology,* 3rd ed. (New York: Holt, Rinehart and Winston, Inc., 1958), pp. 437–47.
11. Stogdill, *Handbook of Leadership,* p. 30.
12. Norman R. F. Maier, "Assets and Liabilities in Group Problem Solving: The Need for an Integrative Function," in *Problem Solving and Creativity in Individuals and Groups* (Belmont, CA: Brooks/Cole Publishing Company, 1970), pp. 438–39.
13. Thomas J. Knutson and William E. Holdridge, "Orientation Behavior, Leadership, and Consensus: A Possible Functional Relationship," *Communication Monographs* 42 (1975), pp. 107–14.
14. Barbara F. Sharf, "A Rhetorical Analysis of Leadership Emergence in Small Groups," *Communication Monographs* 45 (1978), pp. 156–72.
15. Ralph K. White and Ronald Lippett, "Leader Behavior and Member Reaction in Three 'Social Climates' " in Dorwin Cartwright and Alvin Zander, eds., *Group Dynamics: Research and Theory,* 2nd ed. (Evanston, IL: Row, Peterson and Company, 1960), pp. 527–53.

16. Lawrence B. Rosenfeld and Timothy B. Plax, "Personality Determinants of Autocratic and Democratic Leadership," *Speech Monographs* 42 (1975), pp. 203–8.

17. William E. Jurma, "Effects of Leader Structuring Style and Task-Orientation Characteristics of Group Members," *Communication Monographs* 46 (1979), p. 282.

18. Malcolm G. Preson and Roy K. Heintz, "Effectiveness of Participatory versus Supervisory Leadership in Group Judgment," *Journal of Abnormal and Social Psychology* 44 (1949), pp. 344–55; George Graen, Fred Dansfereau, and Takao Minami, "Dysfunctional Leadership Styles," *Organizational Behavior and Human Performance* 7 (1972), pp. 216–36; Norman R. F. Maier and Ronald A. Maier, "An Experimental Test of the Effects of 'Developmental' vs. 'Free' Discussions on the Quality of Group Decisions," *Journal of Applied Psychology* 41 (1957), pp. 320–23; William E. Jurma, "Leadership Structuring Style, Task Ambiguity, and Group Members Satisfaction," *Small Group Behavior* 9 (1978), pp. 124–34.

19. William E. Jurma, "Effects of Leader Structuring Style . . .," pp. 282–95.

20. Fred E. Fiedler, *A Theory of Leadership Effectiveness* (New York: McGraw-Hill Book Company, 1967).

21. James A. Hunt, "Leadership Style Effects at Two Management Levels in a Simulated Organization," *Administrative Science Quarterly* 16 (1971), pp. 476–85.

22. Julia T. Wood, "Alternate Portraits of Leaders: A Contingency Approach to Perceptions of Leadership," *Western Journal of Speech Communication* 43 (1979), pp. 260–70.

23. Cal W. Downs and Terry Pickett, "An Analysis of the Effects of Nine Leadership-Group Compatibility Contingencies upon Productivity and Member Satisfaction," *Communication Monographs* 44 (1977), pp. 220–30.

24. Charles G. Morris and J. R. Hackman, "Behavioral Correlates of Perceived Leadership," *Journal of Personality and Social Psychology* 13 (1969), pp. 350–61.

25. Hugh C. Russell, "Dimensions of the Communicative Behavior of Discussion Leaders," paper presented to Central States Speech Convention, April, 1970.

26. Velma J. Lashbrook, "Gibb's Interaction Theory: The Use of Perceptions in the Discrimination of Leaders from Nonleaders," paper presented to Speech Communication Convention, December, 1975.

27. Norman R. F. Maier and A. R. Solem, "The Contributions of a Discussion Leader to the Quality of Group Thinking: The Effective Use of Minority Opinions," *Human Relations* 5 (1952), pp. 277–88.

28. Franklyn S. Haiman, from a paper given at the Annual Convention of the Speech Association of America, December, 1964.

29. Lawrence B. Rosenfeld, *Now That We're All Here . . . Relations in Small Groups* (Columbus, Ohio: Charles E. Merrill Publishing Company, 1976), p. 76.
30. *Ibid.*
31. A. Paul Hare, *Handbook of Small Group Research* (New York: The Free Press of Glencoe, 1962), chapter XI.
32. Julia T. Wood, "Leading in Purposive Discussions: A Study of Adaptive Behavior," *Communication Monographs* 44 (1977), pp. 152–65.
33. Irving J. Lee, *How to Talk with People* (New York: Harper & Row, Publishers, 1952), pp. 158–60.
34. *Ibid.,* pp. 90–91.

10

observing and evaluating input, process, and output variables

Study Objectives

As a result of studying chapter 10, you should be able to:

1. Explain the benefits of having nonparticipating observers for small groups, and the roles of both reminder and critic observers.

2. Prepare a set of questions to guide your observations of any small group discussion to which you are assigned.

3. Explain ways to make the report of your observations both acceptable and helpful to group members.

4. Select or devise instruments for obtaining postmeeting reactions from group members, to chart the flow and frequency of verbal participation, and to rate groups, individual members, and designated leaders.

5. Make, record, and report actual observations of discussion inputs, processes, and outputs.

Key Terms

Critic-observer   a nonparticipant observer of a small group discussion who evaluates the functioning of the members and the group as a whole; the critic may use any of a variety of observation forms and rating scales in order to provide feedback to the group.

Interaction diagram   a diagram showing seating arrangement of a discussion group, how often each member speaks, and to whom.

Postmeeting Reaction Sheet, or PMR   a form completed by group members following a discussion, on which they evaluate the discussion, the group, and the leader; the responses are usually tabulated and reported back to the group.

Rating scale   a pencil-and-paper instrument, usually completed by a critic-observer, to render an evaluation of some factor involved in the discussion.

Reminder-observer   a nonparticipant observer of a small group discussion who focuses on what is missing or has been overlooked by the group that would be helpful (information, roles, procedures, techniques, etc.), then interrupts to remind the group as a sort of advisor or coach.

Throughout this book the importance of developing a participant-observer focus is stressed. Through reading the book, classroom discussions, and the guidance of your instructor you are developing such an orientation. Even while you have been participating in discussions, part of your attention and energy have been given to observing group inputs and processes. But, as you are undoubtedly aware, one cannot both observe and participate in the substance of a discussion at the same instant, so you have had to shift attention back and forth from the content of the discussion to the processes of the group. You have been able to supply functional behaviors appropriate to the group based on your observations of its processes, and to supply some feedback to reinforce what is going well and to modify what is not so productive. But no matter how skilled you may be as a participant-observer, there are times when you have missed something of importance, and perhaps been puzzled at what happened or frustrated by a lack of goal achievement and member satisfaction. Sometimes the most skillful of us becomes so engrossed in the interaction over an important issue that we lose perspective.

Thus a nonparticipating observer can be of real assistance in helping the group perceive what is going on. Any group of persons trying to understand group dynamics and develop skills as discussion participants and leaders will benefit from the feedback observations of a nonparticipating observer. When serving as a nonparticipant observer, the student of small group communication can see and learn a great deal that would be missed while actively participating. This chapter describes the role of such an observer; suggests how to be most helpful to groups you observe; supplies a variety of forms for recording observations and evaluations of both members and groups; and provides instruments for gathering data directly from participants in discussions. Many of these instruments can be used by groups even when a nonparticipating observer is not available.

The Role of the Observer

Every student of discussion and group processes needs the experience of observing discussion groups at work. As students have remarked countless times, "It looks different when you are sitting outside the discussion." The observer can see clearly what he or she was only vaguely aware of while discussing. After observing other discussants, the observer may be motivated to change his or her own conduct as a discussant. It is therefore suggested that you observe as many discussions as possible. In the classroom, it is wise for you to change frequently from being a discussant in one group to being an observer of another.

A very useful technique is the *fishbowl* arrangement in which a discussion group is surrounded by a circle of nonparticipating observers. These observers may all be focusing on the same aspects of group process and content, or may be assigned to observe, evaluate, and report on different factors (e.g., leadership, process of group problem solving, use of information, roles of members,

Figure 10.1 The fishbowl is a good arrangement for multiple observers.

verbal and nonverbal communication). Observers can be assigned on a one-to-one basis to participants as *alter egos* who make whispered suggestions to the discussant behind whom they sit, or when asked to do so indicate how they think their discussant feels or what he or she means by some action or comment.

When serving as a group observer, there are many things you might want to look for. Considering the group as a system, you will certainly want to be aware of a variety of input, process, and output variables. Although you will be able to pay close attention to only one or a few variables at any one time, you may want to prepare and occasionally scan a mental checklist of items to help you select those that seem most important to the group. Here is a list that you can use as a general guide to observing. You can also use it when preparing more limited lists of questions to answer as observer.

1. Are there clear and accepted group goals? If not, what seems to be hindering the development of an interdependent purpose for the discussion?
2. Are all members aware and accepting of limits on their area of freedom?
3. Are any hidden agenda items interfering with group progress?
4. Are any environmental problems disrupting the group, such as poor seating arrangements, noise, or other distractions?
5. What attitudes toward themselves, each other, and the substance of the discussion are members manifesting?
6. To what degree does the group climate seem to be one of open communication, trust, and cooperation?

7. How well are members listening and trying to understand each other?
8. Are there any communication problems due to the way members encode their ideas verbally and nonverbally?
9. Are any norms interfering with progress and cohesiveness?
10. Do members seem to be adequately prepared with information?
11. Are information and ideas being evaluated, or accepted at face value? Is there any tendency to groupthink and conform to high-status persons?
12. Has some outline, plan, or agenda for the discussion been provided or developed by the group? If so, how well is this being followed and serving the group's needs?
13. If a problem-solving discussion, has the group defined and clarified the problem thoroughly, or has it become solution-centered too soon?
14. How creative is the group in generating potential solutions to its problem? In interpreting information?
15. Has judgment been deferred until solutions have been listed and understood by all members?
16. Do members seem to share the same values and criteria in making decisions, or do they need to clarify their criteria?
17. When evaluating ideas and opinions, is the group making use of the information brought out during earlier discussion?
18. How are decisions being made?
19. If needed, has the group made adequate plans to implement its decisions, including member responsibilities, future meetings, etc.?
20. Are periodic summaries needed to help members recall and maintain perspective on the discussion and move the group to new issues without undue redundancy?
21. If needed, is the discussion being adequately recorded (and possibly charted)?
22. How well is verbal participation spread among all members? Is the pattern of verbal interaction all-channel or unduly restricted?
23. If there is a designated leader, what style of leadership is he or she providing? Does this seem appropriate to the group?
24. Does the role structure provide for optimal inputs from all members? Are any needed behavioral functions missing?
25. Are special procedural techniques such as brainstorming or parliamentary procedure being used in ways that are productive? Could procedural changes benefit the group?

Do not try to observe everything at once. Limit your focus to a few aspects of the discussion, perhaps at first to only one. Later, with experience, confidence, and increased awareness of the dynamics of a group, you will be ready to observe without a definite focus. You will then be able to decide as you watch which characteristics of the group are most important to assess in detail. No observer can simultaneously chronicle the content and flow of interaction, take notice of various group and individual objectives, judge the information and logic of remarks, assess the atmosphere, and note the organization of the discussion. If the observer tries to do so, the result is sure to be confusion that will reduce both personal learning and ability to give feedback to the group.

The nonparticipating observer can do three types of things, sometimes all during a single discussion: learn from the example of others; remind the group of techniques or principles of discussion they have overlooked; supply critical evaluations of the discussion. Responsibilities as reminder and critic to the group will be discussed in the following pages.

The Reminder-Observer

Often group members need to be reminded of what they already know. During interaction they may fail to notice what has been happening or to remember useful attitudes and techniques. To help them, a type of reminder-observer role has been developed. The reminder helps the group without offering any criticism. Many of your classroom discussions will be improved by having one member participate only as a reminder-observer. The reminder role should be changed from one discussion to another in order to give everyone a chance to remind without depriving anyone for a long time of the chance to practice discussion skills. Once you have developed skill in maintaining a participant-observer orientation, you will be able to act as a reminder to nonclassroom discussion groups in which you are a participant. If you serve as a model, gradually you will notice that all members of a continuing group begin to remind.

Designated leaders of group discussion may benefit from the coaching of a reminder-observer. The parliamentarian to a presiding officer of a large assembly serves as an observer-coach. More and more large organizations are employing the services of communication auditors who study the flow of information within the organization, and devise ways to improve it. These persons frequently need to assess a large number of meetings and discussions.

Before serving as a reminder, the following guidelines for reminder-observers should be studied carefully. They are designed to reduce defensive reactions to your observations.

DO:

1. Stress the positive, pointing out what a group or leader is doing well.
2. Emphasize what is most important, rather than commenting on everything you may have observed.
3. Focus on the processes of the group rather than on the content and issues *per se.*
4. Put most of your remarks in the form of questions or suggestions, keeping in mind that all authority for change rests with the group. You have no authority except to remind, report, and raise questions.

5. Remain completely neutral, out of any controversy about either content or procedure. You can do this by asking questions in a deadpan manner, such as, "I wonder if the group realizes that we have discussed _____ , _____ , and _____ in the space of five minutes?" "Are we ready for the consideration of possible solutions?" "I wonder if John and Amy understand each other's points of view?" "I wonder if we all understand the purpose of our committee?" "Is everyone getting an equal chance to participate?" Such questions remind the group of principles of good discussion without leveling specific criticisms.
6. Show trends and group characteristics rather than singling out individual discussants for comment (unless absolutely necessary).
7. Interrupt the discussion only when you believe the group is unlikely to become aware of what is troubling it. First give the group enough time to correct itself.

DON'T:

1. Play the critic-umpire, telling anyone he or she is wrong.
2. Argue with a member or the group. If your question is ignored, drop it.

In addition to serving as reminder during the discussion, afterward a reminder-observer may be able to help the group by leading a discussion of the discussion or by making a detailed report of his or her observations. At this point a reminder-observer can take either of two approaches, depending on what the group wants from him or her and on his or her degree of expertise:

1. A reporter, who describes the meeting without judgment, diagnosis, or suggestions for future meetings.
2. A coach, who offers tentative explanations for the behavior of the group and suggests procedures the group might employ to advantage.

The Critic-Observer

A critic-observer may do considerable reminding, but the primary function is as a critic. Such an observer belongs only in the classroom or training group. In some cases the critic-observer is primarily an advisor, either to the group as a whole or to a designated leader. For example, your instructor may interrupt a discussion to point out what he or she feels is going wrong and to suggest a different technique or procedure. After you have become a proficient observer, you might take the role of critic-observer for a small discussion group in another speech class or perhaps even for a group in your own class.

The critic-observer usually makes a more detailed report after the discussion than does the reminder-observer. In addition to describing and interpreting important aspects of the discussion, the critic will express opinions about weak and strong points of it. He or she may compliment the group, point out where and how it got into trouble, and even place blame or take an individual to task. This must be done cautiously and with tact. Many students hesitate to criticize the participation of others, and some balk at accepting criticism leveled at them. Discussants can be helped to give and accept criticism by reminding them of two points: (1) all criticism should be constructive, objective, sincere, and designed to help; (2) all critiques should include both positive and negative comments, with the good points being presented first.

The critic-observer, of course, will look for the same kinds of group behavior as will the reminder. In general, judgments should cover at least four aspects of the discussion: (1) the group product, including how well it has been assessed, how appropriate it seems to be to the problem, and how well group members support it; (2) the group process, including patterns of interaction, decision making, problem solving, and communication; (3) the contributions and functional roles of individual members; and (4) leadership, especially if a designated leader is present. Different criteria will be needed for public and private groups, learning and problem-solving groups, advisory and action groups. Observation and rating forms can be developed by the student of small groups for various types of discussions and groups. The instruments included in this chapter are suggestive general models that should be modified or used as guides for the preparation of specific forms and rating scales adapted to specific situations in your class or natural groups.

Instruments for Observing and Evaluating Discussions

Any discussion group can improve its processes and outputs by taking time for evaluation. A designated leader is in an especially good position to suggest such a procedure. Most groups will benefit from evaluation sessions scheduled at regular intervals, perhaps after every meeting; there is a danger of not getting to such assessment if it is not scheduled. For this reason, regular times for assessment have been built into the operations of many business, government, and military groups. Also, a systematic review is likely to be more objective than one which is undertaken during a crisis. However, if group evaluation is limited to regular periods following scheduled meetings, much of importance may be forgotten. Also, taking a break for an unplanned evaluation may correct a damaging attitude or procedure before a serious breakdown can occur within the group; therefore, it seems advisable for a continuing discussion group to use both routine and spontaneous discussions of discussion (evaluation sessions).

The rest of chapter 10 is devoted to instruments for observation and evaluation of both groups and their individual members. These forms were developed especially for classes in small group communication, discussion, and leadership.

Postmeeting Reaction Sheets

Postmeeting Reaction Sheets, or PMR's as they are called for short, are frequently used to get objective reactions from discussants. Since PMR's are anonymous, a participant can report personal evaluations without any threat to self. A PMR may be planned by a chairperson or other designated leader, by an instructor, by a group, or by the organizers of a large conference. The PMR's are distributed, completed and collected immediately following the discussion.

A PMR sheet consists of a simple questionnaire designated to elicit frank comments about important aspects of the group and the discussion. Questions should be tailored to fit the purposes and needs of the person preparing the questionnaire. Sometimes the questions concern substantive items, sometimes interpersonal matters, and sometimes matters of technique and procedure. Two or more types of questions may be mixed on a PMR. Three illustrative PMR sheets are shown in figures 10.2, 10.3, and 10.4. These can be used for almost any type of discussion.

Figure 10.2 Postmeeting Reaction Sheet.

Instructions: Check the point on each scale that best represents your honest judgment. Add any comments you wish to make that are not covered by the questionnaire. Do *not* sign your name.

1. How clear were the *goals* of the discussion to you?

| very clear | somewhat vague | muddled |

2. The *atmosphere* was

| cooperative and cohesive | apathetic | competitive |

3. How well *organized and systematic* was the discussion?

| disorderly | just right | too rigid |

4. How effective was the *style of leadership* supplied by the chairperson?

| too autocratic | democratic | weak |

5. *Preparation for this meeting* was

| thorough | adequate | poor |

6. Did you find yourself *wanting to speak* when you didn't get a chance?

| almost never | occasionally | often |

7. How satisfied are you with the *results* of the discussion?

| very satisfied | moderately satisfied | very dissatisfied |

8. How do you feel about *working again* with this same group?

---

eager   I will   reluctant

Comments:

Figure 10.3 Postmeeting Reaction Sheet.

1. How do you feel about today's discussion?

   excellent _____ good _____ all right _____ so-so _____ bad _____

2. What were the strong points of the discussion?

3. What were the weaknesses?

4. What changes would you suggest for future meetings?

(you need not sign your name)

   Specialized PMR forms for learning discussions are presented in figures 10.5, 10.6, and 10.7. The first of these was developed to give evaluative reactions to the leader of a group discussing such products of human creativity as poetry, stories, music, painting, or sculpting. The second can be used to get feedback for almost any learning group; it can be modified quite readily to get any kind of responses you might want. Figure 10.7 is designed to be used during recesses of an encounter group.

Figure 10.4 Reaction Questionnaire.

Instruction: Circle the number that best indicates your reactions to the following questions about the discussion in which you participated:

1. *Adequacy of Communication:* To what extent do you feel members were understanding each others' statements and positions?

| 0 | 1 | 2 | 3 | 4 | 5 | 6 | 7 | 8 | 9 | 10 |

Much talking past each   Communicated directly with
other, misunderstanding   each other, understanding well

2. *Opportunity to Speak:* To what extent did you feel free to speak?

| 0 | 1 | 2 | 3 | 4 | 5 | 6 | 7 | 8 | 9 | 10 |

Never had a   All the opportunity to
chance to speak   talk I wanted

3. *Climate of Acceptance:* How well did members support each other, show acceptance of individuals?

| 0 | 1 | 2 | 3 | 4 | 5 | 6 | 7 | 8 | 9 | 10 |

Highly critical   Supportive and receptive
and punishing

4. *Interpersonal relations:* How pleasant and concerned with interpersonal relations?

| 0 | 1 | 2 | 3 | 4 | 5 | 6 | 7 | 8 | 9 | 10 |

Quarrelsome, status   Pleasant, empathic,
differences emphasized   concerned with persons

Leadership: How adequate was the leader (or leadership) of the group?

| 0 | 1 | 2 | 3 | 4 | 5 | 6 | 7 | 8 | 9 | 10 |

Too weak ( ) or   Shared, group-centered,
dominating ( )   and sufficient

6. *Satisfaction with role:* How satisfied are you with your personal participation in the discussion?

| 0 | 1 | 2 | 3 | 4 | 5 | 6 | 7 | 8 | 9 | 10 |

Very dissatisfied   Very satisfied

7. *Quality of product:* How satisfied are you with the discussions, solutions, or learnings that came out of this discussion?

| 0 | 1 | 2 | 3 | 4 | 5 | 6 | 7 | 8 | 9 | 10 |

Very displeased   Very satisfied

8. *Overall:* How do you rate the discussion as a whole apart from any specific aspect of it?

| 0 | 1 | 2 | 3 | 4 | 5 | 6 | 7 | 8 | 9 | 10 |

Awful, waste of time   Superb, time well spent

Figure 10.5 Postmeeting Reactions for Learning Discussion Leader.

Leader's Name _____

Instruction: Circle number on each scale that best indicates your reaction.

1. *Preparation* for leading the discussion seemed:
   thorough and appropriate   very inadequate

7	6	5	4	3	2	1

2. *Organizing and guiding* the discussion were:
   clear and orderly   rigid or haphazard

7	6	5	4	3	2	1

3. *Spreading of participation* was:
   just right   completely neglected

7	6	5	4	3	2	1

4. The *style* or philosophy of the leader was:
   group centered stimulator   autocratic ("expert")

7	6	5	4	3	2	1

5. *Participating* in the discussion was:
   satisfying and enjoyable   boring or frustrating

7	6	5	4	3	2	1

Comments:

Figure 10.6 Learning Group PMR Form.

1. What did you especially *like* or *dislike* about the discussion?

2. What, if anything, do you believe you learned?

3. What do you most *approve* and *disapprove* of in the leader's behavior?

Figure 10.7 PMR Sheet for Encounter Sessions.

Instructions: Circle number indicating your reaction on each scale.

1. How well was discussion focused on the "here and now" experience of the group?

1	2	3	4	5	6	7

little;
mostly
story telling

totally on
here-and-now

2. How open were members in describing feelings and reactions?

1	2	3	4	5	6	7

no self-disclosure   open, much self-disclosure

3. How descriptive and supportive were members?

1	2	3	4	5	6	7

evaluative and critical,   neutral   entirely descriptive
a "hatchet job"   of reactions and
                                                                  others' behaviors

4. How specific and clear were comments?

1	2	3	4	5	6	7

vague, general and   clear, specific
theoretical   and focussed

5. How much responsibility did members assume for the session?

1	2	3	4	5	6	7

leader dominated, much   members assumed responsibility
dependency behavior   for success of session

Comments:

The results of the PMR questionnaires should be tallied and reported back to the group as soon as possible, either in printed form or by posting on a blackboard or chart. The results then become a guide for review of past practice and for planning new practices. The questions must be designed to produce data that can readily be tabulated, summarized, and reported.

Figure 10.8 PMR sheets can help diagnose problem groups.

Verbal Interaction Diagrams

A diagram of interaction made by an observer will reveal a lot about the relationships among members of a group. The diagram can reveal who is talking to whom, how often each member participates orally, and any dominating persons. A model interaction diagram is shown in figure 10.9. Notice the data at the top of the sheet; the names of all participants are located around the circle in the same order in which they sat during the discussion. Each time a person speaks an arrow is drawn from his or her position toward the person to whom the remark was addressed. If a member speaks to the entire group, a longer arrow points towards the center of the circle. Subsequent remarks in the same direction are indicated by short cross marks on the base of the arrow.

Scales for Rating Group Inputs, Process, and Outputs

Rating scales can be used by critic-observers to record their judgments about any aspect of the group and its discussion, including group climate, cohesiveness, efficiency, satisfaction, degree of mutual respect, organization of discussion, adequacy of information, and the like. A five or seven point scale is sufficiently detailed for most purposes. Members of a class in small group

Figure 10.9 Interaction Diagram.

Frequency and direction of
participation

Group _____

Time _____

    Begin _____

    End _____

Place _____

Observer _____

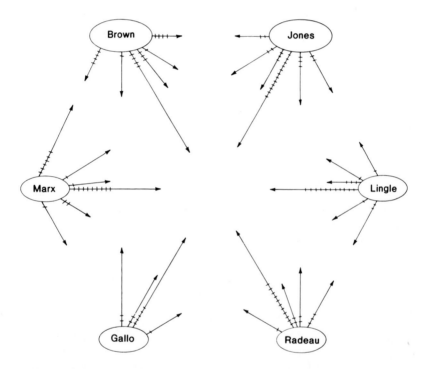

communication can learn much by preparing their own scales to rate both groups and participants on various characteristics; deciding what to emphasize and rate will force you to think through many issues on group process. A sample of the type of instrument you might develop for rating a small group discussion is shown in figure 10.10.

Figure 10.10 Discussion Rating Scale.

Date _____   Group _____

Time _____   Observer _____

Group characteristic	5 excellent	4 good	3 average	2 fair	1 poor
Organization of discussion					
Equality of opportunity to speak					
Cooperative group orientation					
Listening to understand					
Evaluation of ideas					

Comments:

The level of interpersonal trust in a small group can be rated on the scale shown in figure 10.11. Trust is both a process variable and an output variable with strong implications for further group interaction.

Figure 10.11 Level of Trust among Group Members.

7	6	5	4	3	2	1

Complete trust
in each other   Complete distrust
                                                 in each other

The importance of the methods by which decisions are made in a small group is explained in chapter 7. The scale shown in figure 10.12 can be used to report judgments about a group's decision making on substantive issues. With slight modification it can be used as a PMR sheet for feedback when no observer is available. Figure 10.13 is a form on which to record how decisions are made on all issues confronted by the group. It can be used to obtain a tally of how decisions are made on each major type of issue as well as to record exactly how each decision was made.

Figure 10.12 Decision-Making Rating Scale.

Date _____ Group _____

Time _____ Observer _____

Instructions: Circle the number that best represents the degree to which the decision about a solution to the problem discussed (or other substantive issue) meets the criterion of each scale.

Not at all	A little	Moderately	Considerably	Completely
1	2	3	4	5

1 2 3 4 5   1. To what extent does the decision reflect the content of discussion that preceded it?

1 2 3 4 5   2. To what extent are members all in agreement with the decision?

1 2 3 4 5   3. To what extent are members satisfied with and committed to the decision?

1 2 3 4 5   4. How adequate does the solution appear to be?

Figure 10.13 Group Decision-Making Procedures.

Group _____

Date and time of meeting _____

Observer _____

Instructions: Briefly describe each decision and use the appropriate letters to record the type of issue and decision procedure.

Key

Type of issue
A—agenda item
P—procedure to follow
C—criteria to employ
I—interpretation of information
S—solution to problem
AT—action to be taken or
    assignment for member

Decision Procedure
C—consensus or unanimity
M—majority vote
A—averaging
E—expert member decided
L—leader decided

Issue (describe briefly)	Issue type	Decision Procedure

Tally of Types and Procedures
Decision procedures

Issue types		C	M	A	E	L	Sum
	A						
	P						
	C						
	I						
	S						
	AT						
	Sum						

Figure 10.14 is a scale for evaluating the problem-solving procedures of a group. This scale was adapted from one developed originally by Patton and Giffin.[1] A problem-solving group should discuss any deficiencies pointed out by the scale, and how to overcome the deficiencies in the future.

Figure 10.14 Problem-Solving Process Scale.

Instructions: On each scale indicate the degree to which the group accomplished each identified behavior. Use the following scale for your evaluations:

Poor	Fair	Average	Good	Excellent
1	2	3	4	5

Circle the appropriate number in front of each item.

1 2 3 4 5   1. The concern of each member was identified regarding the problem the group attempted to solve.

1 2 3 4 5   2. This concern was identified *before* the problem was analyzed.

1 2 3 4 5   3. In problem analysis, the present condition was carefully compared with the specific condition desired.

1 2 3 4 5   4. The goal was carefully defined and agreed to by all members.

1 2 3 4 5   5. Valid (and relevant) information was secured when needed.

1 2 3 4 5   6. Possible solutions were listed and clarified before they were evaluated.

1 2 3 4 5   7. Criteria for evaluating proposed solutions were clearly identified and accepted by the group.

1 2 3 4 5   8. Predictions were made regarding the probable effectiveness of each proposed solution, using the available information and criteria.

1 2 3 4 5   9. Consensus was achieved on the most desirable solution.

1 2 3 4 5   10. A detailed plan to implement the solution was developed.

1 2 3 4 5   11. The problem-solving process was systematic and orderly.

The productivity and efficiency of a task or problem-solving group can be rated on the scales provided in figure 10.15.

Figure 10.15 Group Productivity and Efficiency.

1. All things considered, how *productive* was the group discussion you observed? Circle the number best reflecting your judgment.

5	4	3	2	1
extremely productive	quite productive	moderately productive	a little accomplished	nothing accomplished

2. How *efficient* was the group in what it accomplished?

5	4	3	2	1
extremely efficient	highly efficient	moderately efficient	only fair	low

Suggestions for increasing accomplishment at future meetings:

It often pays to have more than one observer filling in the same rating scale independently of one another; you could even use a fishbowl arrangement with several observers. The observers can learn by comparing their ratings, and discussing those on which they differ by more than one point.

Evaluating Individual Participants

Almost any aspect of individual participation can be evaluated by preparing appropriate forms. An analysis of roles of members can be made by listing the names of all members in separate columns on a sheet on which the various functions described in chapter 5 are listed in a vertical column at the left side of the sheet (figure 10.16). Each time a participant speaks, a tally is made in the column after the role function just performed. If a member performs more than one function in a single speech, two or more tallies are made. The completed observation form will indicate what functions were supplied adequately, the absence of any needed participant functions, the degree of role flexibility of each member of the group, and the kind of role each took.

Figure 10.16 Behavioral Functions of Discussants.

Date _____ Group _____

Time _____ Observer _____

Participants' Names

Behavioral Functions						
1. Initiating and orienting						
2. Information giving						
3. Information seeking						
4. Opinion giving						
5. Opinion seeking						
6. Evaluating						
7. Clarifying and elaborating						
8. Dramatizing						
9. Coordinating						
10. Consensus testing						
11. Suggesting procedure						
12. Recording						
13. Harmonizing						
14. Tension relieving						
15. Norming						
16. Withdrawing						
17. Blocking						
18. Recognition seeking						
19. Horseplaying						
20. Advocating						
21. Dominating						
22. Attacking						

Figure 10.17 shows a simple rating form that can be completed and given to each participant by a critic-observer. The forms should be filled out toward the end of the discussion so the group does not have to wait while the observer completes them. This form was written by a group of students and has been used extensively to rate students engaged in practice discussions. Although only illustrative of many types of scales and forms that could be used, it has the virtue of being simple and brief, yet focuses on some of the most important aspects of participation. A somewhat more detailed rating scale for individual participants is shown in figure 10.18. This form could be used by a critic-observer, or each participant in a small group might prepare one for each other member of the group.

Figure 10.19 is an observer form for assessing the assertiveness of members of a small group. The observer completes one of these scales for each participant in the discussion. This instrument is different from the other scales in that "Assertive," the optimal position on each scale, is located at the center instead of at one end. A check toward either end of a scale indicates that the participant was either less assertive or more aggressive than seemed desirable to the observer.

All of the previously described observation forms and rating scales can be used to analyze and appraise functional leadership. However, because most discussion groups have a designated leader and because his or her participation is so vital to the group, many special forms have been developed for recording and evaluating the behaviors of designated leaders. The form shown in figure 10.20 is one of the most comprehensive for evaluating designated leaders. The author adapted it from a form originally prepared for rating conference leaders in the United States Air Force.[2]

Figure 10.17 Participant Rating Scale.

For _____ Date _____

_____ Observer _____
(Name)

1. Contributions to the *content of the discussion*? (well prepared, supplied information, adequate reasoning, etc.)

5	4	3	2	1

Outstanding in   Fair share   Few or
quality and quantity   none

2. Contributions to *efficient group procedures*? (agenda planning, relevant comments, summaries, self-discipline)

5	4	3	2	1

Always relevant,   Relevant, no   Sidetracked,
aided organization   aid in order   confused group

3. Degree of *cooperativeness in attitude*? (listen to understand, responsible, agreeable, group centered, open-minded)

5	4	3	2	1

Very responsible   Self-centered
and constructive

4. *Speaking.* (clear, to group, one point at a time, concise)

5	4	3	2	1

Brief, clear,   Vague, indirect,
to group   wordy

5. *Value* to the group? (overall rating)

5	4	3	2	1

Most valuable   Least valuable
Suggestions:

Figure 10.18 Discussion Participation Evaluation.

For _____

Instructions: Circle the number that best reflects your evaluation of the discussant's participation on each scale.

Superior   Poor

1 2 3 4 5   1. Was prepared and informed.
1 2 3 4 5   2. Contributions were brief and clear.
1 2 3 4 5   3. Comments relevant and well timed.
1 2 3 4 5   4. Spoke distinctly and audibly to all.
1 2 3 4 5   5. Contributions made readily and voluntarily.
1 2 3 4 5   6. Frequency of participation (if poor, too low ( ) or high ( ).
1 2 3 4 5   7. Nonverbal responses were clear and constant.
1 2 3 4 5   8. Listened to understand and follow discussion.
1 2 3 4 5   9. Openminded.
1 2 3 4 5 10. Cooperative and constructive.
1 2 3 4 5 11. Helped keep discussion organized, following outline.
1 2 3 4 5 12. Contributed to evaluation of information and ideas.
1 2 3 4 5 13. Respectful and tactful with others.
1 2 3 4 5 14. Encouraged others to participate.
1 2 3 4 5 15. Assisted in leadership functions.
1 2 3 4 5 16. Overall rating in relation to other discussants.

Comments: Evaluator _____

Figure 10.19 Assertiveness Rating Scale.

Discussant _____ Date _____

Observer _____ Time _____

The check mark on each scale indicates my best judgment of your degree of assertiveness as a participant in the discussion.

Behavior	Nonassertive	Assertive	Aggressive
Getting the floor	yielded easily	usually refused to let other take over or dominate	interrupted and cut others off
Expressing opinions	never expressed personal opinion	stated opinions, but open to others' opinions	insisted others should agree with you
Expressing personal desires (for meeting times, procedures, etc.)	never, or did so apologetically	stated openly, but willing to compromise	insisted on having own way
Sharing information	none, or only if asked to do so	whenever info was relevant, concisely	whether relevant or not; long-winded, rambling

Personal Manner			
Voice	weak, unduly soft	strong and clear	loud, strident
Posture and movements	withdrawn, restricted	animated, often leaning forward	unduly forceful, "table pounding"

Eye contact			
	rare, even when speaking	direct but not staring or glaring	stared others down
Overall manner			
	nonassertive	assertive	aggressive

Figure 10.20 Leader Rating Scale.

Date _____ Leader _____

Time _____ Observer _____

Instructions: Rate the leader on all items that are applicable; draw a line through all items that do not apply. Use the following scale to indicate how well you evaluate his or her performance:

> 5—superior
> 4—above average
> 3—average
> 2—below average
> 1—poor

Leadership Style and Personal Characteristics

To what degree did the leader:

_____ Show poise and confidence in speaking?

_____ Show enthusiasm and interest in the problem?

_____ Listen well to other participants?

_____ Manifest personal warmth and a sense of humor?

_____ Behave with objectivity, an open mind to all ideas?

_____ Create a supportive, cooperative atmosphere?

_____ Share functional leadership with other members?

_____ Behave democratically?

Preparation

To what degree:

_____ Were all physical arrangements cared for?

_____ Was the leader's preparation and grasp of the problem thorough?

_____ Were questions prepared to guide the discussion?

_____ Were members notified and given adequate guidance for preparing?

Figure 10.20 continued

Procedural and Interpersonal Leadership Techniques

To what degree did the leader:

_____ Put members at ease with each other?

_____ Introduce the problem so it was clear to all members?

_____ Guide the group to a thorough analysis of the problem before talking about solutions?

_____ Suggest an outline or pattern for group problem solving?

_____ Encourage members to modify the outline or agenda?

_____ State questions so they were clear to all members?

_____ Rebound questions to the group, especially if asking for an opinion?

_____ Facilitate mutual understanding?

_____ Keep the discussion on one point at a time?

_____ Provide the summaries needed to clarify, remind, and move forward?

_____ Encourage the group to evaluate all ideas and proposals?

_____ Equalize opportunity to participate?

_____ Stimulate imaginative and creative thinking?

_____ Control aggressive or dominant members with tact?

_____ Attempt to resolve misunderstandings and conflicts quickly but effectively?

_____ Test for consensus before moving to a new phase of problem solving?

_____ Keep complete and accurate records?

_____ See that plans were made to implement and follow-up on decisions?

Observer-evaluators are not often available outside of the classroom. Designated discussion leaders, if they are to become more proficient, should evaluate their own participation as a means to improvement. The questionnaire in figure 10.21 may be used to evaluate one's own leadership. Many students of discussion and conference leadership have found it helpful to complete this form after practice discussions.

Summary

In this chapter we have examined the role of the nonparticipant observer as an aid to small groups in understanding and improving group discussions. The observer may function primarily as a reminder to the group of what it has overlooked, as a coach to the designated leader, or as a critic whose ratings are used to help discussants discover both their strengths and weaknesses. The student of small group communication is quite likely to learn even more when observing groups than when participating actively in the discussion.

A large number of forms have been provided to help you function as observer of discussion or to get reponses from group members for improving future meetings of the group. You may want to practice using many of these forms, but I want to stress again that you may benefit most by using these as guides in preparing your own unique forms. After extensive experience as observer there may be times when you will prefer to use no forms, but only a note pad to keep a record of your observations.

Enough of reading! Only by getting in the fray as observer will you develop the insights and skills of the competent observer, whether you be called on to remind, audit, coach, or critique small groups.

Figure 10.21   Self-Rating Scale for Problem-Solving Discussion Leaders.

Instructions: Rate yourself on each item by putting a check mark in the "Yes" or "No" column. Your score is five times the number of items marked "Yes." Rating: *excellent*, 90 or higher; *good*, 80–85; *fair*, 70–75; *inadequate*, 65 or lower.

	Yes	No
1. I prepared all needed facilities.	_____	_____
2. I started the meeting promptly and ended on time.	_____	_____
3. I established an atmosphere of permissiveness and informality; I was open and responsive to all ideas.	_____	_____
4. I clearly oriented the group to its purpose and area of freedom.	_____	_____
5. I encouraged all members to participate and maintained equal opportunity for all to speak.	_____	_____
6. I used a plan for leading the group in an organized consideration of all major phases of the problem.	_____	_____
7. I listened actively, and (if needed) encouraged all members to do so.	_____	_____
8. I saw to it that the problem was discussed thoroughly before solutions were considered.	_____	_____

Figure 10.21 continued

9. I integrated related ideas or suggestions, and urged the group to arrive at consensus on a solution. _____ _____
10. My questions were clear and brief. _____ _____
11. I saw to it that unclear statements were paraphrased or otherwise clarified. _____ _____
12. I prompted open discussion of substantive conflicts. _____ _____
13. I maintained order and organization, promptly pointing out tangents, making transitions, and keeping track of the passage of time. _____ _____
14. I saw to it that the meeting produced definite assignments or plans for action, and that any subsequent meeting was arranged. _____ _____
15. All important information, ideas and decisions were promptly and accurately recorded. _____ _____
16. I actively encouraged creative thinking. _____ _____
17. I encouraged thorough evaluation of information and all ideas for solutions. _____ _____
18. I was able to remain neutral during constructive arguments, and otherwise encourage teamwork. _____ _____
19. I suggested or urged establishment of needed norms and standards. _____ _____
20. I encouraged members to discuss how they felt about the group process and resolve any blocks to progress. _____ _____

Exercises

1. Divide your class at random into project groups of five or six members each. If there are both men and women in your class, draw them separately so that no group contains just one man or one woman.

   Each group should select a major term project that it will undertake. These can be limited to questions about small group communication and discussion, or your instructor may permit the groups to undertake any projects selected by the groups. For instance, groups from my classes have planned and held a party for the entire class; studied leadership in various campus groups and reported their findings in a panel discussion and paper; conducted studies of group counseling in area high schools; undertaken experiments in group interaction; participated in the National Contest in Public Discussion; evaluated learning discussion leadership in college classes; developed manuals; studied the jury system; and even written and produced short training films. The purpose and procedures for each project should be evaluated and approved by your instructor, who may be able to supply assistance with resources, ideas, and techniques.

The project groups will need a limited amount of time for meeting in regular class hours, but may need to conduct additional meetings outside of class.

The major purpose is to develop insights and skills as participant-observers. The project group exercise provides an opportunity to study how a group develops from a collection of persons who at first lack any group goal, role structure, or norms. Each student should write a 10–15 page essay describing and evaluating the project group, using the questions at the end of this exerciss as a guide.

Each group will need approximately 30 minutes of class time to report its findings near the end of the term. At this time the evaluation essays are collected and graded by the instructor. In my classes, all members of a group receive the same grades for the written project report and the oral presentation to the class. This is a minor grade, perhaps 5%–10% of the course grade. Each evaluative essay is graded separately; this is a major grade, as much as 30% of the final grade for the course. If your class undertakes this exercise, it should begin not later than midterm so that there are several weeks for the groups to develop, do their work, and prepare their reports.

Guidelines for Essay Evaluating Project Group

The questions below are only suggestions: there may be other issues of importance in examining your particular group, some of these questions may be inappropriate or in need of modification for your essay, and you will need to decide what topics to raise in describing and evaluating your unique small group.

1. What was the *goal* of the group? How did the group develop this as its objective? How adequately did this goal represent the interests and concerns of the members (individual goals)? What *hidden* agendas existed, and how did these contribute to or interfere with the surface agenda?
2. What do you see as the structure of functional member *roles*? How did these emerge? What do you think was the impact of each member on the group, and the group on each member? Were any needed functions missing?
3. What do you perceive as the *leadership* structure of the group? Is there a consensus leader? Who? How did this person emerge or become the acknowledged leader? What types of leadership behavior does he or she contribute? To what degree and in what ways is leadership shared in the group?

4. What *communication network* seems to exist in the group (i.e., who talks to whom)? What issues are talked about? How well do members listen to each other? Have there been problems in communicating, such as ambiguity, bypassing, stoppers, or the mood of dismissal? How did the group handle these? Have adequate records been kept and reports made from meeting to meeting?
5. What *norms* governing individual and group behavior emerged? How did these come about? What effects do they have on group productivity and maintenance? If there were counterproductive norms, were these changed? How? Did you have any problem members? If so, who, and how were these persons handled?
6. What patterns were actually used in *problem solving*? How systematic and productive were these? How were decisions made? How well were all members' resources of knowledge, creativity, reasoning, and skill used? Were meetings adequately planned and organized?
7. What *climate* or atmosphere existed and now exists among the members? How have tensions been handled? Are members committed? Task oriented? Accepting and supportive of each other? Appropriately flexible?
8. *Overall*, how do you evaluate your group and your personal contribution to it? What changes would you make if you could? How, and why?

2. From time to time you may be assigned to observe discussions among members of small groups formed within your class or of groups that exist apart from your class. Use one or more of the forms supplied in this chapter to guide and report your observations.

You may be given the opportunity to serve as a reminder-observer or critic-observer for small groups in other classes, such as fundamentals of speech communication, education, or social psychology. If so, plan carefully, then report the findings and outcomes of your interventions.

With one or more classmates you may be asked to serve as observer of small group discussions outside the university. Much can be learned by observing school boards, city councils, zoning commissions, or other groups whose meetings are open to the public. As a student you may even be granted permission to observe some meetings in private corporations. Tact, courtesy, unobtrusive observing, and disguising the names of those you observe will go a long way in gaining access and keeping the door open to other students who may want to follow you as an observer.

Bibliography

Beal, George M., Bohlen, Joe M., and Raudabaugh, J. Neil, *Leadership and Dynamic Group Action*, Ames, Ia: Iowa State University Press, 1962.

Patton, Bobby R., and Giffin, Kim, *Problem-Solving Group Interaction,* New York: Harper & Row, Publishers, 1973, part IV.

Potter, David, and Andersen, Martin P., *Discussion: A Guide to Effective Practice*, 3rd ed., Belmont, Cal.: Wadsworth Publishing Company, Inc., 1976.

References

1. Bobby R. Patton and Kim Giffin, *Problem-Solving Group Interaction* (New York: Harper & Row, Publishers, 1973), pp. 213–14.
2. Department of the Air Force, *Conference Leadership*, Air Force Manual No. 50–08 (Washington: Department of the Air Force, 1953), pp. 5–6.

11

discussion methods for learning groups, public meetings, and groups in organizations

Study Objectives

You may choose to read only selected parts of chapter 11, using it as a reference for some special techniques or procedures. If you study the entire chapter carefully, you should be able to:

1. Explain the benefits of cooperative learning discussions.

2. List seven guidelines for conducting learning discussions.

3. Write an outline for organizing discussion of a subject, work of art, problem, or personal feelings and values.

4. Conduct a problem census of either problems or issues of concern to members of a small group, and use the results to build an agenda.

5. Explain the "encounter discussion" concept and list eight guidelines for making the feedback during encounter discussion productive of personal growth.

6. Plan and moderate either a panel or forum discussion for a large audience.

7. Conduct buzz groups to involve all members of a large group.

8. List and describe the eight major steps of the Nominal Group Technique.

9. Explain the purpose of parliamentary rules for committees and describe twelve specific adaptations of parliamentary law to committee discussion.

Key Terms

Ad hoc or special committee   committee created to perform a specific task, then disband.

Affective discussion   members of a small group express and explore their feelings, especially fears, in relation to some topic or concept, requiring total acceptance and positive facilitation by leader or teacher of the group.

Buzz group session   large group meeting is divided into small groups of approximately six persons each, who discuss a target question for a specified number of minutes, then report their answers to the entire large group.

Case discussion   learning discussion beginning with consideration of a specific problem or "case" about which group members exchange perceptions, ideas, and possible solutions.

Causal pattern outline   sequence of questions for organizing a learning discussion based on the assumption of a cause-effect relationship among events.

Chronological pattern outline   a series of questions for organizing a learning discussion in which issues are taken up in a time series, such as first, second, and third.

Comparative pattern outline   a set of questions asking the discussants to compare two or more things, institutions, or other concepts on certain criteria or characteristics.

Encounter discussion   open expression of feelings and reactions of members of a group to each other and the group as a whole.

Feedback   description by member of a group of her reaction "here and now" to behavior of another member of the group.

Fine arts pattern outline   a sequence for discussing some product of human creativity beginning with examination of the object, discussion of perceived features, interpretation of the whole, evaluation, and ending with reexamination of the object.

Forum   discussion within a large audience, controlled by a moderator, usually following some presentatation such as a lecture, panel discussion, or film.

Moderator   designated leader of a public discussion such as a panel, group interview, or forum.

Nominal Group Technique (NGT)   special procedure in which six to nine persons work individually in silence to generate ideas, then interact to pool, clarify, and evaluate these ideas until a plan to solve a major problem has been adopted.

Panel Discussion   informal discussion among members of a small group, coordinated by a moderator, for benefit of a listening audience.

Parliamentary procedure (law)   a codified body of rules and procedures governing deliberation in a large assembly, greatly simplified and limited when organizational bylaws mandate it for committee meetings.

Problem census   technique in which members of a small group are polled for topics and problems that are posted, ranked by voting, and used to create agendas for future meetings.

Quorum   minimum legal number of members of a small group who must be in attendance before decisions can be made that affect a parent organization.

Up to now this book has been concerned with the dynamics of small groups as systems and small group communication. Only problem-solving discussion has received special treatment. This final chapter provides a selection of special techniques and procedures for learning discussions, public discussions, and meetings of small groups that report to larger organizations. These techniques and procedures have all proven to be of immense practical value to participants and designated leaders.

Learning Discussion

Learning groups of all types, at all educational levels, formal and informal, sponsored and spontaneous, in and out of classrooms, exist not to reach decisions but for the personal enlightenment and growth of their members. There is an old saying to the effect that if two persons each having one idea apiece give them to each other, then each is twice as rich in ideas as before—this is the very gist of learning discussion. In learning groups there is no need to reach accord on values, beliefs, or courses of action. What is sought is a fuller understanding, a wider grasp of information pertinent to a topic, or consideration of a problem from as many points of view as possible. With no need to reach accord on issues, a pattern of group interaction different from those of problem-solving groups is often needed.

From years of observing learning groups as a researcher, leading various kinds of learning groups, conducting training programs for teachers and study-discussion leaders, and serving as a consultant, I have attempted to distill some principles and techniques for planning and conducting learning discussions.

In addition to classrooms, there are innumerable settings in which learning discussions occur. For example, one evening during what was primarily a social gathering of four couples I enjoyed an impromptu discussion of how homes might be made more energy efficient. An engineer, a statistician, a business professor, and I spent nearly two hours sharing our knowledge and ideas about alternative ways to design, insulate, heat, and cool houses. I left with many new ideas for our "dream" house. Likewise, after watching dogs perform at field trials I have often gotten into informal discussions of their merits, resulting in a gradual change in my criteria for breeding, training, and judging. When members of an informal social gathering discover a common interest, rambling conversation can turn into a deeply satisfying learning exchange.

In recent years much attention has been given to classroom discussion as a means of learning through the sharing of knowledge, beliefs, and feelings. Many schools, colleges, and universities conduct in-service training to help their faculty members learn to lead classroom discussions. In continuing education outside the traditional collegiate structure much learning goes on in discussion groups sponsored by universities, libraries, churches, and other organizations. Encounter and other experiential growth groups can be found in most communities. In these groups members explore new ways of relating and communicating, and how to cope with personal problems. Highly specialized experiential groups exist to help participants cope with problems of alcohol, drugs, weight, and mental health.

Why this great expansion of learning through discussion? For one thing, we have come to view learning as much more than the acquisition of factual information and skills. *Learning* has come to mean any *change* that comes about in a person due to experience; *education* as the structuring of situations in which change will be facilitated. Learning objectives have been organized and classified into three types: (1) *cognitive* or intellectual, ranging from recognition and recall of specific information to abilities in combining and creating; (2) *affective,* having to do with values and feelings; and (3) *psychomotor,* which are primarily about physical skills. Extensive research has shown that active participation in discussion groups is often more productive of higher mental skills and changes of beliefs and values than is any type of lecture, video, or individualized instruction format.[1] The older person, "largely committed to what he is and what he does" and with extensive experience, needs the opportunity to " . . . *think about what he already knows,*" which the " . . . informal study-discussion process attempts to give him."[2]

Many studies have shown that cooperative group interaction is superior to competitive learning structures in reducing racial stereotypes and increasing acceptance of people of different types, provided the discussion is not a one-shot affair.[3] That educational innovations such as individualized instruction, computer-assisted instruction, nongraded and open classrooms, team teaching, and "new" math are not helpful if the quality of interaction in the classroom is not given proper consideration was demonstrated by Hunter. The cooperative relationships established in a discussion *group* approach to learning may be essential if many learning objectives are to be achieved.[4] The following quotation from Johnson and Johnson summarizes well the need for cooperative interstudent relationships:

Beyond all doubt, cooperation should be the most frequently used goal structure. The conditions under which it is effective and desirable are almost too many to list. Whenever problem solving is desired, whenever divergent thinking or creativity is desired, whenever quality of performance is expected, whenever the task is complex, when the learning goals are highly important, and when the social development of students is one of the major instructional goals, cooperation should be used. When a teacher wishes to promote positive interaction among students, a facilitative learning climate, a wide range of cognitive and affective outcomes, and positive relations between himself and the students, cooperative goal structures will be used.[5]

Guidelines for Leading Learning Discussions

Based on the preceding brief summary of research and philosophy of learning through discussion at all levels of education, some guidelines can be formulated for setting up cooperative learning discussions.

1. *Always establish a cooperative group goal.* The outcome to be achieved should always be presented as a *sharing* of individual knowledge and thinking, never as competing for status by giving "correct" answers. Members should be encouraged to listen to understand, to help each other, and to consider each other as partners rather than as competitors in learning.

2. *Give rewards to the group, not to individual members.* This means that praise for good work is directed to the group, not to individuals. Such comments as "I thought we had a very interesting discussion," "I got a lot from all of you," or "That was a really fine discussion" are group oriented, and stress the cooperative relationship.

3. *Keep the focus on common experience.* Effective learning discussion grows out of a common body of experiences. All participants should be reading the same articles or books, looking at the same painting or movie, observing the same group of children, or studying the same problem. Meaningful, enlightening discussions evolve from differing perceptions of such phenomena, supplemented by events or data experienced by one or a few group members. A secret of productive learning discussion is to focus on what has been observed by all discussants. Members of study-discussion groups are more satisfied when discussion is kept relevant to assigned readings than when it rambles to peripheral topics.[6]

4. *Limit the number of issues or topics.* Greater learning and more satisfaction are found in groups where the average number of distinguishable topics per two-hour session is less than eleven than in groups where the average was more than fourteen per meeting.[7] Jumping rapidly from topic to topic should be avoided. Except with younger children, it is unwise to plan to discuss more than three or four basic issues per hour. Of course several subquestions might be discussed under each of these broader issues.

5. *Plan a variety of open-ended questions.* Open-ended questions encourage a variety of answers from different points of view. The contrast between closed or specific-answer questions and open-ended questions is indicated by the following pairs in which the open-ended question occurs first.

   O—Are there any types of acts now classified as crimes that we think should be decriminalized?
   C—What acts does the Chief of Police say should be decriminalized?

O—What does the fifth stanza mean to you?
C—What is the meaning of the fifth stanza?

O—How safe do current nuclear generating plants appear to be?
C—Are nuclear power plants safe?

O—What good is membership in the U.N. to the United States?
C—What did the United States pay into the U.N. last year?

This is not to say that no questions asking for specific items of information should be asked, but they should be used to garner evidence and as follow-up questions to the broad issues of the discussion. Memory questions may bring out needed facts, but the answer itself is not discussable if accepted as correct by the group.

Numerous classifications of types of general questions have been developed. The list of types below may help you in planning questions to stimulate and facilitate learning discussion.

Translation—asking the discussants to change information or statements into their own language. Examples' "How else might we say that?" "What does _____ mean to you?"

Interpretation—the question asks the respondent to determine relationships among facts, generalizations, values, and so on. Discussants are challenged to give meaning to a body of information by such questions. Examples: "How serious is the problem of alienation among students at _____ ?" "Why might the settlers have slaughtered the buffalo?" "What might have motivated Luther to defy the Church?"

Analysis—the group is called on to divide an issue or problem into major components or contributing causes. Examples: "What factors determine the total amount of money you earn on a savings account?" "What other things may have contributed to the rate of illiteracy in the United States?" "When do you most enjoy discussing?"

Value—the respondents are asked to make statements of evaluation, judgment of degree of goodness, rightness, or appropriateness. Examples: "What is the best way to respond if someone calls you a honky or nigger?" "Is it ever right to pollute the air?" "Is capital punishment justifiable as a deterrent to murder?"

Prediction—the discussants are called on to use information in predicting some future trend or condition. Examples: "What energy sources do you think we will be using to heat our houses twenty years from now?" "What do you think will happen to Willy if he doesn't change his behavior?"

Synthesis or *problem solving*—discussants are asked to engage in creative thinking that incorporates information, analysis, prediction, and values in arriving at a conclusion. Examples: "What should you do if you discover a close friend has been shoplifting?" "What should we do to reduce drunken driving?"

6. *Be guided by the nature of the subject.* The pattern for a learning discussion is usually inherent in the subject of discussion and the group purpose in discussing it. Thus if a group desired to understand and appreciate poetry, the pattern would emerge from that purpose and the poem. A group discussing a film might well discuss such characteristics as the truthfulness of the theme, the acting, the staging, the photography, and their enjoyment of the film. A group seeking to understand differences in conceptions of God might discuss Catholic beliefs, various Protestant beliefs, and Jewish beliefs. Or, they might compare each major religion by focusing on images of God, beliefs concerning divine purpose, and the individual's relation to God. A group seeking to understand the problems of securing open and fair housing for all citizens might use a problem-solving outline (even though the discussants would not necessarily seek a solution).
7. *Focus on how the subject relates to interests of the members of the group.* To do otherwise, of course, is not to have a *group* goal but an autocratically determined one. One procedure useful for organizing learning discussion of materials previously examined by all members of a group is to poll the group for questions each wants to explore, writing them all on a board or piece of large paper where all can see. Each person can then vote for 3–5 topics of greatest interest. These questions are then discussed in the order of most to least interest (votes).

It is especially important to plan questions relating a topical discussion to personal concerns and experiences of members of a discussion group. For example, compare the following two sets of questions for guiding a discussion of reactions to Arthur Miller's *Death of a Salesman*. The first set is all too typical of what teachers do to turn students off: ask questions reflecting the interests of the teacher, closed questions, and those that have no connection to the personal lives of the students. The second set encourages the student discussants to relate the play to their personal lives.

1. What method of character introduction is used?
2. Which point of view does the author use?
3. What are some figures of speech used by Miller?

versus

1. What is unhealthy about Willy's inability to face reality?
2. Do we think it was wrong for Biff to quit trying after he surprised Willy in the hotel in Boston? Why?
3. What should we do when someone else fails us, like a teacher we don't like?
4. What does Miller seem to think of the American business world?
5. Should an employee ever take second place to the good of the company?

Patterns for Organizing Learning Discussions

Sometimes there should be no attempt to organize a learning discussion such as an affective discussion or an encounter session. But discussions for many classes and study-discussion groups should be organized, with a designated leader being responsible for developing a set of questions that can be raised to focus and give some order to the group interaction. Many of the same logical patterns used to organize informative public speeches can be applied to discussions.

Topical or Major Issues

This is a common pattern for learning discussions. The group discusses a set of topics or issues, each of which can be phrased as a question. These should be the basic issues that must be understood for members to gain an overall view of the subject matter under study, and to share their differing reactions to it. While a designated leader should prepare a set of questions and subquestions to guide exploration of the major issues, the leader should never insist that the group discuss all of or only the leader's questions. The group must decide what issues will be discussed; the leader can suggest the issues and ask if the discussants want to omit any of them or add others.

Three examples will be presented to show this pattern of organization. The first is from a group that was discussing motion pictures. After seeing each film they used the following outline:

I. What was the reaction to the theme of the picture?
II. How good was the acting?
III. How well was the picture staged and costumed?
IV. How effective were lighting and photography?
V. Would we recommend this picture to our friends?

Following a viewing of the movie "The Poseidon Adventure," a class was divided into small groups for discussion of the following topical outline:

I. How did Scott establish himself as leader of the group that escaped?
II. What role did each person play in the group that contributed to their successful escape?
III. How were these roles established by member and group?
IV. How does this movie relate to leadership in our class?

After reading about the United States and Communism, a group studying American foreign policy discussed the following issues during a two-hour meeting:

I. How feasible is a policy of coexistence?
II. How feasible is a policy of containment?
III. How feasible is a policy of liberation for Communist-dominated countries?
IV. What should be the main tenets of American foreign policy toward Communist states?

These questions were planned in advance by the designated discussion leader. A number of subquestions emerged from the members' reactions to the readings.

Chronological

When discussing an historical trend, the subject can best be dealt with in a time sequence. Consider the following typical outline:

I. How did the United States government treat Indians while the West was being settled?
II. How did it treat them during the heyday of the reservation system?
III. How well are the Federal and State governments treating Indians today?

A series of subquestions were discussed under each of these general issues. They dealt with such topics as treaties, legal contracts, citizenship, finances, discrimination, health, and education.

Causal

The logic underlying this pattern of questions is cause-effect. Since the relationships between events are not so simple as "A caused B," the questions and outline should indicate the complexity of a field of forces leading to some subsequent event(s). If a group were discussing the social problem of sexual assaults, they might be encouraged to follow an outline of questions following a causal pattern.

I. How serious is the crime of sexual assault today?
  A. What kinds of acts do we include as sexual assaults?
  B. How frequent are these crimes?
  C. Who commits them, and against whom?
II. What factors or conditions seem to produce sexual assaults?
  A. Do we have any evidence of physical characteristics that might contribute to being an assaulter?
  B. What personality characteristics may contribute to this crime?
  C. What role do family relationships play in sexual assaults?
  D. Do any social conditions seem to be contributory?
  E. Are there any other factors that seem to us to be contributory?
III. Do we now have any opinions about what produces a rapist?

Comparative

A *comparative* pattern might be used to compare two or more policies, objectives, organizations, and so forth. The group might begin by discussing criteria and goals, or with the first of the topics to be compared. For example, a group of students could discuss the merits of various teaching-learning approaches they have experienced while using the following outline:

I. What are the advantages and disadvantages of lecturing?
II. What are the advantages and disadvantages of discussions?
III. What are the advantages and disadvantages of seminar or tutorial methods?
IV. What are the advantages and disadvantages of programmed instruction?

Organizing Discussion of a Work of Art

Many learning groups, both in and out of the classroom, have found enlightenment and pleasure in discussing such works of art as poetry, paintings, short stories, pieces of sculpture, or architecture. This format has proven to be helpful in countless discussions: (1) the group examines the work of art together; (2) the group discusses what they perceive in the work of art and what it means to them; (3) the group again examines the work of art. Relatively little time will be spent discussing the artist, the artist's motives, or the artist's life. If artistic techniques are considered, they are left until near the end of the discussion.

Literature

The following set of questions can be used to guide discussion of a poem. With appropriate modifications, a similar sequence of questions could be used to organize discussion of any other art form. With any specific work of art, some questions may be fruitless or meaningless, and others may be needed to open up other avenues of perception and interpretation. Previous beliefs of members about how one *ought* to react to a poem or other work should not be allowed to block discussion.

Introduction: A member of the group reads the poem aloud.

I. What situation occurs in the poem?
   A. What is actually taking place? What do you see in the poem?
   B. What other actions are described by the persons in the poem?
II. How does the speaker in the poem feel about the situation he or she is discussing?
   A. At the beginning of the poem?
   B. In the middle?
   C. At the end?
   D. What is the nature and direction of the change of his or her feelings?
III. What kind of person does the speaker appear to be in the poem?
   A. What kind of person would feel like this?
   B. What kind of person would change in this way (or remain unchanged)?

IV. What broad generalizations underlie the poem?
   A. What ideas does the poet assume to be true?
   B. Does he or she arrive at any insights, answers, or solutions?
   C. How do we feel about these generalizations?

Conclusion: A group member reads the poem aloud.

Some of the questions in the general outline above may not fit a particular poem. You must plan questions for the specific poem, depending on what it is about, how it is written, the reactions it evokes in you, and so on. This adaptation is illustrated in the following poem and outline for a discussion of it by a group of college students.

Invictus
William Ernest Henley

Out of the night that covers me,
    Black as the Pit from pole to pole,
I thank whatever gods may be
    For my unconquerable soul.

In the fell clutch of circumstance
    I have not winced nor cried aloud.
Under the bludgeonings of chance
    My head is bloody, but unbowed.

Beyond this place of wrath and tears
    Looms but the Horror of the shade,
And yet the menace of the years
    Finds, and shall find, me unafraid.

It matters not how strait the gate,
    How charged with punishments the scroll,
I am the master of my fate;
    I am the captain of my soul.

  I. What do you think this poem is about?
   A. What might *night* refer to in the first line?
   B. The black pit?
 II. What sort of person does the speaker appear to be to you?
   A. What does the second stanza tell you about the speaker?
   B. What do you think is his or her attitude toward dying?
   C. What do you understand about the speaker's view of life and afterlife?
   D. What do you make out of the last two lines?
III. What beliefs or assumptions underlie the poem?
   A. What does the poet assume to be true?
   B. How do we feel about these beliefs?
IV. Do you like this poem? Why?

A group might discuss a short story, essay, or even a novel in a similar fashion. The following outline was prepared to guide a discussion by a group of persons who had all read *Jonathan Livingston Seagull*.[8]

I. What does the story mean to you?
   A. Is it more than the story of a gull?
   B. Do we find any religious themes in the story?
   C. What do you feel was the high point of the story?
II. What do the leading characters mean to you?
   A. How would you characterize Jonathan?
      1. Is he like anyone you know?
      2. How do you feel about such a character?
   B. What sort of character is Chaing?
      1. What does he represent to you?
      2. Why do you think Bach gave him an oriental name?
      3. Do we have any personal "Chaings?"
   C. What do you think of Fletcher?
      1. What significance do you attach to his crashing into the wall?
      2. What sort of person does he remind you of?
   D. Do any other characters stand out for you? Who and why?
III. What impact do you think Jonathan and his friends would have on the flock?
   A. What do you think happened to the Breakfast Flock after Fletcher's miracle?
   B. How might this affect other gulls?
   C. How does our society view the purpose of life?
   D. How do we view it?
IV. What are our personal feelings in response to *Jonathan*?
   A. Would you want to be like Jonathan in any ways?
   B. Would you have joined his school?
   C. If you had been Jonathan, would you have returned to teach the rest of the flock?[9]

Visual Objects

An outline of questions for discussing a visual object such as a painting, sculpture, clothing, building, or photograph should focus on various characteristics of features of the object, not the whole. The discussants are led to shift the visual focus in this way, and to describe what they see from each new perspective, such as shape, color, line, texture, area, and so on. As part of her work in one of my classes, a student prepared the next outline to lead discussion of an abstract painting.

Introduction: A painting is hung in front of the group seated in a semi-circle, and the group is asked to examine it silently.

I. What different elements do you see?
  A. What do you notice about the texture?
  B. What colors do you notice?
  C. What do you notice about the shapes?
  D. Do you observe anything in the lines?
II. Overall, combining the different elements, what do you perceive?
  A. Does it seem to portray any specific object, idea, or event?
  B. Do your personal experiences or ideas affect your perceptions in any way?
III. What feelings do you experience from looking at the picture?
  A. What emotions does it arouse?
  B. Does it move you to want to take any action?
  C. What seems to be evoking your reaction or arousal?
IV. What does the painting seem to say to you?
  A. Does it have any specific message or theme for you?
  B. What might be the purpose of this painting? Strictly aesthetic?
V. How do you evaluate the painting?
  A. Do you think the artist said what he wanted to say?
  B. Do you feel it was worth saying?
  C. How did the artist achieve this, or what prevented him from achieving it?
  D. Has the painting or our discussion of it revealed anything new or important to you?
  E. Does it have any universality or significance?[10]

Studying Problems

A group wanting to learn as much as possible about a particular problem could use one of the problem-solving patterns without coming to any decisions or solution as a group. The purpose is for each member to achieve a better understanding and have a number of alternatives available. If the members are quite heterogeneous in backgrounds and values, all will learn from the knowledge, perspectives, beliefs, and ideas of each other.

Regardless of the pattern used to organize thinking and talking in a learning discussion, it should reflect the basic purpose, which is learning, reflect the basic issues of the topic or question being discussed, and reflect the particular interests and needs of the group members. To get a better understanding of these principles and how they are applied in a given situation, you may want to prepare a set of leader's outlines on problems and topics to which each type of organization is appropriate, then engage in such discussions with your friends or classmates. Each discussion and outline should be followed by observer and group evaluation.

Special Techniques for Learning Groups

The literature of learning discussion contains many special formats and techniques, some of which can be applied in a wide variety of situations, and some of which have very limited usefulness. Some would be most useful with small children, some with young adults, some with continuing education groups, and some with almost any age level or type of learning group. The techniques presented in this chapter were selected for their adaptability to a wide range of situations.

Case Discussion

Often discussion is desultory when concerned with a vague or general problem. Rather than beginning with a general problem question, the leader can present the group with a specific case as a beginning point. First, this case problem is discussed as if the group were trying to actually solve it, and then the group is asked to generalize from the specific case problem to similar situations they have faced or may face in the future. The following two cases, prepared by students in my classes from their personal experience, may be used for case discussions in your group or class, or you can use them as models in writing your own case problems.

The Teacher's Dilemma

An English teacher in a consolidated, rural high school has had extensive dramatic experience, and as a result was chosen by the principal to direct the first play in the new school. The play will be the first major production for the school. Its success may determine whether or not there will be future plays produced at the school, and if well done can bring prestige to both teacher and the school. As a result, the teacher (a friend of mine) is exhausting every means available to her to make the play an artistic success. She has chosen the cast except for the leading female part. The principal's daughter wants the part, and the principal told the teacher he really wants his daughter to have it. But—she is a poor actress, and would jeopardize the success of the show. Tentatively, the teacher has chosen someone who should do an excellent job in the role, but the principal has implied that if his daughter is not selected, he will appoint another director.

What should I tell my English teacher friend to do?

The Relationship

A close friend of mine recently became engaged to a girl I introduced him to a couple of years ago. Soon after the engagement his fiancée began making extensive plans for the wedding, which is to take place in a few months. She has purchased a gown, groom's ring, and household items. But my friend now feels he is being pushed into a marriage he no longer wants. At the time of engagement he felt deeply in love, but now he says he does not feel ready for the responsibilities of marriage. He told me in confidence that the only attraction he now feels for the girl is a physical one; he does not feel friendship. But he is afraid to reveal his true feelings to her; he thinks she is much in love with him and doesn't want to hurt her. Also, he says it would be hard to end their physical relationship, though they are both afraid she might become pregnant. He says he would be glad to break off the engagement; however, his fiancée reminds him that if he was willing to take her virginity he should be man enough to marry her. His parents are somewhat opposed to the marriage; hers are encouraging it.

My friend feels confused, guilty, and trapped. He has come to me for advice. What should I tell him?

Problem Census

This technique can be used for learning groups in order to elicit agenda items for future discussions. The target question on which the census is conducted must be of interest to the participants, clear, and focussed on a limited range of issues, feelings, beliefs, concerns, or goals. Once when teaching biology in high school I posed the question, "What would you like to learn about human inheritance?" to the class before we began a unit on genetics. We wrote on the blackboard every question presented by members of the class. Then we cooperatively designed our unit to get answers to as many of these questions as possible, using readings, special reports, investigative committees, and guest speakers. Student interest and involvement was the highest I had ever achieved as a teacher. The problem census technique has proven to be of similar value in classes concerned with communication, theatre, and every other subject I have ever tried to teach. Epstein gave the following examples of target questions she found useful in problem censuses designed to get at vital concerns of secondary school students:

What would you like to know about race?

What do you want to know about sex?

What do you want to know about drugs?[11]

It takes acceptance, fairness, objectivity, and complete honesty on the part of a designated leader to conduct a problem census. The issues raised must be based on the real concerns of the group members rather than meet the needs of the leader. Some teachers I have observed failed as census leaders when they tried to impose their interests and beliefs on a class.

Affective Discussion

This term, coined by Epstein, refers to ventilation of feelings among several persons, usually members of a class, but the technique can be used by any learning group at almost any level. The purpose is to express and explore feelings of members of a group, often necessary before persons can make objective and intelligent responses to factual information, ideas, and beliefs different from those they currently hold. The group should consist of 6–10 persons seated in a tight circle. In a traditional classroom the teacher can seat a part of the class in front of the room for affective discussion while other students work at their seats. A rotation system assures that every student has equal time to be in such a group. A college class can be divided into small groups, instructed in the procedure, and each group then allowed to work with the teacher as consultant or observer. I have used it with graduate students in a research class before entering into the study of statistics. These adults get deeply involved in a catharsis of their fears about statistics, and many have testified that ventilation of their feelings made it possible for them to learn math that they had been sure they could not learn. Fears of speaking up in groups or serving as spokesperson for a group in conference or before a large group meeting (stage fright) can be dealt with through affective discussions in speech classes.

An affective discussion begins with the beliefs (assumptions) that all persons have feelings and that any feeling is "okay" to have. The technique is based on the assumption that we need to express our feelings without apology and have them accepted without criticism in order for adequate intra- and interpersonal communication to occur.

When conducting an affective discussion the designated leader plays little part except to facilitate expression and empathic listening. Here are some of the types of responses a leader should avoid because they are likely to arouse defensiveness:

That's right.

That's wrong.

Don't you mean . . . ?

That's not a nice thing to say.

Gasp.

Look it up in your textbook.

We shouldn't use such language here.

I know you didn't mean that.

The facts are that . . .

Don't say such things unless you really know.

Comments such as the following may help to facilitate open and honest expression of feelings and values:

What do *you* think?

How do you feel about that?

Let him finish his thought.

It's all right to say what you feel.

I don't know.

I won't answer questions during this discussion.

It's not a matter of right or wrong, but what you feel.

I hope these examples have helped you to understand the nonevaluative, totally accepting responses needed from the leader of an affective discussion. Present the opening question, then *listen,* perhaps making an occasional facilitative comment showing understanding and acceptance, but *no* evaluation, critical arguing or disagreement, weighing, or questioning of any kind. Here the leader is for once advised to be *laissez faire.* In the classroom this is learner-learner interaction; the teacher is largely an outsider to the affective discussion.

Questions can be on any issue about which group members have shown strong feelings. These issues might come from a problem census, inability to come to consensus on a problem, fantasy chains, or issues raised in a textbook. For example, in a course on small group communication an affective discussion might be generated from such questions as: "How do we feel about members of project groups who are undependable?" or "How do we feel about autocratic leaders?" A lively interchange is likely on any question involving a subject on which students talk a lot:

"How do we feel about parking penalties on campus?"

"How do we feel about interracial dating?"

"How do we feel about being graded?

Learning from Encounter Discussion

The encounter process as a means to personal growth and group development has been described, developed, and employed extensively over the last three decades. *Encounter* means that members explore their reactions to each other, describing openly and honestly what they feel. If done in an honest and caring way, such descriptions by other members of a group of how they are responding to you can be a means for gaining self-insight and self-acceptance. A high degree of interpersonal trust is essential if encounter discussion is to be productive. You will recall Jack Gibb's findings about ways of communicating during encounter discussions (T-Groups) that increased trust, as opposed to ways of communicating that increased defensiveness.

Encounter can greatly expand the area of free communication among group members. When a person reveals private information about self he or she previously kept hidden from others, that person will have energy freed up for constructive work. As some of the mask is slipped aside, others can better understand him as he sees himself. If they accept him and find some identification with his feelings, fears and needs, he is likely to achieve a higher level of self-acceptance and constructive assertiveness. He is also free, if he chooses, to adjust his behavior in order to achieve different responses from others. In a full encounter, nothing of import is left hidden—members reactions to each other are shared as fully as possible. Such encounter discussion should be held only in the presence of a trained and experienced facilitator.

Certain types of limited interpersonal feedback and interpersonal encounter can be used by any group studying small group discussion or enrolled in a speech communication, social psychology, group dynamics, or other course concerned with discussion and small group communication. In this context, *feedback* is defined as information given to a person by another (or others) about how the other has perceived and been affected by him or her. This permits the recipient of feedback to compare the responses of others with the responses expected. Feedback lets you compare your self-image with the image others hold of you; others may see you very differently from how you see yourself. Like a mirror, feedback lets one see how he or she is judged on such dimensions as active-passive, agreeable-disagreeable, dependent-independent, warm-cold, and helpful-harmful. You may think of yourself as warm and friendly, but discover that others feel you are cold and aloof, or everyone may perceive you differently. Since self-images are based on what we *think* others think of us, such feedback can modify your self-concept, perhaps increasing your confidence, reducing dogmatism, and so forth. If so, you are more likely to disclose your feelings and responses, making possible still greater openness and trust among the members of your group.

In feedback sessions among members of a class in group discussion or a working group, comments should be limited to what happens among members of the group while it is in session, excluding talking about other situations members have been in, topical issues, or theorizing—a "here and now" focus, excluding talking about "then and there." Participants should state their remarks as *their personal* reactions and feelings, describing how they feel or felt and what they were reacting to. They should avoid any name-calling, theorizing about why someone acted as he or she did, accusing, or telling another how he or she should behave.

Any extensive period of feedback or encounter in interpersonal relations should be conducted in the presence of your instructor or some experienced group trainer. If no experienced trainer is available, you can still benefit from limited interpersonal feedback. Many variations are possible. The important thing is for each member of the group to be free to invite or not to invite the reactions of others. Comments should be limited to what has happened in the class.

The following guidelines should make a feedback discussion more helpful to the discussants:

1. *Describe rather than pass judgment.* No one should feel condemned as a person. A description of one's own reactions and feelings leaves the receiver of feedback free to react as he or she sees fit. Avoiding the use

of evaluative, emotive, or stigma terms reduces the need for the recipient to react defensively. For example, rather than saying, "You were nasty," one might say, "I felt myself growing very angry when you. . . ." And don't forget to express positive feelings that are sincere.

2. *Be as specific as possible.* To be told he or she is dominating may do a discussant more harm than good. Rather, the recipient should be told what was perceived as an attempt to dominate. Give details, describing what was done and your reactions to it. For example, "When we were talking about how to proceed, I thought you refused to consider anyone else's ideas, so I felt forced to accept your suggestions, face an attack from you, or leave the group."

3. *Consider the needs of the receiver.* What can the receiver hear, accept, and handle at this time? A lambasting to relieve your own tension may do much harm if the needs of the receiver are not sensed and responded to. Usually you should balance negative reactions with any favorable ones you may have.

4. *Deal only with behavior the receiver can change.* For example, you would not tell a stutterer that such hesitations annoy you, or a person with a tic in his cheek that it drove you nuts! However, you might let him know that you feel he has been sulking and you don't like it when he withdraws after his suggestion has been turned down.

5. *Don't force feedback on another.* Let the recipient invite comments (unless you respond immediately after something is said or done). If she indicates she wants to hear no more, stop. She is not likely to accept what you say anyway.

6. *Check to see if your feedback is understood.* Did the receiver understand what you mean? Watch for reactions, perhaps asking him or her to restate your point.

7. *See if the others agree with you.* You may find that other participants do not respond as you did to a particular participant. Questions like, "How do the rest of you feel about that?" should be asked often. When no one else agrees, try to find out why!

8. *Expect slow moments.* At times there will be a lot of hesitation and fumbling. A group may be very hesitant to express its feelings openly. It may take a long time for frank feedback to develop.

Feedback can be especially useful after discussion of a problem directly involving the group, such as, "What should be the date and type of our final exam?" or "By what policy should this class be graded?" Feedback can be helpful between friends and within families, sometimes under the heading of a gripe session. Indeed, no close interpersonal relationship can develop without interchange of this sort.

Public Discussions

All public discussion is conducted for the enlightenment of an audience, not primarily for the sake of arriving at a decision among the discussants or for their learning. Thus all public discussion is a form of public speaking by a group, no matter what format is employed or whether the audience is physically present or listening to a broadcast. As in all public speaking, special concern must be given to planning, organization, and adaptation to the audience. Very precise timing is essential for broadcast discussions, and highly advisable for any public discussion. The cycling, restating, and socializing of a private discussion may tend to bore or confuse an audience. A blend of planned performance and spontaneity is combined in effective public discussions.

The purpose of a public discussion is usually determined by the program committee of some organization, the producer of a broadcasting station, or a group before whom the presentation will be made. A special designated leader called a *moderator* needs to be appointed. To plan and organize the discussion, the moderator would contact the participants and ask each to agree to be a part of the program, telling each the general topic or issue, the purpose of the discussion, the reasons he or she was selected as a participant, who the other participants will be, and who is likely to compose the audience.

Participants in a public discussion should be selected on criteria of expertise, fluency, and diversity. They should be experts on the topic or knowledgeable representatives of special points of view, and able to state their information clearly and concisely. An audience will benefit little from ignorant, misinformed, or incoherent discussants!

A variety of types of public discussion have been developed, but two types are used most frequently: panel and forum.

Panel Discussion

As you will recall, a panel discussion involves a group of specialists interacting informally in front of and for the benefit of an audience. A panel group should represent a variety of points of view, or sides of a major issue. For example, if you were to have a televised panel discussion on how to reduce traffic congestion and air pollution in a city, yet improve transportation, you might want such persons as the following: (1) a city planner who had investigated rapid transit systems; (2) an air pollution control expert; (3) a highway engineer; (4) an urban businessman; and (5) an automotive designer. For a panel on the pros and cons of hunting as recreation before a conservation class you might have: (1) an antihunting lobbyist; (2) a professional game biologist; (3) an articulate sport hunter; and (4) a spokesperson for the National Wildlife Federation.

Figure 11.1 A panel discussion is a form of public speaking.

Public discussions call for special physical arrangements. When staging a live audience public discussion, it is important that all discussants be in view of each other and of the audience at all times. Only with this arrangement can a sense of direct interaction occur. To accomplish this, seat the discussants in a semicircle, usually with the moderator at the center. The audience then faces the panel, and the panelists can alternately face the audience and each other. Panelists should be seated behind a table, preferably with some sort of cover on the front of it. Two small tables in an open V make an excellent arrangement.

A large name card should be placed on the table in front of each panelist. If the room is large and microphones are needed, they should be in sufficient number and so placed that the panelists can largely ignore them. Neck microphones can be used. If a chalkboard or easel is available, display the topic or question being discussed; sometimes the major issues or questions can also be listed. Such visual devices help auditors keep the discussion organized and clear in their minds.

In a very large assembly it may be necessary to have floor microphones for a forum discussion. If so, these should be strategically placed and their use clearly explained to the audience before the forum begins. If not essential, do not use them. They will inhibit some persons, and can lead to much confusion and delay.

The outline for a panel discussion could follow a problem-solving pattern or one of the enlightenment patterns suggested earlier. The moderator should ask each participant in the forthcoming panel to suggest questions for the discussion, then use these in preparing the leader's outline of three to five major questions, each with appropriate follow-up questions or subquestions. This rough draft outline should be sent to each of the participants so that they have a chance to investigate and think of possible answers to each question.

The moderator prepares a special outline with an introduction, the pattern of questions to be raised, and a planned conclusion format. Of course, physical arrangements need to be made by the moderator also, including name cards, possibly a poster with the overall topic or question, seating arrangements, etc. It is the moderator's job to see that the panel is kept organized when underway, summarizing each major topic or having the participants do so, and keeping it moving so that time is well distributed among the major topics on the outline and among the participants. A moderator's outline might look like this:

Introduction
  I. Ladies and gentlemen, the question of whether or not the use of
     marijuana should be legalized and controlled by laws is of significance
     to all of us: young people, medical personnel, parents, law officers, and
     concerned citizens.
 II. Our panel of experts represent different fields and points of view
     concerning marijuana:
     A. Dr. Robert Jones, at my far right, is Professor of Internal and
        Diagnostic Medicine at State University Medical College and
        author of *The Physiology of Marijuana Users*.
     B. Mr. George Ballou is Commissioner of Police for our city and
        former director of the division of narcotics.
     C. Ms. Robin Jones, a master's candidate in chemistry at State
        University, is a spokeswoman for the Society to Legalize
        Marijuana.
     D. Dr. Cedric Hoese is Professor of Sociology, specializing in social
        problems at State University and author of a recent article entitled
        "The Flow of Marijuana in an Urban Complex."
III. Our panel has agreed to discuss the question: "Should the use of
     marijuana be legalized and controlled by the government?" Four
     specific issues on which we will focus are:
     A. Does evidence indicate marijuana to be dangerous to the user?
     B. Are users ever dangerous to society?
     C. If it were to be made legal, by whom and under what conditions
        should use be permitted?
     D. Would legalization increase or decrease the problems facing our
        police and courts?

Discussion

I. Does the evidence indicate that marijuana is dangerous to users? (Here would be the subquestions and the rest of the outline through the four issues mentioned in the introduction.)

Conclusion

I. Let us summarize our agreements and differences on the four major issues: (A.,B.,C.,D.).
II. We should all be better prepared to make our own choices about using marijuana and about what laws we want as citizens.
III. We have time for a few questions from the audience.

Forum

A forum discussion is often conducted following a speech, panel discussion, educational film, public interview, or symposium. To have a satisfactory forum discussion requires strict procedural control by a moderator who understands the purpose of the forum and has mastered techniques for keeping the discussion interesting and fair to all persons involved. A chairperson or moderator should control the forum following a speech, film, or other presentation; the moderator of a panel, symposium, or public interview also moderates any forum following such a group presentation. Follow these guidelines:

1. During the introduction to the panel (or other program) announce that there will be a forum or question and answer period. This allows listeners to be thinking of questions and remarks.
2. State whether only questions or both questions and comments will be permitted.
3. Just before allowing the audience to participate, announce definite rules to assure equal opportunity for all to speak, and insist that they be followed:
    a. Raise your hand and wait to be recognized before speaking;
    b. No one may speak a second time until each person who wants to speak has had the floor at least once;
    c. Comments or questions should be addressed to either a specific panelist by name or to the entire panel;
    d. Remarks must be limited to not more than _____ seconds;
    e. Speak loudly enough to be heard by everyone (or, go to the floor microphone, if one is available).
4. Tell the audience if there will be a definite length of time for the forum; then end it when scheduled.
5. If the audience is large, recognize persons from various parts of the room in a systematic pattern.

6. Encourage different points of view by asking for them: "Does anyone want to present a *different* point of view from that which we have just heard?"
7. If a questioner cannot be heard by all, restate the question clearly and concisely.
8. If a question is unclear, or lengthy, restate it to the originator's satisfaction.
9. When the alloted time is nearly up, state that there is just enough time for one or two more questions (or comments).
10. If no one seeks the floor, wait a few seconds, then thank the panel and audience for their participation and either dismiss the meeting or go on to the next item on the agenda.

Techniques for Groups within Organizations

There are a large number of special discussion techniques for getting small group involvement into a large group meeting and for facilitating communication within small groups that are part of large organizations. Those selected for inclusion in this chapter are all group centered and discussional in nature, and can be of value in a variety of organizational contexts. Any of these techniques or procedures should be explained carefully by the coordinator of a meeting before it is first tried. Often a sheet of instructions is handed to participants in order to explain the purpose and rules of the procedure to be used.

Buzz Groups (Phillips 66)

This procedure is used to organize a large group meeting into many small groups that work concurrently on the same question. The purpose may be to get questions for a speaker or panel, to identify problems or issues, to compile a list of ideas or possible solutions, to develop a list of techniques for implementing and adapting a general solution to local conditions, to get personal involvement and thinking by members of a large class, etc. For example, I was a participant in a workshop of about 500 local education leaders in Kentucky who met to understand and work out techniques for promoting a "minimum foundation program" for public education in that state. Needed was a favorable vote of taxpayers in a special statewide election that would mean state tax support for local schools based on need. This would mean higher taxes overall and a flow of money from the wealthier districts to the poorer. Several times the entire group used the Phillips 66 technique to identify specific local problems, inexpensive advertising and promotional techniques, arguments for the program, etc.[12] These lists were processed in work groups of fifteen to eighteen members each and the final results distributed to all members. Even though the conference was large, every participant was active in discussions and the sense of enthusiasm and involvement was truly remarkable. The procedure:

1. The chairman presents a "target" question to the entire assembly, which may be seated in rows in an auditorium or at small tables. This question should be very concise, limited, and specific. For example:

"What techniques could be used to publicize the MFP to citizens of each county or city?"

"What topics or issues should be dealt with in the next year's convention?"

"What new projects might local unions undertake to help members with social problems?"

"What questions would you like to have Dr. Hanson answer about the effects of narcotics?"

Each question should be written on a card (4″ x 6″ or 5″ x 8″) with one card for each group of six members. It is a good idea to display it also on a large poster or blackboard in front of the assembly.

2. Divide the large group into work groups of six by seating them at small tables, or in an auditorium by counting off by three in each row, then having alternate rows turn to face each other as shown in figure 11.2.

Figure 11.2 Work groups seating.

3. Appoint a recorder-spokesman for each group based on seating, as: "The person sitting in the forward left-hand seat of each group will be its recorder. The recorder should write on the card *all* ideas presented, then have the group put them in rank order." An assistant or assistants then pass out the cards.

4. Next, ask each group to record as many answers to the target question as they can think of in five minutes, then spend one minute evaluating the list to decide if any items should be eliminated and in what order to present them. Thus discussion occurs in groups of six members for six minutes—66!

5. When the five minutes are up, warn the groups and allow an extra minute if all seem involved. Then ask them to evaluate and rank the list.

6. At this point you may do any of several things, depending on the size and plan of the overall meeting.

   a. Collect the cards, which are then edited to eliminate duplications with a tally of the number of times each item was mentioned on cards. The total list is then duplicated and handed to the entire group at a subsequent meeting, presented to some special group for processing or whatever is appropriate; or

b. The chairman asks each recorder to report orally from his seat one *new* item from his card without explanation, or say "pass" if all his items have been presented. A secretary writes all the items on a chart or chalkboard in front of the room. The list is then processed as above or as under the problem census technique.

c. The questions listed are presented in rotation to the speaker or panel.

This technique is also used by teachers in classes studying literature, social problems, political science, psychology, and so on. The buzz groups in a class may have more than six minutes and may even follow a brief outline prepared by the teacher. A number of reports have indicated very little or no difference in the amount of information learned from a more traditional lecture approach, and significantly more creative and critical thinking and modification of values by students involved in discussions. Variations of many types in the buzz group procedure are possible, limited only by the ingenuity of the chairperson or teacher.

The Nominal Group Technique (NGT)

Some of the research into brainstorming showed that persons working individually in the presence of others can generate more ideas for solving problems than will the same number of persons interacting. Interacting groups deciding on a solution by consensus sometimes suppress divergence, producing a group-think outcome. As an outcome of effort to codify the research on small group problem-solving interaction, Delbecq and Van de Ven developed a procedure they call the Nominal Group Technique. It is an alternative to conventional problem-solving discussions.[13] They found that NGT will usually produce more alternatives and a higher quality solution than will discussion in a conventional group session. A nominal group is one in which people work in each other's presence on the same task, but they do not interact verbally. NGT alternates between interacting verbally and working silently in the presence of others. It is *not* recommended for the typical problems that come up in the operation of any organization, but only for such major problems as planning a long-range program; it is not for routine meetings.[14] Delbecq claimed that the superiority of NGT for major program planning resulted from two things: (1) when a question is asked in a group, as soon as one person starts to answer it all others stop thinking; and (2) most persons do not work hard in interactive meetings, but they will when acting individually in the presence of others.[15] As a result, he claimed that different angles, approaches, and possibilities are either overlooked or not brought up (you will recall that the prescriptive developmental outlines for problem solving were developed to offset this tendency). The NGT helps to reduce secondary tension and control conflict, and it virtually eliminates the chance for some members to make speeches to impress or represent outside constituencies rather than to help the group. On the negative side, NGT is not a complete problem-solving process, it does not enhance cohesiveness (and may reduce it), and produces far less member satisfaction than does problem-solving discussion.[16]

The essence of NGT is for several persons (six to nine) to work individually in each other's presence by writing their ideas down on paper, then to record these ideas on a chart as a group, clarify them, and evaluate them by a ranking procedure until a decision has been reached. The procedure may be varied somewhat but should always involve members working silently, then discussion, then silent work, more discussion, and so on. Here are the steps for the leader as outlined by Delbecq:

1. State the known problem elements or characteristics of a situation that differ from what is desired. At this point there should be *no* mention of solutions, and no interaction. Members are seated at a table facing a chart easel. A large group can be divided into several small working groups, each with a leader.
2. Ask the participants to generate a list of features of the problem, considering the emotional, personal, and organizational. Then give a clear definition of the problem. (1 and 2 can be one step, with no discussion as in step 2, with leader presenting the problem and moving group at once into step 3.)
3. Allow the group five to fifteen minutes to work silently. Each person is asked to write down all ideas that he or she can think of on a sheet of paper.
4. In a "round robin" session the results are collected on a sheet of paper (chart) in front of the group where all can see the list.
   a. Ask each person in turn to give *one* item from his or her list. This item is recorded on the chart. No discussion is allowed at this time;
   b. Do not record who suggested the idea, or more than one idea from a person at a time;
   c. Keep going around the group until *all* ideas have been posted on the chart. Additional ideas may occur to members while this is going on; be sure they are stated and listed;
   d. If someone has the same idea as another, put a tally mark by the idea, but don't record it twice;
   e. The leader has also generated a list, and posts his or her ideas in turn just as for the other members.
5. Clarification interaction—anyone may ask another person for clarification of an idea or proposal on the list. Questions such as "What does item 6 mean?" or "Do you understand item 4?" are now in order for discussion. The leader should take the group through the list item by item, but only to clarify and elaborate, *not* to evaluate. At this point allow no lobbying, criticism, or argument for an idea.

discussion methods for learning groups, public meetings,   **313**
and groups in organizations

6. Each person is now given a set of note cards, on which to write the five or so items (all should have same number of cards, one item per card) he or she most prefers. These cards are now ranked (5 being highest, and 1 being lowest rank) and collected by the leader. Sum the ranks for each item, and divide by the number of persons in the group to get a value weight for each solution.
7. Now engage in an evaluation discussion of the several items having the highest average ranks. This should be a full and free evaluative discussion, with critical thinking, disagreement, and analysis encouraged.
8. If a decision is reached, fine. If not, revote, and then discuss further. This process can be repeated several times if necessary until a clear synthesis of a few ideas or support for one idea has emerged. The end result is submitted to the appropriate planners, executive, or other group for action.

This is a "supergun" technique, to be used only for major issues. Obviously you could use variations of this technique in many discussion sessions, by having quiet periods when discussants think silently and jot down their ideas on paper to enrich the ensuing discussion.

The Problem Census

This "posting" technique is useful for building an agenda for future problem-solving meetings, for program planning by an organization, or to discover problems encountered by a group of employees or students that might not be known by a supervisor or teacher. As examples: a university department in which I was employed conducted a problem census that developed into the agenda for a series of future meetings. Different members of the faculty committed themselves to investigate the various problems and to prepare a presentation of information and an outline for each problem as it came up in turn; a group of salesmen for a feed company scattered over two states met with the sales manager to develop a list of problems and programs for a series of monthly meetings; a class in discussion developed a list of questions about how to handle various problems often encountered in committee leadership, and this became the agenda for a series of eight class meetings that included problem-solving discussions, reports, role-played demonstrations, a film, and some lecture; the graduate teaching assistants in my department frequently use this technique to prepare agendas for a series of weekly seminars.

The problem census technique involves a series of distinct steps to be followed by the supervisor or other designated leader of the group:

1. Seat the group in a semicircle facing a chart or chalkboard.
2. Explain the purpose of the technique, which is to bring out all problems, concerns, questions, or difficulties any member of the group would like to have discussed.

3. The leader then asks each participant to present one problem or question, going around the group clockwise. Anyone not ready to present a new problem says "pass" and the next person has the floor. After one complete round, anyone who said "pass" may now add his or her question or problem. The group continues to do this until all problems have been presented.
4. The leader "posts" each problem as it is presented, writing it clearly on a chart or chalkboard where all can see. Each filled chart page can be fastened to the wall with masking tape. The leader must be totally accepting of whatever is presented, never challenging its validity or disagreeing. He or she may need to ask for clarification or elaboration, but always in a way that does not challenge the concern being expressed by a member. Often the leader will need to "boil down" a long question to the core issue, but should always rephrase it and ask if that is what the speaker intended before posting the rephrased question.
5. The group now evaluates the list for priority by voting, usually with each member voting for his or her top three or four choices. But all problems are included on the agenda—this merely gives order to the list.
6. The group may now find some of the questions can be answered or solved at once by other members to the satisfaction of the presenter. Such questions are then removed from the list, and the remaining ones are now in order for future treatment.
7. Each problem is dealt with in turn. Some may call for a factual presentation by a consultant, some may be handled by a brief lecture or other informational technique, some by printed materials; but the core problems should be analyzed and dealt with by the entire group or a subcommittee of it, following one of the appropriate problem-solving patterns presented in chapter 5.

Parliamentary Procedure in Committees

Some organizations require that their committees follow parliamentary procedures, usually specifying that the authority for the rules of procedure shall be *Robert's Rules of Order.* [17] This section is based on the principles and rules laid down in that reference work for committees. Even Robert did not recommend that committees use any more of the elaborate framework of parliamentary law than was absolutely necessary to expedite their work or to make action by the committee legal under the constitution of a parent organization. A rather formal level of parliamentary rules is necessary and useful to accomplish the work of large deliberative groups of 25 or more members. Even in large groups, the amount of detail and formality in parliamentary procedure should be adjusted to the size, sophistication, and amount of conflict within the assembly. The member of a committee (or other small group) who keeps uttering "second the motion," "point of order," "question," or "I move to table the motion" may either be showing off or is ignorant of the basic purpose of parliamentary law and of rules of order that apply to small groups.

Some organizations have a special executive group, known as a "board" or "executive committee," provided for in the bylaws of the society. Such a group has only the authority vested in it by those bylaws or a special vote of the assembly of the organization. A board is usually empowered to act for the assembly between its regular meetings so long as actions of the board do not conflict with those of the assembly or the society at large. Other committees have smaller areas of freedom than a board, usually to investigate, consider alternatives, recommend to the parent organization, or take action in a very limited scope of authority. There are two types of these committees in most large organizations: *standing* and *special.*

Standing committees are established to perform some continuing work or duty, so they exist "permanently" or as long as the assembly authorizes, even though membership of the committee may be changed periodically. Members serve on standing committees until their replacements have been selected. Many organizations have such standing committees as membership, social, and facilities.

Special or *ad hoc* committees are appointed as need arises to carry out specific tasks. When the assigned task has been completed the special committee ceases to exist. Thus when a special committee to investigate and recommend a new meeting place for a large group has made a report to the assembly the committee no longer exists. Members may be elected to such a committee, or appointed by the president or board.

A committee meets on call of its chairperson or any two members. The quorum is a majority (minimum number of members required to be present to carry out business) unless otherwise specified by the parent organization. The chairperson usually acts as secretary of a small committee, but large committees may appoint a separate secretary. If a professional secretary who is not a regular member of the committee is asked to keep records, the chairperson is still responsible for the minutes or other records, and should sign them.

The specific rules governing meetings of boards and committees (as specified by Robert) are considerably less numerous and far more informal than those governing an assembly:

1. Members do not need to obtain permission from the chair by formal recognition before speaking or making a motion. They may speak up whenever they want, so long as they do not rudely interrupt another.
2. Motions do not need a second. A motion is a proposal to take some action as a group.
3. There is no limit on how many times a member can speak on an issue, and motions to limit or close discussion are never appropriate.
4. Informal discussion is permitted with no motion pending. In a parliamentary assembly a formal motion must be made before an issue can be discussed. In committee, usually no motion is made until *after* consensus or at least a majority has been achieved through extended discussion.

5. A vote is taken, often by a show of hands, to confirm a decision already sensed by the group. "Straw" votes can be taken at any time to determine if a majority or consensus exists before taking a binding vote. The leader might say: "Let's see how we stand on this. Would all who favor it please raise your right hand."

6. When a proposal is clear to all members, a vote can be taken and the outcome recorded as a decision even though no motion has been introduced.

7. The chairperson can ask if all members "consent" or agree with an idea or proposal. Then if no one objects, the decision has been made and is reported in the minutes—for example, "It was decided by consent that we should have Jean and Bob draft a resolution to present at the next meeting of the club."

8. Committee chairpersons can speak up in a discussion, taking a stand on a controversial issue, without leaving the chair. They can also make motions and vote on all questions as do all other members of the committee. (In some large committees it may be decided that the chairperson will act as if in a large assembly, and then he or she should do so *at all times,* voting only to make or break a tie, and not participating in the substance of the discussion.)

9. A motion to "reconsider" a previous vote can be made at any time, and there is no limit on how many times a question can be reconsidered. Unlike in a parliamentary body, any person who did not vote with the losing side can move to reconsider. Thus a person who was absent or who did not vote can ask for the reconsideration of a previous decision or vote if the action has not yet been carried out.

10. Formal reports of committees should contain only what was agreed to by a vote of at least a majority of those present at a regular and properly called (notice given each member) meeting at which a quorum was present. Informal reports for in-committee communication were explained in chapter 3.

11. Motions can be amended in committee, but this is best done informally, voting on the proposed change in a motion only if it cannot be decided by consensus in the time available for a meeting.

12. Many of the motions required in an assembly are irrelevant; a member can discuss virtually anything informally in committee sessions, so there is no need for points of order, motions to table, or matters of personal privilege. In short, the bulk of what is called "parliamentary law" is not needed and can even be obstructive to committee deliberations and actions.

Guidance on how to draft committee reports was provided in chapter 6. Usually the chairperson makes formal reports from a committee in writing. In a meeting of the parent body the committee chairperson may give an oral report, then hand the written report to the secretary of the assembly. Reports of less formal motions or work in progress can be made orally. When a committee report includes a recommendation for action by the entire assembly, the spokesperson for the committee presents it as a main motion. No second is required, for at least one other person has supported it within the committee. Robert recommended that the speaker say something like "I move to adopt the report of the _____ committee" when concluding a report that does not include a motion for action as a way of getting endorsement for the report. Such motions to "adopt" and resolutions for action are then treated as any other main motion on the floor of an assembly. Here are some ways of presenting committee reports:

"The Committee on _____ reports that. . . ."

"I move the adoption of the resolution just read."

"The _____ Committee moves that. . . ."

If a committee is unable to reach consensus and a minority of its membership wants to make a report or recommendation different from that of the majority, it usually is permitted to do so as soon as the "majority" committee report has been made. This is not a *right* of a committee minority, but of course during debate under parliamentary rules the members who did not agree with the majority position can speak their opposition. However, no one has the right to allude to what happened during the committee's private discussions unless the entire committee has agreed that this is to be permitted.

In summary, keep business in a committee informal, using only a very minimum of rules of order and precedence. Use votes to show that a legal majority supported all reported findings, recommendations, and actions, but not to shut off discussion or imply that majority is the preferred way of making decisions in a small committee. Write and present formal reports to parent organizations carefully and in good form. Have a spokesperson (usually holder of the chair) speak for the committee; no second is needed when that person speaks for the committee to the parent body. The committee members should be prepared to support the committee's resolutions, and refute arguments that may be made against the committee's well thought out recommendations.

Summary

Discussion methods and techniques for learning discussions, public discussion, and discussions of small groups that exist within large organizations have been presented in this final chapter. Ways to enhance cooperation and the achievement of the common good have been stressed throughout the chapter.

Learnings in the affective area are greatly enhance by cooperative relationships; discussion is uniquely suited to building cooperation. Generally the focus in learning discussion should be on sharing perceptions and interpretations of a limited number of topics emerging from shared experiences. Various formats for learning discussion can be used, depending on the nature of the subject matter and interests of members. Discussion of works of art should be concentrated on the works themselves. Case discussion can be used to explore ideas and feelings about more general types of problems. A problem census can develop an agenda of topics or issues for such discussions. Personal feelings and interpersonal relationships can be dealt with through affective discussion or group encounter.

The most common types of public discussion are panel presentations and large group forums. Special procedures for each of these formats were described in detail. Panel and forum discussions require close control of the procedure by a designated moderator.

Small groups that are part of large organizations often have special problems; special techniques can enhance their productivity. Every member of a large group can be involved directly and actively through the buzz-group technique. Groups doing long-range planning for organizations can often be more productive if the Nominal Group Technique is used, employing a mix of individual work and highly structured group interaction. A problem census can be used to develop an agenda based on member concerns for future meetings of small groups that meet regularly within organizational contexts. Committees are often mandated to adhere to some code of parliamentary law, most often *Robert's Rules of Order*. The rules for committees are far less restrictive and more flexible than those for large assemblies. Robert adapted the code of parliamentary law to the small-group nature of the committee, keeping motions, formality, and voting to the very minimum essential for democratic action.

No matter what special method is employed, it should facilitate member interaction in achieving the common goal.

Exercises

1. Select a poem, short story, brief essay, painting, sculpture, or other work of art that intrigues you. Your class will be divided into several groups of from five to seven members each. If you have selected something written, make a copy for each member of your group. Plan an outline for leading discussion of the work of art; the discussion will be limited to 15–20 minutes. Each member of your small group will in turn lead discussion, using the outline prepared. You may want to have one member sit out as a critic-observer, then lead a brief evaluation discussion.

2. All members of your group or class may view a film or TV program. Together prepare an outline of questions, then discuss the film or show.

3. Conduct an affective discussion either with a group of classmates or some other group, and report the results in a short essay. The target question might come from a previous problem census, or the following list:
   "How do we feel about classmates who don't talk up?"
   "How do we feel about interracial marriages?"
   "How do we feel about capital punishment?"

4. Conduct a problem census on some question, possibly "What do we want to know about small group discussion techniques?" or "What would we like to know about different religions?" After the agenda has been completely rank ordered, have a planning committee develop a schedule to deal with each of the questions, topics, or issues recorded.

5. Following a series of discussions, have a feedback session. On a chart or chalkboard write a set of terms for guiding the feedback. These should be selected by the group, possibly including some of the following: attitudes, preparation, speaking, supportiveness, acceptance of others, self-acceptance, personal insight, openness, warmth.

6. Engage in an encounter session or laboratory, with a trained facilitator to conduct the session(s). Use the guidelines on pages 304–5 as a contract for the members of the group.

7. Plan in detail a panel discussion on a topic of national importance. Imagine that you can select whomever you want as panelists. Select them, giving a rationale for each panelist. Then prepare a moderator's outline.

8. The class can be divided into project groups, each of which will research a problem of interest to it and of importance to all the class. Then the group should prepare and present a panel for the benefit of the rest of the class.

9. Conduct a Nominal Group Technique session in your class. Divide the class into small groups of six to eight persons, and seat each group at a table or in a semicircle facing a chart easel or wall on which are taped sheets of large plain paper for recording results. Your instructor will coordinate and time the exercise, but a student should be appointed to coordinate each working group. Work on some target question such as "How should registration procedures at our college (or university) be revised?" or "How might our highways be made safer?"

10. Form a society or club-like organization of your class. Select as presiding officer a student who has training and experience as a presiding officer (or, the instructor could do this). Then establish such committees as (1) *ad hoc* committee to plan an end-of-the-term party; (2) committee to devise a plan for calculating final class grades; (3) committee to recommend a type of final examination; and (4) committee to recommend a room designed for this course. Each committee should elect its own chairperson, then operate under Robert's rules for committees of an organization. Allow time for committees to work and conduct meetings. Then hold a special parliamentary session of the class at which all committees present their reports and recommendations to be acted on by the entire class.

Bibliography

Beal, George M., Bohlen, Joe M., and Raudabaugh, J. Neil, *Leadership and Dynamic Group Action,* Ames, Ia.: Iowa State University Press, 1962.

Delbecq, Andre L., Van de Ven, Andrew H., and Gustafson, David H., *Group Techniques for Program Planning: A Guide to Nominal Group and Delphi Processes,* Glenview, Ill.: Scott, Foresman and Company, 1975.

Egan, Gerard, *Face to Face: The Small Group Experience and Interpersonal Growth,* Monterey, Cal.: Brooks/Cole Publishing Company, 1973.

Epstein, Charlotte, *Affective Subjects in the Classroom: Exploring Race, Sex, and Drugs,* Scranton, Pa.: Intext Educational Publishers, 1972.

Hunter, Elizabeth, *Encounter in the Classroom,* New York: Holt, Rinehart and Winston, Inc., 1972.

Johnson, David W., and Johnson, Roger T., *Learning Together and Alone: Cooperation, Competition, and Individualization,* Englewood Cliffs, N.J.: Prentice-Hall, Inc., 1975.

Powell, John W., *Research in Adult Group Learning in the Liberal Arts,* White Plains, N.Y.: Fund for Adult Education, 1960.

Rogers, Carl R., *Carl Rogers on Encounter Groups,* New York: Harper & Row, Publishers, 1970.

Robert, Henry M., and Robert, Sarah C., *Robert's Rules of Order Newly Revised,* Glenview, Ill.: Scott, Foresman and Company, 1970.

References

1. See D. W. and R. T. Johnson, *Learning Together and Alone,* (Englewood Cliffs, N.J.: Prentice-Hall, Inc., 1975), pp. 191–92, for a summary of some of this research. See also W. J. McKeachie, "Recitation and Discussion," in O. E. Lancaster, ed., *Achieve Learning Objectives,* 3rd ed. (University Park, Pa.: The Pennsylvania State University, 1963), section F.
2. John W. Powell, *Research in Adult Group Learning in the Liberal Arts* (White Plains, N.Y.: Fund for Adult Education, 1960), p. 3.
3. P. H. Witte, "The Effects of Group Reward Structures on Interracial Acceptance, Peer Tutoring, and Academic Performance" (Unpublished doctoral dissertation, Washington University, 1972); Johnson and Johnson, *Together and Alone,* pp. 193–96.
4. Elizabeth Hunter, *Encounter in the Classroom* (New York: Holt, Rinehart and Winston, Inc., 1972), pp. 1–15.
5. Johnson and Johnson, *Ibid.,* p. 66.

6. John K. Brilhart, "An Exploratory Study of Relationships between the Evaluating Process and Associated Behaviors of Participants in Six Study-Discussion Groups" (Ph.D. dissertation, Pennsylvania State University, 1962), pp. 283–93.

7. *Ibid.,* pp. 275–82.

8. Richard Bach, *Jonathan Livingston Seagull* (New York: Macmillan, Inc., 1970).

9. Adapted from John Hasling, *Group Discussion and Decision Making* (New York: Thomas Y. Crowell Company, 1975), pp. 95–96.

10. Adapted from outline of Connie Chatwood; April, 1973.

11. Charlotte Epstein, *Affective Subjects in the Classroom: Exploring Race, Sex, and Drugs* (Scranton, Pa.: Intext Educational Publishers, 1972), pp. 12–13.

12. This procedure was developed and popularized by J. Donald Phillips, President of Hillsdale College in Michigan, who served as consultant for the Kentucky Conference. The Conference was held in 1954 at Eastern Kentucky State College.

13. Andre L. Delbecq, Andrew H. Van de Ven, and David H. Gustafson, *Group Techniques for Program Planning: A Guide to Nominal Group and Delphi Processes* (Glenview, Ill.: Scott, Foresman and Company, 1975), pp. 7–16.

14. *Ibid.,* pp. 3–4.

15. Andre L. Delbecq, "Techniques for Achieving Innovative Changes in Programming," a presentation at the Midwest Regional Conference of the Family Service Association of America; Omaha, Neb.; April 20, 1971.

16. *Ibid.*

17. Henry M. Robert and Sarah C. Robert, *Robert's Rules of Order Newly Revised* (Glenview, Ill.: Scott, Foresman and Company, 1970), chapter XVI.

author index

Samovar, L. A., 18, 36, 115, 160, 216, 249, 250
Sargent, F., 217
Scheidel, T. M., 93, 111
Schellenberg, J. A., 65
Schlosberg, H., 19, 86
Schutz, W. C., 6, 19, 222, 250
Sharf, B. F., 250
Sharp, H., 189, 211
Shaw, D. M., 86
Shaw, M. E., 19, 46, 55, 63, 64, 173, 174, 209, 210, 250
Shepherd, C., 65
Slater, P. E., 60, 65
Smith, E. B., 60, 65
Solem, A. R., 211, 231
Sommer, R., 68, 86
Starkweather, J., 161
Stech, E., 250
Stephan, E. F., 65
Sternberg, R. J., 190, 211
Stevens, S. S., 115
Stogdill, R. M., 224, 249, 250
Stoner, J. A. F., 166, 174

Tannenbaum, R., 219, 249, 250
Thayer, L., 118, 120, 121
Thelen, H., 21, 40, 60, 65
Theobold, R., 5, 19
Tregoe, B. B., 180, 181, 193, 209, 210, 211
Trodahl, V. C., 65
Tubbs, S. L., 36, 161
Tuckman, B. W., 92, 93, 111

Van de Ven, A. H., 312, 321, 322
Von Bertalonffy, L., 36

Wahlers, K. J., 36
Watzlawick, P., 119
Weinberg, H. L., 160
Weschler, I. R., 219, 249, 250
White, R. K., 250
Whyte, W. H., Jr., 174
Williams, R. M., 65
Witte, P. H., 321
Wood, J. T., 226, 232, 251, 252
Woodworth, R. S., 19

Zander, A. F., 19, 111, 250

subject index

Least-sized group, principle of, 21, 33, 39, 60
Legitimate power, 220
Lieutenants to leader, 102
Listening, 151–54
    actively, 113, 152–53
    consensus and, 167
    exercises, 157–58
    leader, 240, 302
    pitfalls to, 151–52
    pseudo-, 153
"Lost on the Moon," exercise, 168–69

Maintenance behavior (social behavior), 89
Majority
    decision by, 163
    procedure for, 170, 317
Mapping, of a problem, 193–94
Meaning, 126, 129
Members, as input variable, 25, 32
Message components, 128–51
Minority rights, in committee, 318
Minutes, 113, 154–55
Moderator, 288, 308–9
Mutually interdependent purpose, 9

Name tags (tents), 69
Networks of communication
    all-channel, 34
    defined, 89
    exercise, 110
    types, 101–3
Neutrality, as attitude, 53
Nominal Group Technique, 238, 312–14
    defined, 288
    exercise, 320
Nonverbal communication
    codes, 145–51
    cues, defined, 113
    exercises, 158–59
Norming
    behavior, 100
    phase, 93
Norms, 104–7, 136
    defined, 89
    exercise, 109–10
    process variables, 25, 34
Note cards, 75

Objectivity, 39
Observation, as source of information, 76

Observer
    exercise for, 284
    group development and, 245
    need for, 256
    role of, 256–61
Obstacles, in problem, 180–81
One-meeting groups, 91, 222
Openmindedness, 231–32
Open system, 21, 23–25
Opinions
    differences in, and consensus, 168
    evaluating, 81–82
    giving and seeking, 100
    questions of, 143
    stating, 138
Organizations, group techniques for, 310–18
Organizing information and ideas, 83. *See also* Outlines
Orientation
    period of (phase), 191–92
    questions of, 114, 141
Outlines
    causal pattern, 287, 295
    chronological pattern, 287, 295
    comparative pattern, 287, 295
    discussion leader's, 206–7, 238
    exercise, 209
    fine arts, 287, 296–99
    learning discussion, 294–99
    panel discussion, 308–9
    preparation for discussion, 83–84
    problem solving, 73, 201–7
    topical, 294
Output variable, 21, 24, 25

Panel discussion
    defined, 4, 15, 288
    types and guidelines, 306–9
Paraverbal cues, 113, 150
Parent organization, 42
Parliamentary procedure
    committees, 315–18
    defined, 288
    exercise, 320
    group size and, 60
Participant-observer
    defined, 21
    perspective of, 22, 256
Participation
    amount of, among members, 59
    evaluating, 273
    leader rate of, 231
    rating scales, 276–77

Passive (non-assertive), 55
Performing phase, 93
Persuasion in discussion, 56
PERT, 177, 199–200
Phases
 group development, 89, 91–96
 leader emergence, 223
Physical environment, 68–70
Policy, questions of, 114, 144
Population familiarity, as characteristic of
  problem, 177, 184
Post Decision Reaction Sheet, 169
Postmeeting Reaction Sheet, 255, 261–66
Power
 defined, 215
 influence and, 220
 process variable, 25
 types of, 220–21
Prejudice, 39, 57
Preparation
 for discussion, 72–84
 of leader, 235–36
Primary group, 4, 10
Primary tension, 84, 94–96
Problem, 180–82
 census, 288
 characteristics of, 182–86
 defined, 177
 diagrammed, 181
 exercise, 208–9
Problem census
 defined, 288
 exercise, 320
 technique, 301, 314–15
Problem orientation, 53
Problem question, 178, 292
Problem solving
 decision making vs., 164–66
 defined, 178, 180
 discussion, 176–212
 ideal group and, 34
 leader guidance of, 239
 procedures as process variable, 25
 questions, 292
 rating scales, 272–73
Problem solving group, 4, 13
Procedure
 decision making, 166–72
 leader control of, 235
 questions of, 141
 suggesting, 100
Process variable, 21, 23, 24, 25, 91
Pseudodiscussion, 56

Public discussion. *See also* Panel discussion
  and Forum
 defined, 4, 15
 types and guidelines, 306–10
Public interview, 4, 15
Purpose of group, 41–45. *See also* Goal
 achieved as output, 35
 meeting, 236
 understood and accepted by members, 33

Question
 analysis, 292
 answerable vs. unanswerable, 114, 140
 asking, 138
 buzz group, 311
 criteria for, 139
 defined, 113–14
 exercises, 157, 208
 forum, 309–10
 information, 142
 interpretation, 143, 184, 241, 292
 limited vs. open-ended, 140–41
 observers, 257–58
 open-ended, 291–92
 orientation, 114, 141
 panel discussion, 308
 policy, 141, 185
 prediction, 292
 problem, 178, 192
 procedural, 141
 synthesis, 292
 translation, 292
 types of, 138–44, 292
 value, 143, 185, 292
Quorum, 288

Rating scales, 255, 267–80
Reading, in preparation, 76, 291
Recording, 154–56, 233–34
 buzz group, 311
 defined, 100
 exercise, 158
Referent, 114, 129, 130
Referent power, 270
Reflective thinking sequence, 178, 187, 188,
  201–2
Reminder-observer, 255, 259–60
Reports, written, 154–56, 158, 317–18. *See*
  also Recording and Minutes
Resources, 25, 30, 33
Responsibility
 of leader, 233–45
 for success of group, 45–46